Kant's Rational Religion and the Radical Enlightenment

Bloomsbury Studies in Modern German Philosophy

Series Editors:

Courtney D. Fugate, American University of Beirut, Lebanon
Anne Pollok, University of South Carolina, USA

Editorial Board:

Desmond Hogan (Princeton University, USA)
Ursula Goldenbaum (Emory University, USA)
Robert Clewis (Gwynedd Mercy University, USA)
Paul Guyer (Brown University, USA)
Brandon Look (University of Kentucky, USA)
Eric Watkins (University of California, San Diego, USA)
Corey W. Dyck (University of Western Ontario, Canada)
Stefanie Buchenau (University of Paris, France)
Paola Rumore (University of Turin, Italy)
Heiner Klemme (Martin-Luther-Universität Halle-Wittenberg, Germany)

Central and previously overlooked ideas and thinkers from the German Enlightenment Era are showcased in this series. Expanding research into areas that have been neglected particularly in English-language scholarship, it covers the work of lesser-known authors, previously untranslated texts, and issues that have suffered an undeserved life on the margins of current philosophical-historical discussion about eighteenth-century German thought.

By opening itself to a broad range of subjects and placing the role of women during this period centre-stage, the series not only advances our understanding about the German Enlightenment and its connection with the pan-European debates, but also contributes to debates about the reception of Newtonian science and the impact of Leibnizian, Kantian and Wolffian philosophies. Featuring edited collections and single-authored works, and overseen by an esteemed Editorial Board, the goal is to enrich current debates in the history of philosophy and to correct common misconceptions.

Titles in the series include:

Tetens's Writings on Method, Language, and Anthropology
Edited by Courtney D. Fugate, Curtis Sommerlatte and Scott Stapleford

*The Vocation of the Human Being in German Philosophy 1600-1800:
A Critical Reappraisal*
Edited by Anne Pollok and Courtney Fugate

Kant's Rational Religion and the Radical Enlightenment

From Spinoza to Contemporary Debates

Anna Tomaszewska

BLOOMSBURY ACADEMIC
LONDON • NEW YORK • OXFORD • NEW DELHI • SYDNEY

BLOOMSBURY ACADEMIC
Bloomsbury Publishing Plc
50 Bedford Square, London, WC1B 3DP, UK
1385 Broadway, New York, NY 10018, USA
29 Earlsfort Terrace, Dublin 2, Ireland

BLOOMSBURY, BLOOMSBURY ACADEMIC and the Diana logo are
trademarks of Bloomsbury Publishing Plc

First published in Great Britain 2022
This paperback edition published 2024

Copyright © Anna Tomaszewska, 2022

Anna Tomaszewska has asserted her right under the Copyright,
Designs and Patents Act, 1988, to be identified as Author of this work.

For legal purposes the Acknowledgements on p. vi constitute an
extension of this copyright page.

Cover design by Louise Dugdale
Cover image: Immanuel Kant Illustration from 19th century © clu/iStock

All rights reserved. No part of this publication may be reproduced or transmitted
in any form or by any means, electronic or mechanical, including photocopying,
recording, or any information storage or retrieval system, without prior
permission in writing from the publishers.

Bloomsbury Publishing Plc does not have any control over, or responsibility for,
any third-party websites referred to or in this book. All internet addresses given
in this book were correct at the time of going to press. The author and publisher
regret any inconvenience caused if addresses have changed or sites have
ceased to exist, but can accept no responsibility for any such changes.

A catalogue record for this book is available from the British Library.

A catalog record for this book is available from the Library of Congress.

ISBN: HB: 978-1-3501-9584-4
PB: 978-1-3501-9591-2
ePDF: 978-1-3501-9585-1
eBook: 978-1-3501-9586-8

Series: Bloomsbury Studies in Modern German Philosophy

Typeset by Integra Software Services Pvt. Ltd.

To find out more about our authors and books visit www.bloomsbury.com
and sign up for our newsletters.

Contents

Acknowledgements   vi

Introduction   1
1   Towards the radical Enlightenment: Setting the stage for a debate   7
2   Spinoza's God in Kant's pre-critical writings: A departure from theistic metaphysics   25
3   The moral atheist and a *Schwärmer*: Kant's critique of Spinoza   45
4   The primacy of the practical in Kant and Spinoza   67
5   Kant's religious rationalism and Spinoza   89
6   The enlightened church: Kant's contribution to debates on secularization   123
7   The divinity of reason in the *Opus postumum*   143
Concluding remarks   165

Notes   170
Bibliography   197
Index   212

Acknowledgements

This book is a result of research completed within the project funded by the National Science Centre in Poland from 2019 to 2023, titled *Between Secularization and Reform. Religious Rationalism in the Late 17th Century and in the Enlightenment* (grant no. UMO-2018/31/B/HS1/02050). Some preliminary research for the book was subsidized in 2018 by the De Brzezie Lanckoroński Trust run by the Polish Academy of Arts and Sciences. I would like to thank the Institute of Philosophy of the Jagiellonian University in Kraków for their kind and continuous support of my scholarly and academic pursuits. I am particularly grateful to the editors at Bloomsbury for their assistance and collaboration at all stages of the publishing process, and to the reviewers whose critical suggestions benefitted my work a lot. My special thanks, however, go to my family and friends – Hasse, Urszula, Krzysztof, Sari, Natalia, Marta, Magda and Jarosław – for their helpful and supportive presence during the whole process.

Introduction

According to a widespread view, held by representatives of opposite intellectual agendas, the Enlightenment stands at the headwaters of the contemporary processes of secularization.[1] Yet recent research on the topic has parsed the Enlightenment into different currents, depending on various accounts of its relation to religion. Thus, Margaret Jacob has coined the term 'secular Enlightenment' to capture the idea that a significant number of its protagonists 'made the secular world [their] point of departure', attempting to determine 'the purpose of human life… without necessary reference to a transcendent order'.[2] In contrast, David Sorkin has advocated the category of the 'religious Enlightenment' and claimed that 'the Enlightenment was not only compatible with religious belief but conducive to it. The Enlightenment made possible new iterations of faith.' As a result, in the late seventeenth and throughout the eighteenth centuries, 'religion lost neither its place nor its authority in European society and culture.'[3] The religious Enlightenment would be promoted by thinkers who sought the 'middle path' between faith and reason, aiming to reconcile confessional commitments with the advocacy of enlightened tenets: belief in science as a means of improving human life, freedom of speech and conscience, and toleration for different faiths and convictions. Such a description squarely corresponds to what Jonathan Israel featured as the 'moderate Enlightenment' and contrasted with a set of ideas derived originally from Spinoza and his acolytes, called the 'radical Enlightenment'. These ideas, says Israel, comprising 'toleration, personal freedom, democracy, racial equality, sexual emancipation and the universal right to knowledge',[4] would be selectively appropriated by moderate enlighteners and watered down to appear as compatible with the traditional forms of Christianity. For some, the resulting picture would be incoherent. According to Leo Strauss, for example, who defined the radical Enlightenment as an undertaking aimed at the critique of revealed religion,[5] the compromise sought by moderate thinkers resulted in 'self-deception and illusion'.[6]

Kant's critique of reason is often interpreted as a critique of the Enlightenment itself,[7] though his critical philosophy can also be read as an attempt to 'cope with the challenges' generated alongside the decline of the Enlightenment[8] by an 'increasing fragmentation of social and cultural positions' in Prussian society by the late eighteenth century, as Steven Lestition has proposed.[9] Kant's curbing of the cognitive pretensions of reason would thus be accompanied by an effort to safeguard reason's position as the guide in moral and political life. This critical approach to human rational capacities would then be regarded as a commitment to the 'middle path', characteristic of the moderate or religious Enlightenment. For instance, according to Allen Wood, Kant's approach should be described as promoting a reform of religion by confronting it with 'rationalist values', conducive to reconciling faith and reason.[10] Kant enters the path of 'religious reform', avers Wood, which is 'meant to effect a convergence of traditional religion with modern culture, its science and its morality. This process is to deepen and enrich both traditional religious faith and modern culture.'[11] Gordon Michalson, in turn, observes that 'for theologians influenced by the Enlightenment ideal of critical thinking, Kant charts a cause making it possible to embrace the intellectual standards of the day while retaining religious conviction.'[12] Kant's account of rational religion would then provide ideological underpinnings for liberal Protestant – and other Christian and non-Christian – theologies, opening the prospects for fitting in religion within a culture relying predominantly on the authority of science.

This book goes against the grain of this mainstream reading of Kant's views on religion as catering for the moderate Enlightenment theology and engages with the Straussian suggestion that the 'in-between' approaches either end up as inconsistent or veer towards the radical agenda – without pursuing Strauss's hermeneutics, though. Consisting of seven essays, the book seeks to cast light on different aspects of Kant's rational theology and religion against the background of recent debates on Enlightenment and its purported contribution to secularization. These aspects belong to both philosophical theology covering such topics as the existence of God and the relation between human and divine freedom, and philosophy of religion covering topics like the source of religious belief and the justification for religious institutions. I maintain that Kant wavers between offering a new 'rational religion' – that is, a religion originating in reason and justifiable by rational means – and a 'rationalizing' approach to revealed religion, especially in its Christian guise. Thereby his account can be placed among those of heterodox Christian thinkers and radical religious reformers – with all the consequences of this move related to the difficulties in properly assessing the secularizing potential of heterodoxy itself. In what follows, I present an overview of the issues addressed in subsequent chapters.

Thus, Chapter 1 argues that the dividing line between the radical and the moderate Enlightenment cannot be drawn that easily, if at all, and Kant's thought on religion is adduced as an example illustrating the point. Accordingly, several issues in his account are highlighted, such as a critical stance on the epistemic value of Scripture and recognition of the kind of religion that harbours a tendency to perpetuate heteronomous modes of action and foster an authoritarian mindset. It is emphasized that Kant was on the side of religious heterodoxy rather than atheism; thus, defining his position *vis-à-vis* the radical Enlightenment presupposes determining the relation between the Enlightenment radicals and radical religious reformers.

Chapter 2 discusses Kant's pre-critical 'possibility proof' for the existence of God against the background of a debate on some apparently Spinozist implications of the argument. Far from endorsing Omri Boehm's risky suggestion that the God of the young Kant turns into an extended being resembling Spinoza's substance, I propose that Kant's engagement with Spinozism might have contributed to the emergence of the critical philosophy as an alternative to theistic metaphysics. The critical Kant is no longer in a position to accommodate the divine grounding of possibilities (essences, including those actualized by human beings) within the view that makes freedom a prerequisite of moral action. Kant challenges the theistic doctrine of creation insofar as he holds that any kind of causal dependence of reason on God rules out reason's autonomy.

Chapter 3 portrays Kant as a critic of Spinoza by zooming in on two themes: the example of a 'virtuous atheist' in § 87 of the *Critique of the Power of Judgment* and the accusation of '*Schwärmerei*' (usually translated as 'enthusiasm'). Presenting different kinds of unbelief featured in Kant's texts, it argues that Kant makes room within his system for the so-called 'sceptical atheism' – an attitude that expresses itself in the rejection of the theological dogma and which, just like the critical philosophy, envisages morality as independent from religious belief. The virtuous atheist, instantiated by *Kant's* Spinoza, severs the link between theology and morality and, like Kant, prioritizes practical over theoretical rationality. Eventually, Kant even admits that the sceptic can have religion, which suggests that a certain form of unbelief can provide the starting point for developing 'moral faith'.

In Chapter 4, Spinoza's and Kant's views on the relation between theory and practice are compared. *Prima facie*, attributing the primacy of the practical to Spinoza runs counter to the general tenor of his philosophy, which recommends knowledge as a way to an ethical life. Yet for Spinoza the human mind suffers cognitive constraints, which makes it prone to generate 'inadequate ideas' and what could be called metaphysical illusions. Thus, Spinoza does not endorse a model on which cognition is supposed to guide our actions but rather a model on which action and cognition form a unity: it is when we are causally efficient that we entertain adequate ideas. Truth, on such an account, would be conceived as a result of our dynamic relation with reality. Arguably, also Kant's prioritizing practical rationality allows bringing out the constructive aspects in the activity of the human mind.

Chapter 5 situates Kant's philosophy of religion in the context of 'religious rationalism', a tendency to adjust revelation to the requirements of reason, spanning from the late seventeenth century through the Enlightenment era. To trace the junctures at which Kant's religious rationalism intersects with the early modern critique of revelation, some key passages of the *Religion within the Boundaries of Mere Reason* (1793/4) are discussed, such as the metaphor of two concentric circles, the 'definition' of religion and the theory of the prototype of a morally perfect humanity. Moreover, Kant's rationalist views on religion are set against the ideas of two German radical thinkers, Carl Friedrich Bahrdt and Johann Christian Edelmann, and against Spinoza's critique of revelation in the *Theological-Political Treatise*. For all these thinkers, the philosophical reason plays the role of the 'supreme interpreter' (RGV, 6:109) of Scripture.

Chapter 6 engages with Kant's idea of a rational or enlightened church. Despite making morality independent from religion – and providing foundations for secularism by separating religion and politics – Kant does not relegate the church from the so-called public sphere. Nevertheless, his approach is thoroughly revisionist. He does not defend ecclesiastical authority against the attacks of enlightened radicals but puts forward a project of the church as an ethical community – 'the kingdom of God on earth' (RGV, 6:134). The end of this project converges with the end of enlightenment understood as the development of rational autonomy. Kant's construal stumbles upon the apparent incompatibility between human autonomy and theonomy, required for an ethical community in the form of a church. An outline of a solution emerges from the theological fascicles of the *Opus postumum*.

These fascicles are the subject matter of Chapter 7, dealing with apparent contradictions in Kant's post-critical account of the divine and attempting to clarify the purport of what looks like the identification of God with practical reason. This 'deification' of reason results from Kant's retaining both the concept of God as moral legislator and the doctrine of autonomy, and brings about a transformation of his critical theology by challenging the doctrine of the postulates of practical reason. I claim that Kant's identification of God with the moral domain does not render the idea of God superfluous. The idea remains indispensable as part of the theory of practical self-positing (*Selbstsetzung*) and warrants autonomy as the foundation of an ethical community.

1

Towards the radical Enlightenment: Setting the stage for a debate

1.1. Two Enlightenments

Since Margaret Jacob's *The Radical Enlightenment: Pantheists, Freemasons and Republicans* (1981) and Jonathan Israel's *Radical Enlightenment: Philosophy and the Making of Modernity, 1650–1750* (2001), followed by a series of volumes on different aspects of the radical thought in the long 'Age of Lights', Enlightenment scholars have gained extra resources by means of which they could conceptualize the intricate relations between reason and religion in an epoch in which modern culture can be judged to have its roots. The dichotomy between the radical and the moderate Enlightenment, exploited by these scholars, would encourage a picture of the epoch as intrinsically polemical. Religion would figure in the centre of the polemics, with the advocates of the radical Enlightenment seeking to curb or even destroy its influence on morality and politics, and the advocates of the moderate Enlightenment trying to reconcile religion with 'enlightened values'.

With religion in focus, the radical *vs.* moderate Enlightenment distinction parallels the distinction between the secular and the religious Enlightenment, which also enlivens recent debates among intellectual historians.[1] The aim of this chapter is to suggest that, in the long run, the aforementioned dichotomies are untenable as they considerably oversimplify the dynamic of the relation between religion and the Enlightenment. Taking Kant as an example, we shall see that religious criticism, verging on the radical, would mingle with attempts at preserving religion by interpreting or 'reforming' it in light of rational principles, resulting in a new conception of religion as well as its role in private lives and the public sphere.

Characterizing the emergence of the term 'radical Enlightenment', Frederik Stjernfelt has noted that it would initially appear 'as a spontaneous, ordinary language construction', denoting things as diverse as 'deep revelation', 'thorough examination', 'progress' and 'critique of religion'. Throughout the nineteenth and towards the early twentieth centuries, the term 'radical Enlightenment' would develop into 'a more principal concept addressing an anti-religious, science-oriented, critical mode of thinking... exemplifiable in antiquity and the middle ages, and in different religious contexts'.[2] The more recent uses of the term also differ across the wide spectrum of the accounts of the radical Enlightenment. Accordingly, whereas Jacob has emphasized the importance of the 'new science' and 'secret societies' for the emergence of the movement,[3] Israel highlights monist materialism inspired by Baruch Spinoza (see below). For Martin Mulsow, the radical Enlightenment is not only an intellectual, but also a sociological category, designating socially estranged protagonists of 'philosophical micro-history' and marginal, 'often only "experimentally" freethinking' individuals unwittingly made into radicals by the public opinion.[4] Gianni Paganini, in turn, has brought seventeenth-century 'clandestine' manuscripts to the fore, arguing that they were pivotal for the formation of the 'radical' trend as they would target official heterodoxy, both religious and political.[5] Since much of the current debate on the radical Enlightenment has been shaped by Israel's contribution, in what follows we shall take a closer look at his description of the movement.

Israel has captured the key features of the radical agenda as a 'package of basic concepts and values', summarized in 'eight cardinal points':

> (1) adoption of philosophical (mathematical-historical) reason as the only and exclusive criterion of what is true; (2) rejection of all supernatural agency, magic, disembodied spirits, and divine providence; (3) equality of all mankind (racial and sexual); (4) secular 'universalism' in ethics anchored in equality and chiefly stressing equity, justice, and charity; (5) comprehensive toleration and freedom of thought based on independent critical thinking; (6) personal liberty of lifestyle... (7) freedom of expression, political criticism, and the press, in the public sphere; (8) democratic republicanism as the most legitimate form of politics.[6]

According to Israel, the above 'package' can be traced back to the thought of Spinoza, constituting 'a comprehensive and consistent system of naturalism, materialism, and empiricism, eliminating all theism, teleology, miracles, and supernatural agency'.[7] On Israel's proposal, it is due to the influence of Spinoza and Spinozism, a set of ideas propagated by a clandestine, transnational, 'fringe' movement, that reverence for science and the scientific method, to be applied to virtually all domains of human theoretical and practical activity, would replace reverence for religious authority and ethics based on Christian metaphysics.

'For the Radical Enlightenment', Israel contends, 'there is only one source of truth – science and scientifically based scholarship in the humanities – so that "science" understood as *Wissenschaft*... always and inevitably conflicts with and negates religious authority'.[8] Thus construed, the radical Enlightenment is supposed to yield political consequences such as the secularization of the public sphere: 'the elimination of theology from law, institutions, education and public affairs'.[9] In this way, Israel largely recapitulates Max Weber's claim about the development of science as the driving force of secularization that would thrive on the 'disenchantment' of the empirical world.[10] This claim, promoting the idea that the growth of scientific rationality functionally corresponds to diminishing the importance of religious faith, seems to rule out the conception of religion as compatible with rationality, or the idea that the domain of reason and the domain of religion may overlap. Yet the Enlightenment abounds in examples of stances that in one way or another manifest reconciliation between reason and religion.

Israel admits that a number of thinkers intended such a reconciliation, but attributes this attempt to a current he labels 'moderate Enlightenment'. The moderate Enlightenment would constitute a political project aimed at a thorough reform of thought and action on both the individual and the societal levels, to be executed primarily through education. However, despite aiming at a reform of thinking and mores, the moderate Enlightenment would strive to maintain the political and religious status quo, resulting thereby in an internally inconsistent set of ideas. The advocates of the moderate agenda 'aspired to conquer ignorance and superstition, establish toleration, and revolutionize ideas, education, and attitudes by means of philosophy but in such a way as to preserve and safeguard what were judged essential elements of the older structures, effecting a viable synthesis of old and new, and of reason and faith'.[11] Israel says:

> [T]he conservative moral and social theories of Locke, Voltaire, Montesquieu, Hume, and Kant were all expressly intended to avoid forging moral philosophy systematically on the basis of philosophical reason and nature, in the interest of salvaging major elements of tradition, custom, and theology. All these moral philosophers are by definition and by design not just inconsistent but wholly at odds with the consistent naturalism sought by Spinoza, Bayle, Boulainvilliers, Diderot, and d'Holbach. It was the moral theories of the hard-core French High Enlightenment... which follow Spinoza and Bayle in adopting a fully secular and universalist ethic based exclusively on the 'common good', equity, and equality, that were designed to be philosophically coherent and consistent.[12]

Israel charges the moderate Enlightenment with incoherence and attributes this incoherence to a discrepancy between theory and practice, the former based on rational principles and the latter on the ossified traditions of the pre-modern theological framework. In contradistinction to the moderate current, the radical Enlightenment would remain consistent, insisting on the scientific foundations of moral and political practice. Spinoza and Bayle would serve as paradigmatic instances of the radical, consistently rational, attitude, whereas the moderate thinkers would compromise on the requirements of reason, leaving out those domains which could be considered unfit for rationalization.

It seems, however, that Israel's charge results from an oversimplification of what was going on in the relation between Enlightenment and religion. First, his assessment of a certain (heterogeneous) group of thinkers as promoting an incoherent agenda is based on a narrow conception of rationality: a conception which reduces rationality to its scientific breed. Second, integrating religion into the rational foundations of the Enlightenment would not always entail breaking with the 'enlightened values' in order to 'salvage major elements of tradition, custom, and theology'. Rather, within the Enlightenment agenda striving to accommodate religion, or to make it compatible with reason, a breach in tradition would have to be undertaken. Third, and relatedly, Israel builds the distinction between the radical and the moderate Enlightenment on the dichotomy of reason and faith treated as two irreconcilable opposites. Yet, considering the tendency to rationalize religious faith, live among the late seventeenth-century and the Enlightenment heterodox Christians and religious reformers, Kant included, one of the intents of the enlighteners was to challenge the dichotomy. Some of these reformers would be inspired by Spinoza. Moreover, the distinction between reason and faith does not have to reflect the dichotomy of (scientific) knowledge and religion, as Israel is wont to urge; as we shall see in Chapter 5, for some radical reformers, such as Carl Friedrich Bahrdt, (true) religion could be a matter of knowledge, rather than mere faith.[13]

1.2. Does Kant belong to the moderate Enlightenment?

Israel's 'eight cardinal points', excepting those that sound a bit too anachronistic, like point 6 dealing with 'personal liberty of lifestyle', may in fact capture more than the agenda of the radicals alone. At any rate, it seems that even Kant, whom Israel has pictured as one of the leading conservatives in the 'Age of Lights', would subscribe to a significant number of these tenets. For Kant limits legitimate knowledge claims to the domain of scientific cognition, including mathematical truths and historical facts (cf. point 1 on the list of Israel's 'cardinal points'; on the status of historical cognition in Kant, see Log, 9:68 and 72–3). He rejects metaphysical speculation as the source of the cognition of supernatural realities, though without denying the existence of such realities (cf. KrV, A 753/B 781). The moral agency of finite rational beings, rooted in their capacity for self-legislation and in their dignity as 'ends in themselves', underlies the egalitarian tenor of Kant's critical thought (cf. 3; GMS, 4:434–6). Locating the 'supreme principle of morality' in rational autonomy, Kant endorses universalism in ethics (cf. 4; GMS, 4:440) and in the political domain regulated by the principle of innate freedom: 'the only original right belonging to every man by virtue of his humanity' (MS, 6:237).[14] He also defends freedom of thought exercised in the 'public use of reason' and conditioning humanity's 'emergence from… self-incurred minority' (cf. 5 and 7; WA, 8:35–7).[15] Kant's support for republican rule, which guarantees the division of responsibilities between the legislature and the executive, not only lies at the core of his projected conditions of global peace (cf. ZeF, 8:350–2), but is reflected in his tripartite 'moral concept of God' as legislator, ruler and judge (cf. 8; RGV, 6:139; V-Phil-Th/Pölitz, 28:1073).

Yet Israel contends that Kant's views qualify him as an adherent of the moderate Enlightenment. In support of this contention, Israel adduces the opinions of Karl Leonhard Reinhold and Karl Heinrich Heydenreich, who would hold that Kant 'not only crushed atheism, materialism, and Spinozism, but discredited Voltaire's irreverence and Hume's corrosive scepticism'. Accordingly, goes on Israel, quoting Kant's contemporaries, his 'breakthrough meant the philosophical restoration of Christianity and accepted morality to hegemony over learning, science, and the Enlightenment'.[16] Heinrich Heine, in the *History of Religion and Philosophy in Germany* (1833/4), who famously compared Kant to Robespierre, calling him 'the great destroyer in the realm of thought' and executor of the deist God,[17] also admitted that, eventually, Kant had to side with the defenders of Christianity. Feeling for the 'old Lampe', who after all did deserve to have a God, Kant would set out to restore theistic metaphysics under the guise of moral-practical philosophy.[18] Yet, in Heine's ironic description, Kant figures as a radical tormented by scruples, hence insincere in both his radicalism and his attempts to mitigate it. Was he then more radical or rather moderate along Israel's lines? In the remainder of this section, I will explore the second option, while examining the first one has to wait until section 1.4.

Accordingly, Kant's doctrine of postulates (cf. KpV, 5:122–134) – in particular, the existence of God and the immortality of the soul – presupposes the distinction between practical and theoretical reason, with the pretence of the latter to metaphysical cognition being curbed. Theoretical reason, with its ideas and principles, regulates empirical cognition (cf. KrV, A 669/B 697–A 702/B 730), but the fact of its competences regarding the cognition of the supersensible being transferred to practical reason makes it look as if for Kant it was not the case that 'there is only one source of truth – science and scientifically based scholarship'. Kant's 'postulates' are motivated by a 'need' of reason, and the beliefs this doctrine gives rise to are warranted by subjectively but not objectively sufficient grounds (cf. KpV, 5:144–6; WDO, 8:139–141). Against this background, Kant's claim about the primacy of practical reason (KpV, 5:119–121) may seem to involve diminishing the authority of science as the source of cognition. On the other side, the distinction between practical and theoretical reason, and connecting religion with the domain of the practical, has enabled a framework within which religious faith would find its place next to scientific developments. This position, according to Gordon Michalson, would be attractive for modern liberal Christians and 'progressive theologians', because it has provided them 'with a strategy for mediating between Christianity and the powerful new intellectual currents set in motion by the Enlightenment'.[19]

Apart from allowing a defence of the rationality of religion, as well as its relevance for individual lives, Kant's critical thought apparently delivers an argument against secularization understood as separation between religion and the state; that is, against 'the elimination of theology from... public affairs'. The argument assumes that a religious institution may serve as a 'vehicle' for introducing and maintaining 'the pure faith of religion' whose 'true end' consists in 'the moral improvement of human beings' (RGV, 6:106–112). Though Kant clearly sets moral and political laws apart (RGV, 6:95–6), he supports the idea that the 'visible church' promotes an ethical community and, to the extent that the moral and the political states (*Zustände*) overlap, religious institutions 'insert' morality into the public sphere.[20] Of course, this 'Kantian' argument is valid against secularization defined as complete relegation of religion from the public sphere, but not against those kinds of a secular regime that allow some forms of coexistence and collaboration between the 'church' and the 'state' as separate and independent bodies.[21]

If the aim of the moderate Enlightenment was to adjust religion to the progressive outlook based on the development of science and the emancipation of reason from the authority of tradition, this aim may seem to have been accomplished by Kant. Yet, to properly address the question of Kant's relation to the moderate and the radical agendas in the 'Age of Reason', the meaning of radicalism needs to be explicated.

1.3. But what do we mean by radical?

The sense of the 'radical' that informs contemporary debates, through the work of Israel, can be traced back to Leo Strauss. In *Spinoza's Critique of Religion*, Strauss identifies in Spinoza's critical reading of the Scriptures, expounded in the *Theological-Political Treatise*, an example of 'the critique of Revelation as attempted by the radical Enlightenment'. For Strauss, the radical Enlightenment has ancient roots, and Spinoza's historical exegesis of Scripture provides 'only one particular form, one particular stage of the critique of religion which was originated in Greek antiquity',[22] in particular among Epicurus and his followers. Strauss emphasizes the opposition between religion and science; religious criticism, on his account, would be undertaken with a view to replacing 'superstition' with the scientific study of natural causes. Strauss's radical Enlightenment is essentially atheistic, targeting religious orthodoxy and the ecclesiastical establishment. Clearly, setting reason and revelation, or religious orthodoxy, against one another inspires doubts as to the nature and purpose of those attempts to rationalize religious faith, of bringing religion into conformity with reason, that would characterize thinkers representing the 'moderate' side of the fray, such as Kant.

Discussing Strauss's approach to the moderate Enlightenment, Israel points out that the promise to make 'faith and Enlightenment, Christianity and modern philosophy, religion and science' mutually compatible would for Strauss eventually turn out to be 'a form of self-delusion, a means of soothing and comforting the intellectually lazy and feeble of mind'.[23] He would thus hold that 'in-between positions are merely forms of self-deception and illusion or else deliberate evasion and misleading of others, a morally questionable and dubious approach to philosophizing to which he accused Voltaire and Hume of being excessively inclined'.[24] The moderate Enlightenment should eventually acknowledge the superiority of the radical agenda – as long as it claims to be 'Enlightenment' – or abandon the authority of reason for the sake of safeguarding religious orthodoxy. From the Straussian point of view, the irony Heine directed at Kant would be well deserved.

For Epicurus, whose 'criticism of religion', as Strauss says, 'is one source, and the most important one, of seventeenth century criticism of religion', happiness (*eudaimonia*) would be achievable through 'the elimination of all fear of the gods'.[25] The aim of religious criticism is therefore ethical, though among the arguments which form part of radical religious criticism, one can distinguish three kinds: epistemological, moral and political.

The epistemological critique would consist in denying epistemic value to revealed religion. Revelation, in light of the arguments of this kind, does not mediate truth about any reality. The arguments can be found in Spinoza's *Treatise*. For example, carefully analysing the contents of Scripture, Spinoza discovers that the text is full of contradictions and inconsistencies, and that certain books – such as the Pentateuch and the Book of Joshua – could not have been authored by the individuals to whom they have traditionally been attributed: in all likelihood, it was Ezra, not Moses, who compiled the Five Books.[26] A different author, Neoplatonic Porphyry, in a treatise *Contra Christianos*, challenged the truth of the Book of Daniel, otherwise acknowledged by Jesus. Given that God is omniscient, and Jesus did not recognize the dubious character of the Book, how could Jesus be God?[27]

Religious criticism appealing to moral reasons could be summarized by the claim that religion breeds moral harm, that is, evil. Accordingly, Epicurus would argue that religion makes a virtuous life hardly possible because it instils the fear of gods in people's minds, hence it deprives them of tranquillity and of happiness.[28] Religion is a product of imagination that attempts to compensate for the lack of causal explanations of such occurrences as earthquakes, droughts, floods and other natural disasters by inventing stories about gods punishing humans for their alleged wrongdoings. Unable to predict the course of what shall happen to us in the future, yet seeking to obtain such predictions, we imagine that unbeknownst to us transcendent powers control our lives. The solution to the problem raised by the moral critique of religion lies in science: uncovering regularities and laws governing natural phenomena will supposedly put an end to the feats of imagination and diminish uncertainty about the future; thus, once ignorance has been weeded out by scientific investigations, religion will lose its appeal.[29]

Politically motivated arguments against religious orthodoxy would unmask it as a structure devised for the sake of garnering power by a privileged caste of priests, by way of perpetuating the ignorance of the masses and their vulnerability to emotional manipulation. These arguments would also highlight the conflictual potential latent in particular creeds, to be overcome by a rational alternative to revealed religion.[30] Hermann Samuel Reimarus's Wolfenbüttel Fragments depicting Jesus as a teacher of morality whose agenda, overall innocuous, would be exploited by the apostles with a view to political gains, provide a good example of what can be labelled the political criticism of revealed religion.[31]

Now, since in light of the criticism outlined above religion brings neither truth nor the moral and political good, it seems that the most reasonable step one can take is to reject it. Atheism emerges as a response to the requirements of our rationality: the desire for truth and the good.

The critique of revealed religion in the spirit of Strauss is bound to face problems, though. Namely, it seems to ignore the fact that many of the early modern critics of religion did not end up concluding that atheism should be endorsed and propagated. Much of their criticism was indeed religiously motivated – by the desire to 'purify' or 'reform' religion, adjusting it to 'enlightened values'. Besides, the Straussian picture of the radical Enlightenment as a straightforward passage from religious criticism to atheism crudely omits religious heterodoxy. Yet, as Winfried Schröder has argued, conflating heterodoxy with atheism renders an inadequate account of the history of early modern ideas.[32] And then another problem emerges with regard to the meaning of 'atheism'. During the seventeenth and eighteenth centuries, the term acquired distinctively polemical purport. Jakob Friedrich Reimann's *Historia universalis atheismi et atheorum* (1725) testifies to this trend: among the authors accused of the advocacy of unbelief, one can find not only 'Casimir Lyszincki', 'Adrianus Curbachius', 'Matthias Knutzen' and 'J.C. Wachterus', but also Aristotle, Martin Luther and Nicolas Malebranche.[33] In early modernity, the label 'atheist' was distributed generously and usually as a smearword against ideological opponents, critics of orthodoxy or reformers.

The early modern era abounds in the instances of religious criticism, motivated by reformatory zeal and targeting the alliance between the clerical and the state rule,[34] which distinguish themselves from the instances of the advocacy of atheism encountered in clandestine literature, such as *Theophrastus redivivus* and *Symbolum sapientiae*.[35] Yet, given the exposition of the radical Enlightenment as a critique of religious orthodoxy, the question arises which side of the Enlightenment dichotomy should the heterodox critics of religion be assigned to. By placing Voltaire and Reimarus, and many other deistic thinkers, in the same camp with, say, the 'Catholic enlighteners', such as Hugo Kołłątaj and Benedikt Werkmeister,[36] we risk obliterating the distinction between heterodoxy and the kind of religious orthodoxy that would work towards accommodating the key Enlightenment ideas (reform through education, scientific progress, toleration, freedom of conscience, etc.) within a religious worldview. Associating deism with the *atheistic* radical Enlightenment, however, requires a revisionist reading of its protagonists, which has to avoid taking some claims which they made explicitly, at face value. Or should we rather agree with Charles Taylor that 'deism can be seen as a half-way house to contemporary atheism'?[37] The problem with this proposal seems to be that its plausibility depends on adopting the point of view of the orthodox. Moreover, even if deism could agree with atheism in the critique – and rejection – of revelation, there were thinkers, such as the members of 'Spinoza's circle', who questioned the orthodox interpretations of revelation, allied with Spinoza in his critique of the ecclesiastical establishment, yet did not discard revelation as such and did not advance an atheistic position.[38] Does interpreting revelation along the lines of Spinoza's critical exegesis of the Scriptures count as a move towards the radical Enlightenment, or does it still qualify as adherence to the moderate mainstream? The radical enlighteners would espouse a secularizing agenda, but so did the Christian dissenters inspired by Spinoza, like Jarig Jelles and Lodewijk Meijer, who severed their ties with the organized religion and practiced their faith in a group of like-minded friends.[39]

In light of the foregoing, the following dilemma emerges: (1) If we associate heterodox thinkers with the radical Enlightenment, then the radical Enlightenment will no longer constitute an atheistic movement, *pace* Strauss (and Israel). (2) If the heterodox thinkers are included among the representatives of the moderate Enlightenment, the differences between orthodoxy and heterodoxy will be obliterated. Strauss would solve the dilemma by divorcing the 'in-between positions' from the Enlightenment agenda, the choice being left between unbelief and orthodoxy.[40] But could not the scope of the 'radical' be expanded so as to comprise heterodox thinkers without denying the essentially religious character of their views?

1.4. Rethinking Kant in light of the radical Enlightenment

Keeping in mind the doubts concerning the scope of the radical Enlightenment, we can now return to Kant. As we shall see below, all three kinds of arguments spelled out in the previous section as featuring the critique of revealed religion can be found in Kant in one form or another.

Thus, as much as for Spinoza, revealed religion for Kant does not yield any cognition of supernatural realities, though it can provide us with the cognition of 'teachings that are ethical and hence related to reason' (RGV, 6:156). The reason why revelation does not produce knowledge of the divine, according to Kant, is that due to our epistemic constraints, we are cut off from the possibility of knowing objects that cannot be represented as belonging to the domain of appearances. This is precisely the outcome of Kant's critique of dogmatic metaphysics, undertaken in the Transcendental Doctrine of Elements of the first *Critique* (cf. KrV, A 707/B 735). The epistemic restrictions we face call for the necessity to posit the distinction between faith and knowledge, a project Kant adumbrates in the second-edition Preface and in the Doctrine of Method (KrV, B xxx, A 822/B 850–A 829/B 857). Though he does not deny the mere *possibility* of divine revelation, Kant's rational faith rules out the possibility to *experience* the divine: 'if God should really speak to a human being', avers Kant in *The Conflict of the Faculties*, 'the latter could still never *know* that it was God speaking,' hence it is for us 'impossible' to 'apprehend the infinite' and '*be acquainted with* it as such' (SF, 7:63). Consequently, we cannot read Scripture as mediating truths about supernatural realities, because we cannot 'dare to have unlimited trust in every word' of the Gospels as a historical account (Br, 10:178).

There are also moral arguments challenging revealed religion that can be found in Kant, though they are differently motivated than the Epicurean arguments recounted by Strauss. First, by being religious, in one of the senses of the term, one can come into conflict with morality. A person who would be religious in this morally contentious sense would be one who places her principal motive of action in the will of God. Yet to follow the divine will as such means for Kant to let one's actions be motivated by an object external to one's own will. Now, a will motivated by an object external to it is a will that is motivated heteronomously – a condition which precludes moral action (cf. KpV, 5:64). Thus, by encouraging people to follow the divine will, religion would perpetuate heteronomous modes of acting and hence undermine morality.

Second, revealed religion may encourage taking 'morally indifferent actions', such as 'festivities, professions of faith in revealed laws, and the observance of precepts that belong to the form of the church' (RGV, 6:106) – that is, that should serve as a 'vehicle' of moral faith and so be treated as a means – for the essential content of religious faith. Replacing genuine service to God which, in Kant's view, consists in the fulfilling of 'their duties toward human beings (themselves and others)' with manifestations of 'passive obedience' to God (RGV, 6:103), a religious person ends up embracing a morally corrupting 'mercenary faith'. Kant describes this faith as follows:

> The faith of a religion of service is... a slavish and mercenary faith (*fides mercenaria, servilis*) and cannot be considered as saving, because it is not moral. For moral faith must be a free faith, founded on pure dispositions of the heart (*fides ingenua*). The one faith fancies to please God through actions (of *cultus*) which (though laborious) yet possess no moral worth in themselves, hence are actions extracted only through fear or hope, the kind which also an evil human being can perform.
>
> (RGV, 6:115–16)

Thus, there is a form of religion based on revelation, which Kant refers to as the 'religion of service', that promotes conduct entirely void of moral significance. Conflating the religion of service with 'a purely moral religion' (RGV, 6:103) is detrimental to morality because it reassures believers that morality does not form the essential part of religion. If morality is not essential for religion, being immoral might well be compatible with being religious; thereby the 'religion of service' invites immorality.

Political arguments levelled against revealed religion can also be found in Kant's texts. For he acknowledges the conflict-generating potential of religion, observing that 'the so-called religious struggles, which have so often shaken the world and spattered it with blood, have never been anything but squabbles over ecclesiastical faiths' (RGV, 6:108). Kant assigns to 'ecclesiastical faith' the role of a 'vehicle' of 'pure religious faith' and emphasizes its 'statutory' character (cf. SF, 7:37). Misunderstanding the role of the ecclesiastical faith, contingent upon particular circumstances of history and culture, has contributed, as he notices in the essay on *Perpetual Peace* (1795), to divisions between individuals and societies that stand in the way of the possibility of global peace (ZeF, 8:367). The root cause of this misunderstanding is ingrained in the ecclesiastical faith itself. Kant identifies it as 'spiritual despotism' (RGV, 6:176n.; cf. WA, 8:40) and characterizes as attempts to constrain the church members' free use of reason by, for example, setting up 'a permanent religious constitution not to be debated publicly by anyone' (WA, 8:39). The authoritarian bent he recognizes in religion manifests itself in the tendency of religious authorities to compete with the authorities of the state for the rule over society (cf. WA, 8:40). This tendency to enforce 'authoritarian patterns of belief', as James DiCenso has put the point, and thereby to inculcate moral heteronomy, can in turn be exploited by governments to reinforce political despotism.[41]

From the arguments outlined above we can see that Kant was a critic of revealed religion himself. Does this qualify him as an adherent of the radical Enlightenment, or is he nevertheless committed to the apparently inconsistent moderate agenda? The answer may hinge on the interpretation of Kant's concept of rational religion – as well as its relation to historical faiths based on particular 'revelations'. Does the 'religion of reason' provide an alternative to a certain revealed religion, namely Christianity, or does it rather constitute an attempt at 'reforming' that religion along rationalist lines? Or are these two options ultimately reducible to one another? Clearly, unlike Spinoza on Strauss's and Israel's reading, Kant does not strive to replace revealed religion with science. Rather, 'pure moral faith' and scientific cognition in tandem are supposed to compensate for the deficiencies of religion which the critical approach to revelation has made manifest.

1.5. Kant and Spinoza

As said, according to Israel, the ideas traceable to Spinoza provided the driving force behind the radical Enlightenment, an initially clandestine 'sect' that was to expand into a movement whose subversive ideas 'would ultimately transform the world'.[42] Israel contends:

> Spinoza's contribution was arguably the most crucial in crystallizing what is here termed Radical Enlightenment, primarily because his thought goes further than that of the other six [*scil*. Bacon, Descartes, Hobbes, Locke, Bayle and Leibniz – A.T.] in undermining belief in revelation, divine providence, and miracles, and hence ecclesiastical authority, and also because he was the first major advocate of freedom of thought and the press as distinct from freedom of conscience and the first great democratic philosopher.[43]

Accordingly, given the pivotal role of Spinoza in the emergence of the radical Enlightenment, to be able to locate Kant in relation to the movement, we should investigate whether and if so, then to what extent he engaged with Spinozist ideas.

Many sources, both old and new, confirm Spinoza's relevance for the German Enlightenment. For example, Moses Krakauer, a nineteenth-century rabbi and author of a dissertation on the history of Spinozism in Germany, wrote: 'one can say of Spinozism that, apart from the Kantian system, it is the most notable for taking part in the struggles for spiritual development in Germany'.[44] According to Walter Sparn, a contemporary scholar, 'it is exactly in confrontation with Spinoza that the capacities of the Protestant orthodoxy reached their limits. This confrontation with Spinoza belongs to the most important processes that brought this orthodoxy to its historical end.'[45] Manfred Walther explains that around 1700 in Germany Spinoza was gaining popularity not only among 'educated intellectuals who worked outside the universities' but also among church officials and academics who 'were shocked by Spinoza's naturalism but attracted by the rationalist approach', which they would find helpful in promoting 'free research and liberty of expression'.[46] Despite the pervasiveness of Spinoza's ideas in German philosophical and theological culture, Kant is believed not to have had much acquaintance with them. Friedrich Heman, an early twentieth-century interpreter of Kant and Spinoza, adduces the words of

Georg Hamann, who was to report that 'Kant confessed... that he had never thoroughly studied Spinozism'.[47]

Kant may not have studied Spinozism *thoroughly*, yet there are traces of his engagement with Spinoza's ideas present throughout his philosophical output, although he would not always render these ideas adequately and he would avoid directly referring to the Dutch thinker. I will discuss some of the instances of Kant's references to Spinoza in more detail in subsequent chapters of this book, especially in Chapters 2, 3 and 7; here, a brief overview of them should suffice.

Accordingly, in the pre-critical period, Kant offers an argument for the existence of God as the necessary ground of possibilities. Given that he does not specify what exactly the grounding relation consists in, there remains an option to construe the relation in terms of God instantiating certain basic realities, such as extension or space. Despite Kant's express denial of an extended nature to God (cf. BDG, 2:85) in *The Only Possible Argument in Support of a Demonstration of the Existence of God* (1763), in an earlier essay, titled *Universal Natural History and Theory of the Heavens* (1755), he compares eternal 'manifestations of the highest being' to 'the infinity of space' and identifies 'the basic matter itself, the properties and forces of which underlie all changes' as 'a direct consequence of the divine existence' (NTH, 1:310).

In a note dated late 1770s or early 1780s, Kant diagnoses that Spinozism forms 'the true conclusion of dogmatic metaphysics' originating from Plato's theory of ideas (HN, 18:434–6). From this point of view, given that the *Critique of Pure Reason* promises to 'make room for faith' (KrV, B xxx) by curbing the aspirations of reason in the area of theoretical cognition, followed by a rebuttal of the arguments of dogmatic metaphysics, Spinoza would be the main adversary of the critical philosophy. Omri Boehm has even argued that in the Antinomy of Pure Reason (KrV, A 405/B 432–A 567/B 595) it is Spinoza – and not Leibniz – that represents the rationalist side of the contention.[48]

In the *Critique of Practical Reason*, Kant makes use of Spinozism to argue for transcendental idealism as the only way to safeguard freedom, the necessary condition of morality (KpV, 5:101–2). In the *Critique of the Power of Judgment*, he involves Spinoza – a 'righteous atheist' (KU, 5:452) – in an argument which aims to show that rejecting belief in God leads to practical inconsistency, '*absurdum practicum*' (V-Phil-Th/Pölitz, 28:1083). Fending off accusations of Spinozism in an essay *What Does It Mean to Orient Oneself in Thinking?* (1786), which voices Kant's position in the controversy between Friedrich Heinrich Jacobi and Moses Mendelssohn on Gotthold Ephraim Lessing's rumoured pantheism, Kant contends that an unbridled use of reason, which he calls 'lawless', will likely bring about reason's self-destruction, with consequences for morality and political life (WDO, 8:145–6).

Finally, in an unfinished draft of a work titled 'Transition from the Metaphysical Foundations of Natural Science to Physics', published as the *Opus postumum*,[49] the name of Spinoza surfaces more frequently than in any of Kant's earlier writings. Kant juxtaposes there Spinoza's 'transcendental idealism' with his own: whereas according to Spinoza, we are supposed to 'intuit everything in God' (OP, 22:56), thus God serves as the condition of the possibility of our cognition, according to Kant we need the idea of God to be able to refer to ourselves as moral agents (OP, 21:80–1; 21:93) – members of the 'kingdom of ends' adumbrated in the *Groundwork of the Metaphysics of Morals* (GMS, 4:433–6) and/or the 'ethical community' introduced in the *Religion* (cf. RGV, 6:94f.). For the late Kant, God plays the crucial part in the doctrine of 'practical self-positing', that is, the way in which we constitute ourselves as moral agents.

As this cursory overview of textual evidence spanning all stages of Kant's philosophical career shows, Kant treats Spinoza as an important point of reference for his critical thought, albeit an adversary. Yet, given that his picture of Spinoza captures no more than a 'spectre', invoking associations with materialism, atheism, determinism and monist metaphysics, this may also testify to no more than that Kant, like many others in his time, would – for merely polemical or self-advertising purposes – invent 'a Spinozism that would go beyond the letter of Spinoza'.[50] As Max Grunwald metaphorically put it, 'so colourful was the attire of the master that among those who believed to have taken on his colours, one can find diverse elements in an array.'[51] Spinozism would appear in a number of guises and eventually create an ideological patchwork: whereas John Toland read Spinoza as a pantheist, Grunwald observes, Bayle and Voltaire ascribed to him materialism in metaphysics and Epicureanism in ethics. Thus, as much as there is a Spinoza of Toland, Bayle and Voltaire, there can also be Kant's Spinoza.

Remarkably, Kant does not appeal to Spinoza in any of his arguments in the *Religion*. This might be due to the character of his work which presupposes 'only common morality... to understand the essentials of this text, without venturing into the critique of practical reason, still less into that of theoretical reason' (RGV, 6:14). Instead, Spinoza would appear in those texts of Kant in which methodological issues are dealt with, issues relevant for other philosophers but not for the general public. Yet this explanation of Kant's being silent about Spinoza in the *Religion* ignores the fact that it is in this work that salient commonalities emerge between the two thinkers in their approach to religion. Several such features seem particularly evident; namely, as much as Spinoza, Kant defies the idea that faith includes an epistemic component, such as *knowledge* about the existence and/or nature of God (cf. RGV, 6:154n.). Essentially, for Kant and Spinoza alike, faith has a practical dimension: whilst the former makes clear that religion needs no 'assertoric knowledge', the latter argues that 'simple obedience is a way to salvation'.[52] Furthermore, both thinkers place the core of faith in a universal, reason-based ethic which can also be traced back to the Scriptures. Spinoza acknowledges that at its core Scripture mediates the uncorrupted 'Word of God' inscribed in our hearts or minds and enjoining us 'to obey God with all one's heart by practicing justice and charity'.[53] Kant, in turn, adducing passages from Matthew to corroborate the unity between revelation and rational faith, writes about a teacher who 'was the first to advocate a pure and compelling religion' based on morality and 'made this universal religion of reason the supreme and indispensable condition of each and every religious faith' (RGV, 6:158). Finally, like many heterodox Christians influenced by Spinoza – the circle of Collegians,[54] radical pietists such as Johann Christian Edelmann or rationalists like Carl Friedrich Bahrdt[55] – Kant proffers a reinterpretation of the Christian dogma which imbues it with ethical meaning while ignoring its suprarational dimension.

There are also interpreters who see more than superficial affinities between Kant and Spinoza. Thus, according to Yirmiyahu Yovel, in his writings on religion Kant would resort to the kind of the strategy of subterfuge that could be attributed to Spinoza as well. 'Spinoza's work and letters', avers Yovel, 'provide ample proof of his mastery of what Strauss called "the art of writing within persecution". And the language of Kant's *Religion* must be read like Spinoza's'.[56] Following Yovel's suggestion, one could explain Kant's silence about Spinoza in his main work on religion as part of the strategy. Kant could then be perceived as acting analogously to 'Spinozist' preachers involved in the public spread of heterodoxy, tacitly mediating Spinoza's ideas.[57] The problem with Yovel's remark, though, is that Kant quite openly expresses his non-orthodox interpretations of the Christian revelation. This pertains to his critique of the practical relevance of the trinitarian dogma (cf. SF, 7:39), of the doctrine of the hereditary nature of original sin (RGV, 6:40–1) or of vicarious satisfaction (RGV, 6:116–117) (Kant thinks that these doctrines remove from us the burden of responsibility for our own evil and for moral regeneration).

Thus, Kant's avoidance of mentioning Spinoza can be motivated differently than by willingness to hide his genuine views. First, as noted earlier, he might not be sufficiently familiar with Spinoza's ideas on religion advanced in the

Theological-Political Treatise. Second, even supposing that he was aware of these ideas, he could consider them largely unproblematic while rejecting the view that these ideas need to be grounded in one-substance naturalist metaphysics expounded in the *Ethics*. The affinities between Kant's and Spinoza's views on religion would then indicate that there is a kind of religion that can be endorsed irrespective of one's theoretical or metaphysical commitments. One could dub the religion of this kind a rational religion.

2

Spinoza's God in Kant's pre-critical writings: A departure from theistic metaphysics

2.1. Introduction

In the second-edition Preface to the *Critique of Pure Reason*, Kant states that 'through criticism alone can we sever the very root of materialism, fatalism, atheism, of freethinking unbelief, of enthusiasm and superstition, which can become generally injurious, and finally also of idealism and skepticism, which are more dangerous to the schools and can hardly be transmitted to the public' (KrV, B xxxiv). This statement belongs to his manifesto featuring critical philosophy as a project which aims to 'deny knowledge in order to make room for faith' (KrV, B xxx). But he also specifies the objective of his critique, of which the idealism of Descartes and Berkeley and the scepticism of Hume constitute but a part. As the first half of the above quote tells us, the critical philosophy is supposed to provide a remedy against the pernicious influence on the general public of what would be associated with Spinozism in Kant's times.

For the critical Kant, Spinozism epitomizes dogmatic metaphysics (cf. HN, 18:436), and, as we shall see in more detail in Chapter 3, he even considers Spinoza's philosophy to be conducive to enthusiasm (*Schwärmerei*), a label which has predominantly negative purport. Yet, the *early* Kant was himself a dogmatic metaphysician: for he had not yet recognized the transcendental ideality of space and time (cf. KpV, 5:102). Does his drawing the connection between Spinozism and dogmatic metaphysics imply that he admits having embraced Spinozism in his early writings? Michela Massimi, for instance, thinks

---

Earlier versions of this chapter appeared as: Anna Tomaszewska, 'Spinoza's God in Kant's Pre-Critical Writings: An Attempt at Localizing the "Threat"', *Kant Studies Online* (2015): 65–102, and Anna Tomaszewska, 'Bóg Spinozy w pismach przedkrytycznych Kanta', in *Filozofia Oświecenia. Radykalizm – religia – kosmopolityzm*, ed. Justyna Miklaszewska and Anna Tomaszewska (Kraków: Wydawnictwo Uniwersytetu Jagiellońskiego, 2015), 305–29.

that Kant's appeal to Spinozism as the consequence of dogmatic metaphysics marks a rhetorical strategy devised to bolster the authority of the critical philosophy as the only safeguard of reason against its own erratic tendencies.[1] Omri Boehm and Andrew Chignell, on the other side, tend to regard Kant's appeal to Spinozism as a diagnosis of the turn taken by his pre-critical philosophy itself.[2] When Jacob Freudenthal, Spinoza's late nineteenth-century biographer, discussed Kant's solution to the problem of the possibility of the interaction of substances, he would also encounter 'the spirit of Spinozism' at the beginning of Kant's philosophical career.[3]

This chapter does not provide a definitive answer to the question whether Kant endorsed Spinozism in his pre-critical writings. Rather, it makes an attempt to see in what way Kant's engagement with some ideas that can be considered representative of Spinozism might have encouraged the emergence of the critical philosophy and Kant's own position as an alternative to dogmatic metaphysics (2.4). It also traces various modes of Spinoza's presence in Kant's early thought: as both the latter's possible corollary and a negative point of reference. I start with an outline of the 'possibility proof'[4] as developed in *A New Elucidation of the First Principles of Metaphysical Cognition* (1755; henceforth: *Nova Dilucidatio*) and *The Only Possible Argument in Support of a Demonstration of the Existence of God* (1763; henceforth: *Beweisgrund*) (2.2), and then proceed to discuss some possible Spinozist consequences of the argument (2.3).

2.2. The possibility proof

In chapter 3 of the 'Second Book of the Transcendental Dialectic', Kant lists three kinds of arguments for the existence of God, which he strives to refute: physico-theological, cosmological and ontological. He closes with the remark that 'there are no more of them, and there also cannot be any more' (KrV, A 591/B 619). The 'possibility proof' is not on the list. The reason for this might be that Kant would not consider this argument a 'proof', but at most a 'ground for a proof'. In a note dated early 1780s, he refers to the argument as a proof, and 'one which affords us the most satisfaction', yet he adds that the argument 'cannot establish the objective necessity of an original being but establishes only the subjective necessity of assuming such a being'. As such, Kant continues, 'this proof can in no way be refuted, because it has its ground in the nature of human reason.' One needs to assume 'a being which is the ground of everything possible, because otherwise [one] would be unable to know what in general the possibility of something consists in' (V-Phil-Th/Pölitz, 28:1034). This need to assume the ground of possibility reflects reason's quest for 'the unconditioned', which it 'necessarily and with every right demands in things in themselves for everything that is conditioned' (KrV, B xx). Thus, Kant's mature judgement is that although the 'possibility proof' does not establish the existence of God, it expresses the intrinsic tendency of human reason to inquire into the sufficient ground of phenomena.

The 'possibility proof', as formulated in the *Nova Dilucidatio* and the *Beweisgrund* essay, moves through the following steps: First, (1) Kant distinguishes between possibility and existence and characterizes existence in terms of 'absolute positing' (BDG, 2:73–4). Then, (2) he introduces two kinds of possibility: logical and real (BDG, 2:77–8). The logical possibility of an object means that the object can be conceived in a contradiction-free way. An object is really possible if something exists which the object is related to as its consequence or otherwise (BDG, 2:78). Further, (3) Kant considers the consequences of the assumption that nothing exists (BDG, 2:79). In this counterfactual scenario nothing would be really possible and the thought that nothing exists would also be empty of content. Hence, the thought that nothing exists proves to be self-invalidating. Thus, (4) the mere possibility of any scenario requires that something exist and therefore something must exist necessarily. Now, since *all* that is possible requires that something exist, there has to be one necessary being which grounds everything that is possible (BDG, 2:82–3). Kant thinks that (5) such a being must be identical with God, from which he draws the conclusion that God exists necessarily (i.e. is a necessary being) (BDG, 2:84–9).

Thus outlined, the argument seems to contain gaps, especially in its passage from (4) to (5). In what follows (2.2.1–3), we shall go through the stages of the argument more closely.

2.2.1. Existence

Already in his pre-critical argument, Kant abandons the key assumption of the ontological proof in its Cartesian or Leibnizian version, stating that 'existence is not a predicate or a determination of a thing' (BDG, 2:72; cf. KrV, A 598/B 626). To justify this move, Kant employs an example from Leibniz's *Discourse on Metaphysics*, that is, Julius Caesar, enjoining:[5]

> Draw up a list of all the predicates which may be thought to belong to him, not excepting even those of space and time. You will quickly see that he can either exist with all these determinations, or not exist at all. The Being who gave

existence to the world and to our hero within that world could know every single one of these predicates without exception, and yet still be able to regard him as a merely possible thing which, in the absence of that Being's decision to create him, would not exist.

(BDG, 2:72)

Kant's reference to Leibniz is not incidental; it evokes the doctrine of complete concept, that is, the concept that comprises all the predicates that can be attributed to a particular object, which shall yield true judgments about the object. The complete concept expresses the (particular) essence of the object to which it applies and allows the identification of the object across possible worlds.[6] Now, suppose that there are two countable sets of predicates – $\{P, Q, R, E\}$ and $\{P, Q, R\}$ – associated with the essences of two different objects: C_1 and C_2, respectively. Suppose, also, that predicate E stands for 'existence'. Given these suppositions, if God decides to create C_2, C_1 and C_2 will turn out to be identical. But this cannot be the case because, as has been assumed, they have different essences. Thus, if existence is a predicate, God cannot create an object without changing the object's essence and the idea of possible worlds is not plausible because whenever we try to think about possible scenarios involving actual objects, we will refer to different, even if significantly analogous, objects.[7] Therefore, if one subscribes to the doctrine of complete concept and seeks to maintain the distinction between actuality and possibility, one should drop the idea that existence is a property that can enter the concept of a thing. Instead, Kant suggests, existence should be conceived in terms of 'absolute positing' (*Setzung*) of an object (cf. BDG, 2:73). Yet, since 'the concept of positing or setting is perfectly simple' and 'identical with the concept of being in general', it cannot be analysed into simpler concepts and, as such, has no definition.[8] The concept of existence, then, is '*almost* unanalysable' (BDG, 2:73–4; italics A.T.), being explained merely in terms of positing.

2.2.2. Possibility

The distinction between two aspects of possibility – logical (formal) and real (material) – is illustrated by another example in the *Beweisgrund* essay. Kant says:

> A triangle which has a right angle is in itself possible. The triangle and the right angle are the data or the material element in this possible thing. The agreement... of the one with the other, in accordance with the law of contradiction, is the formal element in possibility. I shall also call this latter the logical element

in possibility... The something, or that which stands in this agreement, is sometimes called the real element of possibility.

(BDG, 2:77–8)

The formal element of possibility, an object's being logically possible, consists in the concept of the object being free from contradiction. As Kant explains in the *Nova Dilucidatio*, the material element of possibility amounts to something being 'given' (PND, 1:395), or posited, in the concept of the object. This something could be called the content of the concept. Accordingly, 'triangle' and 'right angle' furnish the conceptual content of 'right-angled triangle'. To test whether a concept is contradiction-free, one should analyse it by splitting the concept into its constitutive elements and examining the relations between them. Since without concepts having content one would not be able to carry out this test – for there would be nothing 'available for comparison' (PND, 1:395) – the 'material element' of possibility seems to be epistemically prior to the formal one. Thus, the lack of contradiction and content-possession jointly imply conceivability; a concept without content would be empty, not inconsistent, and could not express any thought (cf. KrV, A 51/B 75).[9] Of course, we can conceive of things for which it is impossible to exist, such as a human being made of ice from Peter Yong's example,[10] but as long as such things are conceivable, their concepts must relate to something existing *via* the material element of possibility which they express.

However, a difficulty awaits with regard to what in the *Beweisgrund* essay would be called real possibility. Namely, if real possibility is explained in terms of conceivability (i.e. the lack of contradiction *and* content), how can we account for the possibility of transition from mere conceivability to existence? Hence, Chignell proposes to add a third condition of real possibility, which he calls 'real harmony'.[11] The human being made of ice does not fulfil this condition, because 'being human' and 'being made of ice' cannot be jointly exemplified in an object, that is, they cannot harmoniously coexist. According to Chignell, 'the metaphysical harmony of two or more (non-intentional) predicates... can only be explained or grounded by the *non-intentional* predicates of some actual being.'[12] In other words, to see why a set of properties contained in the concept of an object satisfies real harmony, one needs to be able to trace the instantiation of the properties to an existing object. Yet Chignell's proposal runs the risk of making 'real harmony' dependent on a random fact that itself calls for a further explanation.

To avoid the problem that Chignell's real harmony condition might generate, we can replace this condition with an alternative one, namely the requirement that the existence of an object be compatible with particular domain-specific laws. Kant's example of two 'opposite motive forces' helps to clarify the point:

The motive forces of a body in one direction and an equally strong tendency in the opposite direction do not contradict each other.... However, one motive force annihilates the real consequences of the other motive force; and since the consequences of each motive force by itself would otherwise be a real movement, the consequence of both together in one subject is nought.... From this it is also apparent that real opposition is something quite different from logical opposition or contradiction, for the result of the latter is absolutely impossible.

(BDG, 2:86; cf. NG, 2:203)

The reason why the effects of two opposite motive forces affecting an object annul one another, that is, generate 'a real repugnancy' (BDG, 2:86), should be sought in the laws of dynamics (here: Newton's first law), rather than in the fact that the coexistence of opposite forces, without mutual cancellation of their effects, has not been instantiated in an object. Consequently, real possibility would imply concordance with laws specific for a particular domain of objects. This means that the human being made of ice would not be really possible not because nothing could jointly instantiate the properties of being human and being made of ice, but because the instantiation of these properties jointly is precluded by the biological laws for living beings such as humans.

However, the subordination to domain-specific laws, though presumably fit for replacing the condition of real harmony, does not provide the ultimate explanation of the real possibility of a thing or state of affairs, either, as the 'fiery body' example (BDG, 2:80) makes clear. For real possibility has to eventually be 'grounded' in the existence of a thing that either exemplifies or causally accounts for the reality of an object or state of affairs, such as the fiery body or two opposite motive forces. Adducing the example, Kant says:

[T]he agreement of the predicate, fiery, with the subject, body... is inherent in the concepts themselves.... But I proceed to ask: is then a body itself possible in itself? Not being permitted to appeal to experience, you will enumerate the data of its possibility, namely extension, impenetrability, force... You must, however, give me an account of what entitles you so readily to accept the concept of extension as a datum.... Suppose that you can now no longer break up the concept of extension into simpler data in order to show that there is nothing self-contradictory in it... then the question will be whether space and extension are empty words, or whether they signify something.... *If space did not exist, or if space was not at least given as a consequence through something existent*, the word 'space' would signify nothing at all.

(BDG, 2:80–1; italics A.T.)

Accordingly, to probe into the real possibility of a fiery body, one should first analyse the concept 'fiery body' into its constituents until one arrives at 'simple notions',[13] like the notion of space, further unanalysable. The content of such notions must then be determined by what they refer to. There are two options with regard to what a simple notion may refer to: it may designate either an existing object or a consequence of the existence of an object. The real possibility of a fiery body would thus depend on *either* the actual instantiation of extension or space by an existing object, *or* the existence of something that could account for the possibility of extension or space. Consequently, two models of grounding real possibility emerge: in the first, grounding would consist in certain basic properties being instantiated by something that exists, and in the second, grounding a real possibility would require that something exist which causally underlies this possibility.

2.2.3. The necessary being

In the next stage of the argument, Kant assumes that nothing exists – an assumption that seems to capture a logical possibility (cf. BDG, 2:81–2). However, he continues, if 'I cancel all existence whatever and the ultimate real ground of all that can be thought therewith disappears, all possibility likewise vanishes, and nothing any longer remains to be thought' (BDG, 2:82). For if nothing exists, the simple notions that one would arrive at in the course of the analysis of a concept which expresses a particular possibility do not refer to anything. Since the claim that nothing exists annuls all possibility, Kant contends that it is 'absolutely necessary' that something exist if anything is to be possible. In other words, the existence of something is the necessary condition even of the conceivability of any state of affairs and any meaningful employment of concepts. Without certain basic notions bearing referential properties, no meaningful thought could ever be formulated: the very act of predication expressed in a judgement requires that something exist.

But, having established that it is necessary that something exist if anything is to be possible, Kant makes an apparently unwarranted leap to the existence of the necessary being, claiming that 'there exists an absolutely necessary being' which 'contains the ultimate real ground of all other possibilities' (BDG, 2:83), that is, God, characterized as 'one in its essence… simple in its substance… a mind according to its nature… eternal in its duration… immutable in its constitution; and… all-sufficient in respect of all that is possible and real' (BDG, 2:89). Kant summarizes his argument thus:

All possibility presupposes something actual in and through which all that can be thought is given. Accordingly, there is a certain reality, the cancellation of which would itself cancel all internal possibility whatever. But that, the cancellation of which eradicates all possibility, is absolutely necessary. Therefore, something exists absolutely necessarily.

(BDG, 2:83)

The claims: (a) 'Necessarily something exists' and (b) 'There exists a necessary being' are not equivalent, though, as the range of the modal operator is different in both cases. In (a) the operator ranges over the entire proposition, whereas in (b) it is embedded within the proposition; hence the difference between (a) and (b) could be captured by means of the *de dicto vs. de re* modality distinction, respectively. Claims (a) and (b) have different truth-conditions: for (a), it suffices that there exist a universe *A* consisting of a series of objects that come into being consecutively, with the incipient existence of one object and the perishing existence of the other object overlapping just for a millisecond. Since the existence of *A* hinges on there always being in it a finite, contingent object, it is the case that necessarily something exists in *A*. The truth-conditions of (b) require the existence of a universe *B* containing a necessary being, that is, a being that cannot cease to exist and thus exists eternally, uncreated, without a beginning or an end. In both universes *A* and *B*, (a) is true; what (a) says is the case with regard to *B* because there can be no point at which the necessary being would cease to exist. But scenario *A*, in which something exists of necessity, does not imply the existence of a necessary being, for the objects existing in *A* can be contingent.

One may conjecture that what motivates Kant's conflation of (a) and (b) – but does not properly justify transition from one claim to another – is his reliance on the rationalist 'harmony of reason and nature',[14] on which there would occur correspondence between the contents of a proposition and the reality it represents, or on the principle of sufficient reason,[15] on which the existence of any object or state of affairs would have to be 'grounded' ultimately in the existence of a necessary being. But these motivations are far from fully satisfactory. For, first, if the main difference between (a) and (b) is captured in terms of the *de dicto vs. de re* distinction, such a difference is metalinguistic and does not represent the properties of the objects which each proposition is supposed to refer to. Second, Kant indeed rejects the alternative in which possibilities would be grounded by transient, contingent beings, or even a plurality of necessary beings (cf. BDG, 2:84), for on this alternative, relations between such beings would be in need of a further ground. Thus, to avoid infinite regress, the existence of one necessary being grounding all realities, as well as relations between them, should be posited. Still, such an account might generate the problem of grounding with regard to the relation between the necessary being and other realities – a version of Plato's third-man argument. Michael Della Rocca has therefore suggested that the idea of grounding should be dropped, yet this may lead to abandoning the principle of sufficient reason.[16]

Interestingly, there might be one more way to explain what looks like Kant's conflation of (a) and (b). Namely, we can think of the *series* of consecutively existing objects making up universe *A* as one with the necessary being, subject matter of claim (b). In an alternative universe *C*, the necessary being would be identical with the sum total of all contingent beings coming into and out of existence. The key difference between this scenario and the scenario in *A* is that *C* unlike *A* satisfies Kant's requirement for the ground of relations between the plurality of objects and therefore also the principle of sufficient reason. Yet, and importantly, to identify the necessary being with the sum total of contingent beings is to invite the conception of God that – in its Baylean interpretation that some have considered an oversimplification[17] – would be widely attributed to Spinoza in Kant's times.

Though, as we shall see, Kant denies allegations of Spinozism and formulates anti-Spinozistic arguments, this may not suffice to drive Spinozism away. For even if he does not identify the necessary being with a congeries of finite objects, significant aspects remain under which Kant's necessary being may be viewed as approximating the God of Spinoza. First, as Yitzhak Melamed has argued, Spinoza's God is 'nothing but existence';[18] so is Kant's necessary being insofar as existence is required to ground real possibility. In other words, whatever attributes Kant's God might have, the possibility argument itself does not seem to warrant assigning to God more than existence, which is barely analysable, other features of the divine entity (cf. BDG, 2:89) being derived from the philosophical and theological tradition Kant would partake of. Second, since the very conceivability of things hinges on whether something exists, and ultimately on the existence of the necessary being, the divine existence accounts for what Kant has called the material or real element of possibility. This material element of possibility would be given together with the existence of God. Kant's God would therefore embody, as he frames it in the first *Critique*, 'an All of reality (*omnitudo realitatis*)' and 'a transcendental substratum, which contains as it were the entire storehouse of material from which all possible predicates of things can be taken' (KrV, A 575/B 603–A 576/B 604). Or, as he puts it metaphorically in a much later essay on the 'real progress of metaphysics' (1793/1804), the necessary being would 'contain the wherewithal for the creation of all other possible things, as the marble quarry does for statues of infinite diversity' and as such would 'fall very much under the suspicion (despite all protestations against Spinozism), that as a universally existing being He is identical with the universe' (FM, 20:302). These formulations clearly recall Spinoza's conception of God; in what follows, Spinoza's trail in Kant's pre-critical theology will be followed more closely.

2.3. Spinoza at Kant's door

At the close of the third part of his comparative essay on Kant and Spinoza, Friedrich Heman remarked that though one cannot rule out the possibility that Kant's philosophy, 'as much as Leibniz's, contains elements which can be interpreted as conducive to Spinozism and cognate with it', it has been 'proven that Kant was not in any case aware of them, that he protested against them and would not allow Spinozism into his system.'[19] This remark is rather misleading with regard to Kant's awareness; for he must have realized at least the possibility that his argument could be read as a proof for the existence of Spinoza's God. This is because he took pains to distinguish his conception of God from the conception in which 'God, the necessary and infinitely perfect being, is indeed the cause of all things that exist, *but he does not differ from them*', which Bayle attributed to Spinoza.[20]

To fend off possible charges of Spinozism, Kant stresses that God is 'a mind according to its nature' (BDG, 2:89) and has understanding and will which are incompatible with extension: 'The impenetrability of bodies, extension and such like, cannot be attributes of that which has understanding and will' (BDG, 2:85). Furthermore, he says, the world cannot be 'an accident of God, for there are to be found within [it] conflict, deficiency, changeability' (BDG, 2:90–1), that is, imperfections which one cannot attribute to an all-perfect being. Also, the pre-critical Kant subscribes to a version of the argument from design when he says that due to its perceivable order and beauty, the world must originate from 'an intelligent creator' and a 'Wise Being' (BDG, 2:123–5). Suggesting that the occurrence of order and beauty follows from the existence of a being that thinks and has good will, thus that possesses intentional properties, Kant insists that 'from the point of view of its possibility, extensive harmony is never adequately given in the absence of an *intelligent ground*' (BDG, 2:124; italics A.T.). Moreover, he explicitly rejects ontological monism, saying that 'God is not the only substance which exists; all other substances only exist in dependence upon God' (BDG, 2:91).

Later, in lecture notes on the *Philosophical Doctrine of Religion*, collected in Kant's critical period, we can also find criticisms of Spinoza's 'faulty definition of substance' as an entity whose existence does not need the existence of another entity (*'cuius existentia non indiget existentia alterius'*) and the claim that this misconstrual brought Spinoza to an absurdity according to which 'God and the world were one substance and that apart from the world there is no substance anywhere' (V-Phil-Th/Pölitz, 28:1041). On Kant's proposal, substance is defined not in terms of *'aseitas'*, but as a being that 'exists for itself, without being a determination of any other thing', a notion that our own experience of ourselves as agents is supposed to make clear (V-Phil-Th/Pölitz, 28:1042).

Despite the above textual evidence, Boehm contends that in the critical period Kant would realize that he had been committed to Spinozism, because '*he had made extension an attribute of God*'.[21] Yet, given an alternative account of grounding, which we shall discuss in 2.3.2, the claim about the early Kant attributing extension to God, albeit unwittingly, might not be entirely correct and Boehm's reading seems to rely on much of Chignell's view of grounding as instantiation. In 2.2.2 we could see that Kant left the possibility open to think of grounding in terms of causation rather than the instantiation of basic properties.

On the other hand, Boehm is right when it comes to Kant's self-attribution of Spinozism, or so a number of his critical reflections on the theme seem to suggest. Accordingly, in the *Critique of Practical Reason*, Kant presents Spinozism as a consequence of not endorsing transcendental idealism with regard to space and time (KpV, 5:102). In a similar vein, in *Metaphysik Pölitz*, one can read: 'If I assume space to be a being in itself, then Spinozism is irrefutable, i.e., the parts of the world are parts of the divinity. Space is the divinity; it is united, all-present; nothing can be thought outside of it; everything is in it' (V-Met-L2/Pölitz, 28:567). However, when it comes to the corollaries of his pre-critical theology, Kant seems to be concerned more about human freedom than the nature of God. For he insists that unless one endorses the transcendental idealist account of space and time, one runs the risk of turning human freedom into an illusion and the human being into 'a marionette or an automaton, like Vaucanson's' (KpV, 5:101).

Thus, the critical Kant appeals to the 'threat' of Spinozism to argue for transcendental idealism as the only safeguard against Spinozist determinism. Kant's argument can be outlined as follows: (1) Unless one opts for the ideality of space and time, one will end up attributing divinity to the world or its parts. (2) 'Deifying' the world or its parts thwarts the possibility of human freedom. Therefore, (3) salvaging the possibility of human freedom requires that transcendental idealism be endorsed. *Pace* Boehm, this argument does not identify the *main* problem entailed by Spinozism, potentially flawing the theology of the early Kant, in the conception of God as an extended being. Rather, Kant's critical argument targets the transcendental realist conceptions of space and time, and that regardless of the way in which the grounding relation would be construed. The sources of Kant's self-attributed Spinozism must therefore lie elsewhere than Boehm has located them. This issue will be brought back to the fore in section 2.4.

2.3.1. Grounding possibilities

According to Kant's transcendental idealism, space and time constitute *a priori* modes by means of which we can represent empirical objects, rather than being properties of these objects themselves, that is, as they would be independently of the epistemic relation (cf. KrV, A 369; A 491/B 519). On this account, spatial and temporal properties of objects should be traced back to the structures of the human mind. Kant calls the view which denies this claim and offers an alternative explanation of space and time transcendental realism. Accordingly, if he held, in the *Nova Dilucidatio* and the *Beweisgrund* essay, that spatial and temporal properties have their source in God's 'grounding' real possibilities, he clearly subscribed to transcendental realism. But what would grounding possibilities by God consist in on such an account?

The notion of grounding is spelled out both in Kant's published works and in the lecture notes, some of them also recounting the views of other authors, discussed by Kant. To begin, let us look into a passage from the *Beweisgrund* essay: 'Since the necessary being contains the ultimate real ground of all other possibilities, it follows that every other thing is only possible in so far as it is given through the necessary being as its ground. Accordingly, every other thing can only occur as a consequence of that necessary being' (BDG, 2:83). The German word rendered as 'consequence' is *Folge*. This word can mean both the result of a causal process and the conclusion of a reasoning. Consequently, we can understand by grounding either a causal or a logical relation, or – given the conflation of reasons and causes, following the rationalist assumption about the 'isomorphism' of thought and being[22] – probably both. A bit more specific description can be found in the notes from Kant's lectures on Baumgarten's metaphysics, collected by Herder (1762–64):

> Now properly no substance can contain the ground of the accident in the other, if it does not at the same time contain the ground of the substantial power and of the existence of the other. I cannot become the ground of a thought in another if I am not at the same time the ground of the power that produces the thought: in this manner God is the ground.
>
> (V-Met/Herder, 28:52)

Herder's note suggests the following conception of grounding: To say of an object x that it contains the ground of an accident A of an object y does not mean to say solely that x causes y having A. Rather, to be a ground of A in y also means for x to endow y with a 'power' whereby y can itself produce A. Thus construed, grounding would consist in bringing about the causal efficacy of an object. One could then call it second-order causality. More precisely, grounding would come down to a kind of double causality since it would manifest itself in both causing an object and bringing about, or contributing to, the object's causal efficacy.

The above description of grounding can be read as expressing an insight into the nature of creation, whereby God endows finite beings with 'powers' (essences) which they will then develop and use in affecting other finite beings in determinate ways. Thus, in the act of creation some of the divine power would be transferred onto finite beings in such a way that God would remain the further or remote cause of the effects brought about by creatures. Thinking of grounding in terms of creation is entirely legitimate in light of Kant's picture of God, presented in the *Nova Dilucidatio*, as 'the creator, the ultimate ground of effects, and the fertile ground of so many consequences' upon which, once it is posited, 'other grounds follow, and others from them, down through the ages which follow, in accordance with an ever constant law' (PND, 1:339). Accordingly, to say that God grounds possibilities means to attribute to God the role of the first cause or rational explanation of the realization of possibilities: the source of the causal efficacy of created objects through which possibilities can be actualized.

In *Metaphysik Pölitz* (early 1790s), the distinction appears between logical and metaphysical ground, of which the latter is said to belong 'under the concept of causality'. The distinction is accompanied by definitions of ground as 'that upon which something follows in a wholly necessary way', 'that upon which something follows according to necessary rules' and 'that whereby, when it is posited, another thing is determinately posited' (V-Met-L2/Pölitz, 28:548–9). The ground can be connected with its consequences either in the way of subordination, or coordination. We can trace this distinction back to the Inaugural Dissertation (1770), where Kant claims that as a 'necessary substance' God can be related to the world exclusively as a cause (MSI, 2:408). The world is subordinated to God and therefore God must be an *'ens extramundanum'* (V-Phil-Th/Pölitz, 28:1041). Objects in the world remain instead to one another in the relation of *commercium* (*Wechselwirkung*), that is, mutual interaction (V-Met-L1/Pölitz, 28:196; cf. V-Phil-Th/Pölitz, 28:1043).[23] Logical grounds are based on the principle of identity, whereas real grounds on the principle of causality, according to which 'something is posited or canceled' (V-Met-L2/Pölitz, 28:549). The distinction between logical and real grounds reflects two notions of necessity – associated by Kant in the critical period with analytic and synthetic judgements – and marks Kant's departure from his earlier conflation of reasons and causes.

2.3.2. Grounding Spinoza's God

Though the pre-critical Kant tends to explain grounding as a causal relation, argues that the relation between God and realities should be described as one of subordination, and rejects the Spinozist idea of the cause of itself (*causa sui*) (cf. PND, 1:394),[24] his account of the relation between God and possibilities evokes pantheistic associations. These associations emerge from passages such as the following:

> [T]he data for anything which can be thought must be given *in* the thing of which the cancellation is also the opposite of all possibility; and... therefore, that which contains the ultimate ground of one internal possibility also contains the ultimate ground of all possibility whatever (BDG, 2:84–5; italics A.T.).

> The data of all possibility must be found *in* the necessary being either as determinations of it, or as consequences which are given through the necessary being as the ultimate real ground. It is thus apparent that *all reality is*, in one way or another, *embraced by the ultimate real ground* (BDG, 2:85; italics A.T.).

Kant's idiom echoes Spinoza's, in which the latter describes the relation between substance (God) and modes as inherence of the latter in the former.[25] If the 'data of possibility' inhere in God, according to Kant, they must be divine determinations, or properties, analogously to Spinoza's modes that are determinations of substance which he equates with God. Yet Kant talks about possibilities not only as determinations of the divine being, but also as consequences which follow from the divine existence.

Boehm thinks that the distinction between determinations and consequences is spurious. His argument is that had Kant considered consequences self-subsisting, the possibility proof would be equivalent to a cosmological argument, which it nevertheless is not. According to Boehm, 'consequences, like determinations, are properties of the necessary being; they inhere in it. In this sense all possibility depends on a single being – it is in this sense that if that being didn't exist, nothing would be possible.'[26] The problem with Boehm's reading, though, is that besides not taking Kant's protestations against Spinozism seriously, it misconstrues the sources of what looks like Kant's pre-critical Spinozism (for an alternative reading of these sources, see 2.4.). To challenge Boehm's interpretation, it seems sufficient to explain grounding in terms of an *intentional* relation between God and possibilities. However, such a construal does not suffice to dispel the Spinozist 'threat' running at a deeper level of Kant's pre-critical metaphysics and identified by Kant himself in his later writings. In the remaining part of this subsection, an answer to Boehm's challenge will be discussed, and in section 2.4 we shall see why even successfully dealing with this challenge fails to clear the early Kant of the accusation – or indeed self-accusation – of Spinozism.

On a reading alternative to Boehm's, which can be labelled intellectualist, possibilities grounded by God can be conceived as ideas in the divine mind. Textual evidence adduced at the beginning of section 2.3 shows that for Kant God is a spiritual, not a material or extended being: an infinite mind exercising understanding and will. Relatedly, elaborating on the divine wisdom as the ground of the beauty and order of nature, Kant says that in 'a Wise Being, in the absence of which none of these natural things would themselves be possible', there inhere '*the essences of . . . natural things*' which 'are united into such regular relations' (BDG, 2:125–6; italics A.T.). Thus, as divine ideas, possibilities can be 'given' together with and 'follow' from God's existence as its consequences without this necessitating that God instantiate such properties of the empirical world as extension or space. According to Yong, who supports the intellectualist reading, 'Kant seems to believe that an intellectual order can be grounded only by an intellect. . . . it is precisely such an order that constitutes the domain of possibility.'[27] In a similar vein, Noam Hoffer identifies Kant's real possibilities with essences in the divine mind.[28]

The intellectualist reading encounters a difficulty, though. Recall Kant's doctrine of simple notions. According to this doctrine, there are certain fundamental properties, such as extension or space, yielding the 'matter' of possibility, and either instantiated by the ground of all possibilities or following from it as the consequences of its existence. Should space be instantiated by God, it would have to inhere in the divine substance as modes inhere in Spinoza's God or Nature. If it were to be explained by a more basic constituent of reality, extension or space could not be designated by a simple notion.

The above concern has been addressed by the advocates of the intellectualist interpretation. Accordingly, Christopher Insole places spatial relations outside God as the consequences of the essences following from the divine mind: in the picture he proposes, spatial relations would emerge as a result of the dispositional properties of substances. Insole attributes to Kant the position that 'although God can choose whether or not to create a particular substance, and whether or not to place it in connection with other substances, God cannot choose all the relational properties of a substance, some of which are fixed by its essence.'[29] On the intellectualist reading, spatial properties are generated as consequences of relations between objects that are created by God and whose essences are determined by the divine understanding. God grounds possibilities in that he provides a unitary framework for interactions between substances (*commercium*). The intellectualist construal seems thus to concur with the interpretation of grounding, discussed in section 2.3.1, as double causality which would consist in God's 'empowering' a thing to exercise its own causal capacities. Still, the above-mentioned difficulty has not been addressed, because it seems that the intellectualist solution requires renouncing the simplicity of some fundamental notions, like extension or space, by making them derivative of something more basic, such as the relations between objects and the laws of geometry by means of which these relations can be described.

2.4. Transcendental idealism, divine creation and human freedom

In light of Kant's view on his earlier work, expressed in the critical period, it is rather clear that the intellectualist reading does not suffice to dispel the 'threat' of Spinozism. According to the argument outlined in section 2.3, Kant associates Spinozism with transcendental realism, which he considers unfit for safeguarding the possibility of freedom. 'Spinozism' thus epitomizes determinism and Kant employs the label to discredit the position of his philosophical adversaries, in particular Leibniz (cf. ÜE, 8:225).[30] To see why failing to endorse the ideality of space and time is for Kant conducive to determinism, we should first investigate what kind of view on human freedom can be associated with Kant's pre-critical account of God as the ground of possibilities.

On the intellectualist reading, God provides the ground of possibilities by creating substances endowed with the intrinsic properties (essences) that enable them to enter into relations with other substances, and thus to generate relational properties. For example, the intrinsic properties of physical objects make it possible for the objects to enter causal relations, as a result of which space emerges as a field of interactions between substances. Spatial properties would then be contingent upon the existence of bodies and their properties such as force. The empirical world construed in this way must be deterministic throughout, with space and time presupposing causal relations between objects. Since human beings belong to the empirical world, only God being transcendent to the causally determined spatio-temporal framework, human freedom would have to be exercised in the midst of empirical constraints.

Indeed, in the pre-critical period Kant holds freedom to be compatible with a deterministic stance, more specifically, with human actions being 'regarded as determinate' and 'their opposites… excluded' (PND, 1:400) insofar as the actions follow from 'an inner principle' (PND, 1:404), namely one's desires or inclinations. 'To act freely is to act in conformity with one's desires', says Kant, 'and to do so… with consciousness. And that is certainly not excluded by the law of the determining ground' (PND, 1:403). Thus, according to the early Kant, freedom consists in acting in accordance with one's nature or essence 'designed' in the divine mind: 'the ultimate ground… of the internal possibility of things' (BDG, 2:100). (Noteworthy, Kant distinguishes two kinds of dependence on God: moral, whereby an object's existence depends on the divine will, and non-moral, whereby an object's essence depends on the divine intellect.)

Yet, thus construed, the idea of freedom espoused by Kant in the pre-critical period strikes a Spinozist note. For to be free, on Spinoza's definition in Part One of the *Ethics*, means to exist and act in conformity with one's nature: 'That thing is said to be free [*liber*] which exists solely from the necessity of its own nature, and is determined to action by itself alone.'[31] Spinoza thinks that in this sense only God is genuinely free. Since at the time of authoring the *Nova Dilucidatio* and the *Beweisgrund* essay Kant was committed to what he later termed transcendental realism, he had no resources to think of our exercise of freedom outside the empirical, causally determined world. In this picture, whichever action one considers free must also be regarded as possessing underlying physical causes, and freedom consists then in no more than the possibility to describe occurrences in space and time in a way that involves reference to mental states.

From Kant's critical perspective, though, developed in the *Groundwork* and the second *Critique*, the compatibilist account of freedom does not suffice to safeguard morality, and that for two reasons: First, it makes no room for the idea that human action is free if and only if its springs transcend the spatio-temporal framework (on Kant's pre-critical compatibilist account,[32] reasons and causes would be one and the same thing under two different descriptions). Second, the idea that an action is free if it is a consequence of the God-given nature of the agent does not cohere with autonomy (self-legislation) as the principle of all moral actions. In the critical period, Kant thinks that if the principle of one's actions were outside practical, morally legislative reason, one's actions could not have proper moral motivation, hence in the end they could not be moral (cf. GMS, 4:442–4).

Kant's pre-critical theology invites a thoroughly deterministic framework within which subjects are supposed to act. Yet in what way does transcendental idealism succeed in transforming this framework into an indeterministic one? Let us consider two scenarios, corresponding to Kant's pre-critical and critical accounts of freedom, respectively. In the first scenario, God creates physical objects and finite rational beings and imparts causal power to them; the objects, in turn, generate relational properties such as spatial and temporal determinations, and finite rational beings act in accordance with the nature with which they have been equipped, thus following their inclinations and desires. In the second scenario, God creates finite objects and rational beings, and equips them with particular capacities, but now the features of the empirical world hinge on the cognitive setup of the human mind: things in themselves are neither causally determined nor spatial and temporal. Causality bifurcates thus into the empirical and the noumenal kind,[33] the former being dependent on the human mind and the latter on God. The second scenario would allow for thinking of actions as determined by non-empirical grounds and thereby would make room for freedom as 'an absolute causal spontaneity beginning from itself a series of appearances that runs according to natural laws' (KrV, A 446/B 474; cf. KrV, A 803/B 831).

The concern remains, though, that even in the second scenario moral autonomy cannot be salvaged. This concern has to do with the account of grounding as double causality, discussed in 2.3.1. On this account, grounding consists in bringing about both the existence of an object and the object's causal efficacy. Thus, even if the subject had the capacity to begin a new series of events 'from itself', which freedom as 'causal spontaneity' comes down to for Kant, this capacity would have to be imparted to her in the act of creation by God. Thus, even if the subject's actions were not empirically determined, their 'ultimate' ground would be located outside the subject, that is, in the divine will or intellect.

Kant was aware of this difficulty: in a passage of *Religion within the Boundaries of Mere Reason*, inquiring into the compatibility of divine creation with the religion of reason, he expresses doubts as to whether divine creation and human autonomy as the ground of moral action can be put together. It is worth quoting the passage in extenso:

> It is... totally incomprehensible to our reason how beings can be *created* to use their powers freely, for according to the principle of causality we cannot attribute any other ground of action to a being, which we assume to have been produced, except that which the producing cause has placed in it. And, since through this ground (hence through an external cause) the being's every action is determined as well, the being itself cannot be free. So through our rational insight we cannot reconcile the divine and holy legislation, which only applies to free beings, with the concept of the creation of these beings.
>
> (RGV, 6:142)

The above quote evidences that the critical Kant recognized the 'threat' of what Kimberly Brewer and Eric Watkins refer to as 'theological determinism'.[34] The problem of theological determinism does not seem to disappear once transcendental realism about space and time has been replaced by transcendental idealism. The problem originates in Kant's pre-critical theology, or more generally, in the rationalist metaphysics which he would subscribe to back in that period, and in light of which the divine grounding was spelled out in terms of what we have called double causality.

The question of Kant's views on the relation between God and human freedom is a complex one (I return to this question in 7.4); Insole, for example, observes that 'when Kant worries about the question of how a being who is "derived from another" [i.e. created – A.T.] can be free, he takes the view that God is an alien cause on the creature'.[35] This seems to imply that Kant may think that it is impossible to accommodate human autonomy within a theistic picture. Somewhat paradoxically, having eliminated (by introducing transcendental idealism) the kind of 'Spinozism' that would consist in 'deifying' space – an accusation that also Newton's conception of space as 'divine *sensorium*' had to face[36] – Kant would fall into the kind of 'Spinozism' that would require denying God's creation on pain of thwarting the possibility of human autonomy.

Yet the passage quoted above does not have to be read as implying that much, the more that Kant employs the concept of creation throughout his critical writings, for example when he describes humanity as the end of *creation* (cf. RGV, 6:6, 60). The passage, quoted above in extenso, derives from the 'General remark' closing Part Three of the *Religion*, in which Kant explicates 'three mysteries revealed to us through our reason', the first of them being 'the mystery of the *call*' of rational beings to an ethical community (RGV, 6:142). Kant argues there that we cannot explain our 'citizenship' in the ethical community, which has God as its sovereign, by relying on the traditional Christian doctrine of God's creating finite rational beings. The doctrine is incomprehensible, according to Kant, since the existence of free and rational agents escapes explanation in causal terms. It is thus a 'mystery' of reason that we remain under divine legislation, and so in a sense, depend on God, even though our relation to God cannot be traced back to any act establishing an ontological dependence of finite rational beings on their 'creator'. The doctrine of creation should therefore be put aside to the realm of mere 'speculation' (RGV, 6:143).

There are some 'radical' consequences which can be drawn from Kant's denial of the comprehensibility of creation, though. First, as unfathomable for human reason, there is no need that this theistic doctrine, especially in its credal format, pass for an indispensable element of rational faith. Second, if construing the relation between God and human beings in terms of the creation of the latter as rational and free by the former surpasses our rational capacities, there have to be alternative ways of thinking of the dependence of human beings on God, more fit for our rational capacities. We will explore these ways in some of the subsequent chapters, especially 6 and 7, examining the suggestion that Kant could locate the relation at issue in human rationality.

3

The moral atheist and a *Schwärmer*: Kant's critique of Spinoza

3.1. Preliminaries

In the first-edition Preface to *Religion within the Boundaries of Mere Reason*, Kant famously claims that although morality 'in no way needs religion... but is rather self-sufficient by virtue of pure practical reason' (RGV, 6:3), nevertheless it 'inevitably [*unumgänglich*] leads to religion, and through religion it extends itself to the idea of a mighty moral lawgiver outside the human being' (RGV, 6:6). Since religion is not a prerequisite of morality, being religious does not guarantee that one will also be moral. Yet the reverse seems to hold: being moral is supposed to be conducive to religiosity. Hence, an irreligious person should at the same time be immoral. Kant makes this point clear in the first *Critique*, where he declares that should he ever lose faith, based on moral grounds, he would become 'contemptible in [his] own eyes', because the moral principles on which the faith rests would be 'subverted' (KrV, A 828/B 856).

However, in § 87 of the *Critique of the Power of Judgment*, he introduces the figure of a moral atheist, whom he equates with Spinoza – a 'righteous man... who takes himself to be firmly convinced that there is no God and... also no future life' (KU, 5:452). In light of his claims opening the *Religion*, there being such a figure as 'Spinoza' amounts to a paradox, if not a contradiction in terms; it may as well form part of a thought experiment in an argument that proceeds like an indirect proof.[1]

Kant's argument in the third *Critique* defends the practical untenability of atheism and shows that a rational agent should rather endorse faith in God. But, as will be argued in this chapter, Kant's attitude to the lack of religious belief is more complex than the outcome of his argument seems to suggest. The figure of the righteous unbeliever can be traced back to Pierre Bayle's entry 'Spinoza' in his *Dictionnaire historique et critique* (1697). The righteous unbeliever may engender a paradox, but given that Spinoza did exist, invoking the figure cannot be reduced to a thought experiment for the sake of an indirect proof. In fact, Kant's statements about particular cases of unbelievers are not as negative as his enunciations concerning atheism as such, and sometimes not negative at all. Thus, arguably, there is a form of what Kant refers to as atheism that the critical philosophy can accommodate. The question is what the kind of unbelief that would be compatible with the critical philosophy would amount to.

This is a relevant question, especially in the context of the debates outlined in Chapter 1, and addressing it might help us better determine Kant's relation to the radical Enlightenment. For example, it can be plausible to claim that Kant is closer to the radical side of the fray if there are genuine and essential differences between his and, say, John Locke's attitude to atheism. Locke would argue that atheism should fall out of the scope of tolerated views because by refusing to work towards their own salvation, the unbelievers compromise their moral principles and 'exclude themselves entirely from the community'.[2] Locke's atheists are unequivocally immoral. There are echoes of the Lockean argument in Kant, but as we shall see, there are more essential divergences between both philosophers' accounts.

In what follows, sections 3.2–3.4 are dedicated to the analysis of Kant's views on atheism and the argument that he eventually makes room for a certain type of unbelief within his critical philosophy. Section 3.5 fleshes out his ambiguous attitude to enthusiasm (*Schwärmerei*). Both issues – atheism and enthusiasm – are connected in the person of (Kant's) Spinoza, to whom Kant attributed these attitudes.

3.2. The moral atheist in Bayle and Kant

The way Bayle features Spinoza as a moral atheist illustrates his outlook on the relation between theory and practice. As Michael Czelinski-Uesbeck recounts, in Bayle's view, 'religion and morality, in general ideology and morality, are to be separated from one another'.[3] This is because, according to Bayle, our actions are not in fact guided by the beliefs we entertain, but rather by passions that, in order to be curbed, require political authority regulating human behaviour, rather than religious precepts. It is thus not the task of religious authorities to make people moral and it is not up to the state to control what beliefs people profess – clearly a stub of an argument for separation between church and state. Bayle describes Spinoza as a 'systematic atheist',[4] at his deathbed 'completely convinced of his atheism'[5] and prone to endorse 'monstrous absurdities' as his theories.[6] At the same time, Spinoza's moral standing would find high esteem among his contemporaries. Says Bayle:

> Those who were acquainted with him, and the peasants of the villages where he had lived in retirement for some time, all agree in saying that he was sociable, affable, honest, obliging, and of a well-ordered morality. This is strange; but, after all, we should not be more surprised by this than to see people who live very bad lives even though they are completely convinced of the Gospel.[7]

According to Bayle, Spinoza's righteousness, together with a number of morally impeccable lives of other atheists, like Diagoras, Theodorus, Nicanor, Hippo, Euhemerus, Stilpo, Epicurus and Vanini,[8] and societies such as the Chinese,[9] provide examples supporting the independence of morality from religious faith. Thus, whatever views one holds, one can act morally, because action need not be guided by theoretical belief. Two things merit attention. The first is Bayle's association of religious faith with theoretical belief and the second – his cutting off the connection between belief and action, which typically marks a sceptical stance (in its Humean rather than Cartesian version). Two types of atheists illustrate this lack of connection between theory and practice. Accordingly, practical atheists are 'people who live with no fear of God, but not without some conviction of his existence', yet despite their proclaimed theistic faith they do not act morally. In contrast, theoretical atheists, such as Diagoras, Vanini and Spinoza, are those 'whose atheism is attested to either by historical or by their own writings', but in whom Bayle admits not to have found 'indications of... evil life'.[10]

Let us now proceed to *Kant's* Spinoza. This is an individual who despite abiding by the moral law 'takes himself to be firmly convinced [*sich fest überredet hält*]', that there is no God and no future life, thus who subscribes to the autonomy of pure practical reason but rejects its postulates. What is the ground of the moral atheist's rejection of God's existence and the immortality of the soul? Kant's text contains a hint at an answer, which can easily be overlooked due to a misleading translation of the fragment. Note that the words 'sich fest überredet hält', which Kant uses in KU, 5:452 to describe the epistemic stance of the moral atheist, are translated by Guyer and Matthews as 'takes himself to be firmly *convinced*' (italics A.T.). But 'überredet' is a cognate of 'Überredung', that is, 'persuasion', and not 'Überzeugung' which translates as 'conviction'. Meredith and Walker render the fragment more adequately as 'who considers himself firmly *persuaded*' (italics A.T.). Kant clearly distinguishes between conviction and persuasion. 'Conviction' captures the sense of 'taking something to be true' (*Fürwahrhalten*, usually rendered as 'assent') following the kind of justification that 'is valid for everyone merely as long as he has reason' (KrV, A 820/B 848). In contrast, persuasion 'has its ground only in the particular constitution of the subject', a ground that 'cannot be communicated' (KrV, A 820/B 849);[11] therefore, persuasion guarantees no more than 'the merely private validity of the judgment' (KrV, A 821/B 849). Kant explains that persuasion occurs when the subject conflates subjective and objective grounds, or entertains beliefs 'based on grounds, without investigating whether they [i.e., the grounds – A.T.] are objective or subjective' (V-Lo/Dohna, 24:747, cf. Log, 9:73, V-Lo/Wiener, 24:889). He even comes to qualify persuasion as 'a kind of delusion' (V-Lo/Blomberg, 24:144) and 'the illusion of conviction' (V-Lo/Dohna, 24:732), emphasizing that 'all persuasion is false as to form (*formaliter*), namely, insofar as an uncertain cognition appears here to be certain' (Log, 9:73).

Given the above distinctions, Kant's Spinoza, being 'firmly persuaded' that there is no God and no future life, presents himself as undergoing cognitive delusions, and one who dedicates insufficient amount of reflection to the grounds of his beliefs. Perhaps his experience has taught him that there is too much evil in the world that theists – and their deistic allies – depict as created by the most perfect being; or he may have never experienced God's caring hand in his life. Whatever the atheist's motives, considering the merely private validity of his reasons not to believe in God, he represents a position which, on Kant's tenets, we cannot expect each rational agent to adopt. The grounds for not believing in God, not being universally shareable, cannot convince anyone to abandon faith – and ultimately, they cannot be convincing even to the atheist himself insofar as he has a mistaken view about their validity. Thus, Kant's atheist proves eventually to be a harmless, though errant solitary. Why then does Kant characterize atheism as a morally pernicious attitude?

3.3. Kant's case against atheism

Contrary to what has been suggested above, there are places in Kant's corpus in which he expresses the view on atheism as socially pernicious. Thus, in the second-edition Preface to the *Critique of Pure Reason*, he lists 'atheism' and 'freethinking unbelief' among positions 'which can become generally injurious' and to which 'criticism alone' can provide a remedy (KrV, B xxxiv). In the *Religion*, he suggests that atheism breeds political harm, describing the position as 'more dangerous to the state' than even 'the coarsest polytheism' (RGV, 6:111). Also, in the Pölitz lecture notes on religion, we can encounter a statement accusing the atheists of immorality, urging that a person who denied faith in God 'would have to be a scoundrel' (V-Phil-Th/Pölitz, 28:1083). Moreover, Kant decidedly condemns a dogmatic atheist, who 'directly denies the existence of God, and… declares it impossible that there is a God at all', because in such an individual 'all the incentives of morality have been broken down' (V-Phil-Th/Pölitz, 28:1010).

The above statements support the suggestion, contained in the second Preface to the *Religion*, that if morality implies religious faith 'inevitably', then denying religious faith must indicate that one has also abandoned morality. Yet being religious is understood in this text as a *consequence* of being moral, not as its precondition, because morality is independent of religion and rests on the autonomy of practical reason alone. I act morally if I follow the moral law, that is, do my (moral) duty for duty's sake. The moral law binds me unconditionally, regardless of whether God exists or not. I also ought to acknowledge the binding force of the moral law irrespective of whether I believe in the existence of God or not. Accordingly, having completed, in § 87 of the third *Critique*, 'the moral proof of the existence of God' (KU, 5:447–450), Kant explicitly denies that 'it is just as necessary to assume the existence of God as it is to acknowledge the validity of the moral law, hence that whoever cannot convince himself of the former can judge himself to be free from the obligations of the latter'. Even without belief in God, 'every rational being would still have to recognize himself as forever strictly bound to the precept of morals; for its laws are formal and command unconditionally' (KU, 5:450–1).

If one ought to act morally regardless of the existence of God and/or one's belief in this existence, it should also be possible, given Kant's 'ought implies can' principle (formulated, for example, in RGV, 6:45, 50), for one to act morally whether one believes in God or not. Why then does Kant perceive unbelief as a threat to morality? To address this issue, we need to look at the moral argument in the third *Critique*. (There are different versions of the argument scattered through Kant's major critical writings – see, e.g., KrV, A 806/B 834–A 815/B 843; KpV, 5:124–6; WDO, 8:139–140; RGV, 6:5–7, 139[12] – but since the 'moral atheist' example originates from the *Critique of the Power of Judgment*, we shall focus primarily on the 'proof''s formulation in this work.)

Accordingly, the moral law 'determines for us' as rational beings in the world '*a priori*, a final end', which it is therefore our duty to pursue, namely 'the highest good in the world possible through freedom'. This highest good contains two ingredients: happiness, which is the 'subjective condition' of our end-setting

(KU, 5:450), or the 'subjective final end' of our actions (RGV, 6:6n.), as Kant puts it in the *Religion*, and morality 'as the worthiness to be happy' (KU, 5:450). Yet these two ingredients are not connected in a necessary manner, for Kant does not subscribe to the Stoic view that virtue is necessary and sufficient for happiness.[13] Nor can nature as such guarantee the connection; experience teaches us all too well that nature does not 'respond' to moral reasons, if one may so put it – in the empirical world, there is no match between being morally good and being happy (or the match occurs occasionally and contingently). Thus, to be able to think of the connection of the two components of the highest good as really possible – or to 'give objective reality to the concept of the highest good' and thus 'prevent it... from being taken merely as a mere ideal' (WDO, 8:139) – and thereby to think of our pursuits in the promotion of the highest good as feasible, 'we must assume a moral cause of the world (an author of the world)' (KU, 5:450). In other words, only if we assume the existence of God, can we think of the 'realm of nature' and the 'realm of freedom' as actually harmonized in such a way that the former becomes 'responsive' to the demands of the latter. In a world ruled by God, nature would not thwart our moral strivings but would encourage them by supplying an extra component – happiness – properly suited to our efforts.

Thus, the moral person who denies the existence of God – such as Kant's Spinoza – 'would certainly have to give up' the end, which his practical reason presents to him as a human being, 'as impossible' (KU, 5:452). Hence, as Bernd Dörflinger has noticed, the moral atheist must suppress his 'need for a comprehensive realization of his moral-practical rationality',[14] a need that morality effects in him (RGV, 6:6). But since as a moral being the unbeliever is obliged to 'promote' (*befördern*) this end, he will get into a practical inconsistency, attempting to pursue a goal that is in fact unachievable. According to Gabriele Tomasi, a person who commits herself to morality while not endorsing faith in God will have to hold two inconsistent beliefs: first, the belief that 'the moral law imposes upon her a final end as a duty' and, second, the belief that 'the world in which that final end should become real is such that its realization is impossible'.[15] It is not difficult to foresee that this inconsistency will impede the atheist's moral motivation – think about any goal which you are obliged to pursue while knowing that the goal is not within your reach, such as working to meet a too tight deadline, which you have to meet on pain of being fired, for example. From the psychological point of view, the practical inconsistency of the unbeliever is bound to 'weaken the respect, by which the moral law immediately influences him to obedience' (KU, 5:452). Confronted with the adversities of life, which he encounters both as a natural being and in human society, he will fall into despair upon realizing the absurdity of a life in which one's efforts to do good do not really matter. Here is how Kant describes the plight awaiting the righteous unbeliever:

> Deceit, violence, and envy will always surround him, even though he is himself honest, peaceable, and benevolent; and the righteous ones besides himself that he will still encounter will, in spite of all their worthiness to be happy, nevertheless be subject by nature, which pays no attention to that, to all the evils of poverty, illnesses, and untimely death, just like all the other animals on earth, and will always remain thus until one wide grave engulfs them all together (whether honest or dishonest, it makes no difference here) and flings them, who were capable of having believed themselves to be the final end of creation, back into the abyss of the purposeless chaos of matter from which they were drawn.
> (KU, 5:452)

To sum up: in § 87 of the third *Critique*, Kant argues that rejecting belief in God inevitably leads to thinking of the highest good, and so the end of our moral strivings, as unfeasible. Thinking of the highest good as unfeasible shall weaken our moral motivation by making us realize that morality demands that we pursue goals that cannot be achieved. Conceiving of the highest good as unachievable may also trigger despair because it can make us realize that living a virtuous life makes no difference – both to us and to the world. From this point only one step needs to be taken to renouncing all moral pursuit.

The above argument has been challenged by attempts to exonerate the moral atheist from the charge of practical inconsistency. Lara Denis, for instance, suggests a 'historical conception of the highest good' as an alternative to theistic accounts.[16] Denis bases her alternative on Kant's description of the highest good in KU, 5:451 as 'a happiness of rational beings that harmoniously accompanies their compliance with moral laws'. An atheist endorsing the historical conception would still be motivated to promote the highest good by acting morally because he would hope that his moral action will contribute to bringing about a better world anyway. He could, for example, believe that the world can become more just – so that the virtuous would be 'rewarded' by living happy lives – as a result of social and political reforms, or, we could add, implementing the 'package' of values and ideas defining the radical Enlightenment, on Israel's account (see 1.1). According to Denis, the atheist could also adhere to a different conception of nature than Kant's: 'he could think of the natural world as part of a necessary, self-creating and self-sustaining system, elsewhere in which virtue is rewarded by happiness.'[17] Such a conception of nature would approximate Spinoza's.

Lawrence Pasternack challenges the 'secular' conceptions of the highest good, of which the historical conception forms a variety, and defends an account which he labels 'theological'.[18] Crucial to this account is the 'Principle of Proportionate Distribution' (PPD) that regulates the way in which virtue is supposed to be conjoined with morality in the ideal of the highest good. For the PPD to obtain, both employing the resources of nature in apportioning the suitable share of happiness to agents and assessing the agents' worthiness to get their share must be possible. This last condition for the PPD to obtain, Pasternack emphasizes, can be met only upon the presupposition of the existence of God because, as Kant argues in the *Religion*, only God can know our hearts (RGV, 6:99) and adequately assess our moral worthiness.[19] Pasternack insists, besides, on the non-empirical meaning of the concept of 'world' in the context of the highest good.[20] The secular or historical conceptions, on his account, fail to make the right sense of the PPD. For if proportioning happiness to virtue is to make any sense, the existence of an intelligent agent – a just judge – needs to be assumed on pain of the two components of Kant's moral ideal being conjoined randomly and contingently, that is, in a way that defies any notion of a just world.

Without having to subscribe to Denis's proposal, one could observe that at least in the third-*Critique* moral argument, and given Kant's conception of nature as morally indifferent, Kant seems to take the concept of 'world' in the empirical rather than noumenal or metaphysical sense – as he did, for example, in his Inaugural Dissertation (1770), where he used the phrase '*mundus intelligibilis*'. Moreover, the moral atheist (or an advocate of the secular conception of the highest good)[21] could maintain that the theological conception is incoherent or unconvincing as a proposal that would aim to inspire conversion in an unbeliever. At least, the idea of God as apportioning what *we* regard as happiness, and what *we* desire, as partly sensible and partly rational beings belonging to the empirical world, seems to be carved too much 'in the image of man'. Also, it looks like the worthiness to be happy is bound to be assessed in accordance with *our* – human – standards because this worthiness consists for Kant in the fulfilment of one's moral duties. But why should we think of God as distributing happiness in relation to virtue in a way which *we* would find appropriate? An apophatic theologian, like Pseudo-Dionysius the Areopagite, might claim that though God is just and benevolent, divine justice and benevolence far exceed what we know as justice and benevolence: our justice and benevolence are not the same as God's. Thus, we can think of God as rewarding with happiness even those agents that fail to practice moral virtue in the Kantian sense. And, of course, God might be thought as rewarding those who believe in him without being virtuous or those whom he chooses to reward, in which case only the secular conceptions of the highest good could warrant hope for the realization of *Kant's* moral ideal.

Be that as it may, the moral atheist could also question Kant's conclusion from the unachievability of the highest good to his moral motivation being impaired as a result. He could claim, for example, that genuine moral virtue does not require additional, non-moral incentives in order to be practicable – and human beings, as moral agents, should not contaminate their moral motivation by mixing happiness with the moral law. The virtuous unbeliever could accept the moral indifference of nature – the fact of there being huge amounts of underserved and unjust suffering in the world – and sacrifice his desire for happiness for the sake of morality; he would thus abide by his moral commitments, come what may.

However, by way of a rejoinder, the atheist's confidence in his moral capacities could be regarded as unrealistic, demanding a heroic or super-human attitude. As John Hare has put the point, 'we human beings are, for Kant, free beings who bind ourselves through our reason to unconditional law. In a word, we are autonomous. But we are not *only* such beings. We are also creatures of need. If we were purely rational, we would not need the idea of another being over us to help us do our duty.'[22] On Hare's account, the righteous atheist harbours a hubristic, hyper-rational attitude and overlooks the constraints inherent in rational *human* nature. But hyper-rationality falls short of rationality proper. Being hyper-rational compromises the rationality of the moral unbeliever no less than entertaining practically inconsistent beliefs. The problem with the moral atheist, on Hare's construal, is that by rejecting belief in God as a way to strengthen the agent's commitment to the moral law, he ignores the pull of incentives competing with the moral law, as well as the human propensity to prioritize those incentives over the moral law. Kant has called this propensity radical evil (RGV, 6:34, 37–8, 72). The unbeliever may think, for example, that the right kind of moral education should suffice to extirpate individuals' drive to flout the moral law for the sake of non-moral inclinations, yet such a belief does not adequately render Kant's position: the evil that stains our moral, hence intelligible nature, cannot be blotted out by empirical means.

The problem of radical evil deserves separate discussion, and we shall return to it in Chapter 5. For now, we can imagine the atheist critic of Kant's moral argument replying to Hare, somewhat along the Nietzschean lines, that Kant makes belief in God contingent upon certain facts about human beings. Rational finite beings that would be less vulnerable to the incentives of sensibility would not need to resort to God; hence it is particularly the human weakness that generates the need for faith. And in a counterfactual scenario, absent the weaknesses of human nature originating in the fact that we are not only rational but also sensible beings, we would be able to live up to the requirements of morality without believing in God. If faith is meant to be a prop in our moral life, as it is in the picture sketched by Hare, one may also inquire whether the prop is to stay with us permanently, or shall we throw it away upon entering a higher stage of moral progress, should such progress be within our reach.[23]

3.4. Making room for Spinoza

Kant's moral argument for the existence of God can be questioned, as we have seen, also from Kantian – or, shall we say, revisionist Kantian – positions. However, some of Kant's statements, especially those about particular cases of unbelievers, also encourage the idea that the critical philosophy can accommodate unbelief, at least in a certain form. The aim of this section is to find out what kind of form it might be.

In Collins's lecture notes on moral philosophy, Kant entertains the idea that atheism is a metaphysically erratic position, yet such that does not have to exert a negative impact on the moral life of its advocate. Those atheists whose understanding is corrupt, but not the will, can worship God in their actions. Spinoza provides an example of an atheist whose 'heart was good, and could easily have been brought to rights; he merely had too much trust in speculative argument' (V-Mo/Collins, 27:312). Echoing Bayle, Kant comments on practical atheists, whom he clearly distinguishes from the theoretical breed, that they manifest 'shameless wickedness', which has nothing to do with their theoretical views (V-Mo/Collins, 27:327). In addition, in his review of Schulz's[24] *Doctrine of Morals for All Human Beings Regardless of Different Religions*, Kant praises the author – who otherwise promotes materialism and fatalism – for 'good intentions' which he thinks accompany his attempt to 'vindicate the wisdom and kindness of God through the progress of all his creatures toward perfection and eternal happiness though on various paths, to lead religion back from unproductive beliefs to deeds' (RezSchulz, 8:12). Kant recognizes in Schulz's work an attempt at founding a religion on moral grounds. Concluding the review, he contends that since 'the practical concept of freedom has nothing to do with the speculative concept' and to act, it suffices to entertain the *idea* of freedom, even while denying its metaphysical reality, the fatalist has to act '*as if he was free*', and even if 'he is not otherwise able to bring his practical principles into harmony with [the] speculative' ones, 'not much' is eventually 'lost' (RezSchulz, 8:13–14).

Thus, in the examples adduced, Kant seems to hold a weaker position on the relation between belief in God and morality than is suggested by the conclusion of his moral argument in KU, 5:447–450. According to this weaker position, the lack of faith may but does not have to impair morality.

How can these divergences in Kant's attitude to atheism be explained? Addressing this question, we should keep in mind the historical context within which his position would take its shape. This context would be provided, among other things, by the controversy that followed an exchange between Friedrich Heinrich Jacobi and Moses Mendelssohn on the supposed Spinozism of Gotthold Ephraim Lessing. The controversy, known as *Pantheismusstreit*, would touch on the question concerning the relation between reason and faith. Kant strove to navigate between extremes: the Scylla of rationalism, represented by Mendelssohn and assimilating faith with knowledge, and the Charybdis of fideism, proclaimed by Jacobi who would recommend a 'leap' into faith as a remedy for the excesses of rationalism.[25] Kant's intent, expressed in the Orientation essay, was to defend reason, and hence enlightenment, against 'hyper-rationalism', on the one side, and irrationalism, on the other.[26]

Accordingly, Kant concurs with the Baylean sceptic (or 'Spinoza' in the guise of the 'righteous unbeliever'), mentioned in 3.2, in rejecting the rationalist demand that knowledge be necessary to provide reasons for action, yet he contends that action can be based on non-epistemic grounds which can underlie the attitude he calls 'belief' or 'faith'. Importantly, knowledge for Kant does not consist in justified true belief, as in contemporary post-Gettier analytic epistemology, but rather in a form of assent (*Fürwahrhalten*, 'taking something to be true', see 3.2 above), warranted by 'subjectively and objectively sufficient' grounds (KrV, A 822/B 851). A subjectively sufficient ground is one that can be adduced by the subject who takes a particular proposition to be true, and an objectively sufficient ground – one which derives as a result of the subject's relation to the object to which a proposition refers. Andrew Chignell distinguishes two kinds of subjective sufficiency: one consisting in the subject's readiness to cite a certain ground as her ground for assenting to a proposition, and one that amounts to an assent carrying 'nonepistemic merits' for the subject.[27] Regarding knowledge, it should also be added that it is marked by both conviction and certainty: unlike persuasion (cf. section 3.2), one can expect that one's taking something to be true in the mode of knowledge entails the obligation of other rational beings to assent to it in the same way.

Also 'belief' or 'faith' (*Glaube*) has a different meaning for Kant than in contemporary epistemology, and the term 'faith' does not designate religious faith exclusively, but also 'moral faith' and 'theoretical belief',[28] and is not the opposite of 'reason' (as, for example, Jacobi would contend). The Kantian 'belief' or 'faith' consists in assenting to a proposition for which one does not have objectively but only subjectively sufficient reasons. Thus, a belief is not supported by a deductive or inductive reasoning, or empirical evidence, acquired in relation to a given object of inquiry. The kind of subjectivity that is involved here, though, does not pertain merely to a ground's being available to the subject (in the sense of the subject's being able to justify her belief), but rather consists in the belief having what Chignell terms 'nonepistemic merits', that is, 'a property of an assent that makes it valuable or desirable for a subject – given his or her needs, interests, and goals – but which does not do so by way of directly indicating that the assent is true.'[29] Thus construed, belief or faith rests on non-epistemic grounds which can be valid for everyone given the universality of the needs or goals of human nature.

The non-epistemic nature of its grounds also distinguishes belief from 'opinion' (*Meinen*), held upon insufficient grounds, both objective and subjective. Also, as we read in the *Jäsche Logik*, belief can turn out to be 'firmer than all knowledge'; for 'with knowledge one still listens to opposed grounds, but not with belief, because here it does not depend on objective grounds but on the moral interest of the subject' (Log, 9:72). Thus, opinion can be abandoned once the subject accumulates evidence confirming the truth of a proposition he assents to, and transform into knowledge – and knowledge can turn out to be backed by insufficient evidence and slip back to opinion, a feature called fallibility in contemporary epistemology 'after Popper'. But neither can replace or be replaced by belief. (Mark that the last point concerns the modes of assent, i.e. something like attitudes to propositions and not propositions themselves.)

Let us give some examples of the modes of assent Kant distinguishes. Accordingly, based on historical evidence contained in chronicles and recording the testimonies of witnesses, I can know that the Prussian Tribute took place in 1525. Historians and laypeople, forming hypotheses about the causes of the 9/11, hold various opinions which evidence may not suffice to entitle them to, nor which they themselves have to be particularly strongly committed to (they would abandon the hypotheses upon acquiring stronger evidence of a different kind). So far, we can see that both 'knowing' and 'opining' are a matter of collecting evidence or constructing a proof supporting one's attitude to a proposition. This is not exactly the case with 'belief'. Consider the following mundane situation: if I undertake to go home through a road frequented by people letting their dogs run around unleashed, I must believe that the dogs are tame enough not to thwart my completion of the goal. Here, I do not form a conjecture that the road is safe, which will then be tested, and I am not really interested in getting to know whether the proposition is true or false; all I need is to arrive home safely and if I want to pass a road swarmed by unleashed dogs, I need to assume that it is safe – otherwise I would have to stop paralysed by fear.

We can now turn back to Kant's issue with the moral atheist. Surely, Kant and the moral atheist share the idea that we cannot base our belief in God, that is, consciously assent to the proposition that there is a God, on the grounds that would suffice for knowledge: empirical evidence, *a priori* reasoning, or the 'tidings' of revelation. In the *Critique of Pure Reason*, Kant invalidates all speculative arguments – the so-called proofs – for the existence of God. Having refuted the arguments of transcendental and natural theology,[30] he states that 'all attempts of a merely speculative use of reason in regard to theology are entirely fruitless and by their internal constitution null and nugatory' and that 'the principles of reason's natural use do not lead at all to any theology' (KrV, A 636/B 664). A 'sceptical atheist', likewise, 'disputes only the proofs for the existence of God and especially their apodictic certainty'. Yet the sceptical atheist's antispeculative stance does not divest him of the possibility of 'having religion' because, says Kant, 'he sincerely admits that it is even more impossible to prove that there is no God than to prove that there is one' (V-Phil-Th/Pölitz, 28:1010). Elsewhere, Kant describes an atheist belonging to the '*sceptical order*' as one who 'adopts the maxim that, though God's existence may be unprovable, it is best after all to presuppose it as a hypothesis, since the moral laws find a surer entry thereby, and are more easily followed'. Hence, says Kant, 'to be a sceptical atheist, an unbeliever, is not punishable. For his doubts are guiltless. The certainty of God's existence is impossible to bring to conviction, in the logical sense. Such a person cannot, therefore, persuade himself of theism, or the reality of God; though the impossibility of God is equally incapable of demonstration' (V-MS/Vigil, 27:530–1).

Thus, according to Kant, the sceptical atheist does not deny the possibility of the existence of God and even accepts the theistic hypothesis as a reinforcement of his commitment to morality. Kant's use of 'hypothesis' in this context is telling. In the first *Critique*, he characterizes hypotheses as expedient in the regulative use of reason (KrV, A 647/B 675) and contends that they are not meant to explain 'things in nature' (KrV, A 772/B 800), but rather to be employed polemically against certain 'transcendent pretensions' of reason (KrV, A 781/B 809). Thus, a person who proffers the hypothesis of the existence of God to his adversary does not thereby establish that God exists, but rather tries to safeguard reason against falling into the opposite side of the dogmatic conflict. Also, hypotheses are like theoretical assumptions endorsed for their beneficial consequences for the unity and systematicity of cognition; as examples of hypotheses Kant mentions the 'incorporeal unity of the soul' and the 'existence of the highest being' (KrV, A 774/B 802), which he calls 'assertions of reason', though having non-dogmatic (and non-epistemic) purport. Yet, although he emphasizes the moral significance of the theistic hypothesis, formed by the sceptical atheist, and even entertains the idea that hypotheses are 'assertions of reason', eventually he does not equate them with beliefs, *pace* Chignell,[31] but rather classifies them as 'problematic judgments' which can be neither refuted nor proven. He concludes then that 'one must preserve them [i.e. the hypotheses – A.T.] in this quality and indeed carefully make sure that they are not believed in themselves and as having an absolute validity, and that they do not drown reason in fictions and deceptions' (KrV, A 782/B 810). Consequently, a theistic hypothesis must be distinguished from theistic belief or faith based on moral grounds. Though we are guided by our theoretical interest when adopting hypotheses, as much as we are guided by the need of reason, or our practical interest, when endorsing theistic belief, the latter enjoys the kind of (practical) certainty which allows taking it as true. The 'moral theist', who represents the position Kant sides with, 'is ... firmly convinced of the existence of this being [i.e. God – A.T.], and he has a faith beyond all doubt based on practical grounds.' '[H]is faith in God built on this foundation', avers Kant, 'is as certain as a mathematical demonstration. This foundation is *morals*, the whole system of duties, which is cognized a priori with apodictic certainty through pure reason' (V-Phil-Th/Pölitz, 28:1011). The sceptical atheist's hypothesis, concerning the possibility of the divine existence, does not generate a similar conviction.

We can now formulate a few conjectures regarding the source of the divergences between the moral theist and the sceptical atheist – and try to determine the identity of the sceptic. First, the moral theist and the sceptic would differ in their conceptions of theistic faith: whereas for the moral theist the need of reason to ensure the possibility of the realization of its *a priori* moral ideal suffices to legitimate his belief in the existence of God, the sceptic may hold that faith should be based on or at least reinforced by epistemic grounds. Having established the insufficiency of the epistemic grounds for belief in God which philosophers and theologians have so far come up with, the sceptic resolves to abandon the theistic faith. We may call this individual a Disappointed Thomist, because of his conception that faith needs to be accompanied by theoretical arguments.

Second, the sceptic may claim that the only way to make him convert from unbelief to faith would be to present him with a proof of God's existence, such that becoming acquainted with this proof would guarantee that we *know* that God exists. He would thus, unlike the moral theist, find the doctrine of postulates far too insufficient to ensure the certainty of the theistic conviction; he would also not be satisfied with the practical cognition (*Erkenntnis*) of the divine existence, as opposed to theoretical knowledge (*Wissen*) about it,[32] because he would hold that it is illegitimate to transition from mere awareness of an object (an idea in the mind) to the existence of this object outside the mind. On this construal, the sceptic would hold what Antony Flew has termed the 'presumption of atheism':[33] he would stipulate that unless the theist demonstrates that God exists, the atheist is entitled to nourish doubts concerning God's existence. Since the sceptic would entertain the possibility that such a proof exists, though so far he has not come across any, he can be called a Would-Be Cartesian Rationalist, because of his supposition that the certainty of faith should be based on rational argumentation producing knowledge about the existence of God.

Third, the sceptical atheist may be motivated to act morally by the assumption that it is possible that one day a convincing proof for the existence of God will be found. Thus, as much as the moral theist's, his conduct would be fuelled by hope in the existence of God and divine justice.[34] Yet his hope would have primarily epistemic underpinnings. Since this sceptic satisfies the conditions of entering Pascal's wager (by not excluding the possibility that God exists and commitment to the moral law), one may label him the Addressee of Pascal's Wager.

Finally, one could think of the sceptical atheist as one who has moral faith indeed – recall that Kant even attributed religion to him – for he acts morally, accepts 'a *problematic* assumption (hypothesis)' that God exists and hence must have '*the idea of God* which must occur to every morally earnest (and therefore religious) pursuit of the good, without pretending to be able to secure objective reality for it through theoretical cognition' (RGV, 6:154n.). The sceptical atheist of this breed might be called a Simple Kantian, because he fails to have conceptualized all the intricacies of Kant's account of faith while instantiating an attitude of a person living by the requirements of this faith, as a matter of fact. Like the Disappointed Thomist, the Would-Be Cartesian Rationalist and the Addressee of Pascal's Wager, he can also have an un-Kantian conception of faith, perhaps due to being raised in a culture which favours the defence of theoretical arguments and dogmatic tenets over plain moral life as a manifestation of theistic faith. This individual might also consider himself an atheist in opposition to those who claim to possess knowledge of God based on reason and revelation, and assess their arguments as weak. Thus construed, 'sceptical atheism' seems to be eligible for being integrated into Kant's critical philosophy.

On a final note: the moral atheist, like Kant, would prioritize the practical over the theoretical kind of rationality, despite entertaining a different conception of what faith in God should amount to. For both the moral theist and the righteous unbeliever, knowledge of the existence of God is not requisite for moral action; hence they discard the necessary connection between theology (in its speculative guise) and morality. Their positions also tend to converge on the relevance of theistic faith for moral practice; for, according to Kant, faith in God, as we have seen in 3.1, is to follow from moral action, as its corollary or consequence, and reinforce the agent's perseverance in her efforts towards the good – without conditioning their possibility, though. Arguably, the difference between the moral atheist and the moral theist could capture different stages in their moral development; the former would have just started on the moral path. Somewhat paradoxically, atheism, conceived as the denial of all theoretical construals of theistic faith, furnishes a precondition of acquiring theistic faith based on moral grounds. This way, it represents a stage in the development of the critical philosopher – that is, Kant himself.

3.5. An excursus on enthusiasm

A recurring accusation levelled by Kant at Spinoza is expressed by the claim that Spinoza's philosophy leads to 'enthusiasm' (*Schwärmerei*). The word 'enthusiasm'[35] has a rich history and Kant's attitude to what it connotes is sometimes ambiguous. According to Gregory Johnson, Kant manifests a 'volatile mixture of attraction *and* revulsion toward enthusiasm' throughout his 'mature critical project'.[36] Oftentimes, he uses it as a 'combat concept' against positions with which he contrasts his critical philosophy: 'a kind [of] a diagnostic catch-all, with ample room for madness, melancholy, mysticism, biblical literalism, excessive introspection, traditional metaphysics and "lazy free-thinking"', as listed by Anthony La Vopa.[37] In Kant's philosophical vocabulary, there are three terms which can be rendered as 'enthusiasm', all of which capture a bit different attitude to the phenomenon: *Fanaticism* (negative), *Enthusiasm(us)* (moderately positive) and *Schwärmerei* (expressly negative). '*Enthusiasm(us)*' denotes a state in which one is influenced 'beyond the appropriate degree by some principle, whether it be by maxim of patriotic virtue, or of friendship, or of religion' (GSE, 2:252n.), or overcome by 'the passion of the sublime' (HN, 20:43).

The 'fanatic' kind of enthusiasm manifests itself as a 'delusion' leading to 'the moral death of the reason' (RGV, 6:175) and consists in replacing commitment to morality with what one experiences to be an immediate presence of God (or so one claims). The philosophical *Schwärmerei*, of which Kant accuses Spinoza, is a cognate of 'fanaticism'.

In Kant's *Reflections* from the late 1770s/early 1780s, notes can be found in which the meaning and origin of 'philosophical enthusiasm' is spelled out (HN, 18:434–8). Accordingly, we can read that the road to enthusiasm starts when a thinker claims to possess the capacity to cognize things by means of ideas in the mind of God. But to cognize ideas in the mind of God means to cognize objects outside spatiotemporal determinations, in the way in which an infinite intellect, not limited by the forms of sensible intuition, would cognize them, that is, as things in themselves, using pure intellect alone to acquire cognitions of objects. Kant contends that it was Plato who gave rise to the idea of philosophy as knowledge of things in themselves (HN, 18:434–5). The Neoplatonics would go further, introducing spiritual intermediaries in intellectual cognition, such as '*genii*, astral spirits, eons'. All this 'raving enthusiasm' would culminate in Spinozism, that is, 'theosophy by means of intuition'. Although the Aristotelian philosophy strove to 'suppress this delusion' (HN, 18:435), for it recommended to start one's inquiry from experience, it would also end up in Spinozism, since the *a priori* concepts which it came up with would be employed outside the boundaries of empirical cognition. Here is how Kant presents this development:

> Now the subjective conditions of reason... began to be held objective conditions of things in themselves, and since reason is not satisfied until it has grasped the whole, conquests in the supersensible world began to be made.... one finally also had to take away from all things their individual and separate possibility of existing... and leave to them all merely inherence in one subject.
>
> (HN, 18:435–6)

Conflating the subjective conditions of cognition with the objective conditions of things outside the mind generates enthusiasm, which would attain its most express shape in Spinoza and which would come out in three degrees (note the pantheistic imagery):

> The highest degree of enthusiasm is that we are ourselves in God and feel or intuit our existence in Him. The second: that we intuit all things in accordance with their true nature only in God as their cause and in his ideas as archetypes. The third: that we do not intuit them at all, but rather derive them from the

concept of God and thus infer from our own existence and our rational concepts of things directly to the existence of God, in which alone they can have objective reality.

(HN, 18:438)

The polemical edge of Kant's critique of enthusiasm is turned against his contemporaries – Emanuel Swedenborg, Christian Wolff, Johann Gottfried Herder, Johann Georg Hamann, Maria von Herbert, Johann Caspar Lavater, Friedrich Heinrich Jacobi and Heinrich Jung-Stilling[38] – though primarily it forms part of his critique of speculative reason. The conflation of the subjective with the objective, a defining trait of the enthusiastic frame of mind, evokes the 'transcendental illusion' which Kant unmasks in the first *Critique*. The 'transcendental illusion' occurs when 'the subjective necessity of a certain connection of our concepts on behalf of the understanding is taken for an objective necessity, the determination of things in themselves' (KrV, A 297/B 354). A definition of enthusiasm in one of the notes of the *Opus postumum*, as a mental state which arises when 'that which is in man is represented as something which is outside him, and the product of his thought represented as thing [*Sache*] in itself (substance)' (OP, 21:19), echoes Kant's description of the 'transcendental illusion'. An enthusiastic state of mind also resembles the state Kant characterizes as persuasion (cf. 3.2 on Kant's Spinoza), in which one's private grounds for assenting to a proposition are regarded as objective; indeed, persuasion as such might be the root of enthusiastic mental states.

To issue judgements about objects that surpass the boundaries of experience, we need a maxim guiding our use of reason; otherwise, Kant warns in *What Does It Mean to Orient Oneself in Thinking?*, 'instead of thinking we would indulge in enthusiasm' (WDO, 8:137). Spinozism gets thinking off the right track in that it makes use of notions which, as Kant contends, can neither be found in the *a priori* furnishing of the human understanding nor acquired by it in experience, such as 'thoughts which themselves think' and 'an accident that simultaneously exists for itself as a subject'. Thus, it exceeds not only the boundaries of experience but also those of intelligibility. Moreover, it makes illegitimate claims about the 'impossibility of a being the idea of which consists solely of pure concepts of the understanding, which has been separated from all conditions of sensibility, and in which a contradiction can never be met with' (WDO, 8:144n.). Kant's statements not being particularly lucid here, we can limit ourselves to the observation that the kind of thinking that Spinozism authorizes is for Kant detached from empirical reality and betrays ignorance of the capacities of the human mind, and therefore constitutes a paradigm of philosophical abstraction. This attitude culminates in 'an unbelief of reason' (*Vernunftunglaube*) which jeopardizes both morality and public order because it robs them of rational guidance (WDO, 8:146).

Depicting Spinozism as a doctrine that encourages the misuse of reason and engenders anti-rationalist reactions, Kant presents himself as a defender of enlightenment, who by delimiting the boundaries of reason, protects it against the 'extremes' which it tends to fall into when used in an unbridled or lawless manner.[39] Thus, Kant's critique of enthusiasm does not constrain itself to demarcating the criteria of philosophically legitimate thinking, but carries implications that can be deemed to have political significance.[40] Critiquing the misuse of reason by those who want to market their private insights, based on incommunicable grounds, as objectively valid claims, Kant warns against dissent and partisanship as the corollaries of philosophical *Schwärmerei*.

Several aspects of Kant's critique of Spinoza as a *Schwärmer* can be found puzzling, though. First, on Kant's account, Spinoza's ideas prove to be subversive for the Enlightenment agenda insofar as the Enlightenment is supposed to acknowledge the guidance of reason. As an 'enthusiast', Spinoza approximates religious fanatics and mystics, to be encountered across the wide spectrum of secret societies and the Christian heterodoxy. How does this picture fit with the account of Spinoza as the founding father of the radical Enlightenment, presented in Chapter 1?

Second, since according to Kant enthusiasm encompasses a broad range of phenomena: from religious fanaticism to Spinoza's supposed denial of God's existence, one may wonder what these diverse phenomena have in common. It is indeed the case, from the historical point of view, that Spinoza was regarded both as an atheist and as a divinely inspired mystic, the latter by Herder and other authors of the *Goethezeit*.[41] But what would explain these divergences in perception, at the same time allowing to exhibit a common feature of atheism and mysticism?

Third, in light of a recent interpretation by Stephen Palmquist, the question arises how sincere Kant was in his critique of 'enthusiasm' understood as a state in which one enters a 'mystical' union with God. In *Kant and Mysticism* (2019), Palmquist argues that 'Kant himself develops a special *Critical* type of mysticism.'[42] Kant's 'mystical experience', says Palmquist, would involve an immediate and personal 'encounter' with God, which 'lies at the very heart of the Critical philosophy'.[43] In this construal, Kant's critique of *Schwärmerei* would not target mysticism as such, but only attempts to build a system of *knowledge* of the supersensible, to make into the object of knowledge that which lies at the ground of the possibility of any articulate thought and judgement.

The first two concerns can be addressed jointly. Thus, as Margaret Jacob points out in her *Radical Enlightenment*, pantheism, with its roots in Spinoza's philosophy, 'although so profoundly secular in its orientation, could slip, long before the Romantics got hold of it, into the language and metaphor of mysticism'.[44] In Jacob's picture, pantheism was the new 'religion' of the radical Enlightenment, practised, for instance, by members of masonic lodges. The 'religion' would be tainted by ambiguity: after all, equating God with nature or attributing corporeality to the divine being can express both an atheistic and a religious, or mystical, outlook – depending on one's conception of divinity. For one who believes that everything is divine, there is no space for the *personal* God of theism. Yet atheism could be defined as a rejection of any divinity, however conceived, in which case denying the personal God of theism would not qualify as endorsing an atheistic stance. Regarding Kant's use of 'enthusiasm' as an umbrella term designating phenomena as different as religious fanaticism and unbelief, this parallels his use of 'dogmatic metaphysics' in reference to opposite positions, such as those presented by the thesis and the antithesis in each 'conflict of the transcendental ideas' in the Antinomy of Pure Reason (KrV, A 426/B 454–A 460/B 488). Rooted, like the dogmatic metaphysics, in the 'propensity' of the human mind to hypostatize subjective representations into mind-independent realities, enthusiasm represents the practical, socially pernicious side of dogmatic thinking.

Let us proceed to the third concern. One may concur with Palmquist that Kant's life exhibited traits, such as ascetic self-discipline, which mark the lives of mystics.[45] Moreover, if the Critical mysticism is spelled out as a doctrine which posits some foundations of thought and action that escape discursive grasp, then Kant's position can indeed be seen as inviting this kind of 'mysticism'. In the first *Critique*, Kant contends that underlying our experience of objects ('appearances'), there are 'things in themselves' about which we cannot legitimately make objectively valid claims, but which ensure our reference to the objects of experience (cf., e.g., KrV, B xxvi–xxvii). In the second *Critique*, he speaks about the rational *feeling* of respect for the moral law ('moral feeling') (KpV, 5:75f.; TP, 8:283; MS, 6:399–400) which he holds to have an 'inscrutable source' (MS, 6:400). The third *Critique* discusses the *feeling* of the sublime which we are supposed to experience when encountering a reality that transcends our representational capacities (cf. KU, 5:244–6). According to Palmquist, 'Kant's account of the sublime is one of his key examples how we *encounter* the hand of God in nature.'[46] In the *Religion*, Kant refers to the *ground* of freedom as 'a mystery' because it is 'inscrutable to us' and '*not given* to us in cognition' (RGV, 6:138). Finally, in the *Opus postumum*, there are passages suggesting that Kant regards the existence of God to be directly deducible from the awareness of the moral law in the form of the categorical imperative (cf. OP, 22:127), as if moral awareness were to provide us with direct access to the divine.[47]

Yet the above examples may not suffice to unequivocally demonstrate Kant's commitment to the claim that, as Palmquist puts it, '*immediate* and *personal* religious experience' constitutes the basis of the critical philosophy.[48] Palmquist's argument is based on the premise, which he formulated as a result of studying Kant's discussion of Swedenborg in the *Dreams of a Spirit-Seer*, that Kant does not rule out the possibility of mystical experience, but only denies that such an experience could 'properly be interpreted through reason'.[49] Thus, the suggestion that mystical experience provides the foundations of the critical philosophy can be read as a plausible hypothesis concerning these foundations. Now, the crucial aspect of a mystic's experience is its directedness at an object which far surpasses our cognitive capacities, but which is also transcendent to these capacities. A mystic's experience is not supposed to be generated by something 'from within' but rather by something 'from outside' the experiencing subject. This is at least how Kant himself understands the term. For example, in *The Conflict of the Faculties*, he calls a 'mystical solution' the idea that 'a moral metamorphosis of the human being' could be effected by a 'supernatural influence' (SF, 7:54–5), such as 'grace' (SF, 7:54–5, 57). Also, in his notes, adduced above, mysticism is associated with 'intuiting in God' (HN, 18:437), hence with the idea that our cognition is enabled by a union with the divine mind and mediated by God in whom our minds only 'participate'. Briefly, in a mystical experience, it is God that 'speaks' to the human being. However, in both the feeling of respect for the moral law and the feeling of the sublime it is reason that provides the source of these states: in the first case, by presenting us with the idea of duty (KpV, 5:76f.) and in the second – with 'ideas of reason, which, though no presentation adequate to them is possible, are provoked and called to mind precisely by this inadequacy, which does allow of sensible presentation' (KU, 5:246). In any case, according to Kant, the origin of both kinds of feelings is 'rational', hence it would be difficult to trace them back to an 'encounter' with God without presupposing God's 'presence' 'in' human reason.

Besides, it seems that another key feature of mystical experience must be the surety accompanying the awareness of the divine presence, due to the immediate character of this experience, emphasized by Palmquist. However, given the epistemic restrictions that the critical philosophy imposes upon our capacities, how is such surety supposed to be gained? In other words, even if it were possible to experience the divine, how could we recognize that the experience we are currently undergoing is a mystical experience? Nothing short of a judgement of reason would suffice to ensure that what we happen to be acquainted with is of divine nature, for the required certainty can be arrived at neither through sensible intuition nor through feeling. Kant makes this clear in the Orientation essay, where he says:

> The *concept* of God and even the conviction of his *existence* can be met with only in reason.... If I come across an immediate intuition of such a kind that nature, as I am acquainted with it, could not provide that intuition, then a concept of God must serve to gauge whether this appearance agrees with all the characteristics required for a Deity.... in order to judge whether what appears to me, what works internally or externally on my feelings, is God, I would have to hold it up to my rational concept of God and test it accordingly – not as to whether it is adequate to that concept, but merely whether it does not contradict it. In just the same way, even if nothing in what he discovered to me immediately contradicted that concept, nevertheless this appearance, intuition, immediate revelation, or whatever else one wants to call such a presentation, never proves the existence of a being whose concept... demands that it be of *infinite* magnitude as distinguished from everything created; but no experience or intuition at all can be adequate to that concept, hence none can unambiguously prove the existence of such a being.
> (WDO, 8:142–3)

The above-quoted lengthy fragment does not challenge the *possibility* of an '*immediate* and *personal*' 'encounter' with the divine, yet it makes clear that such an 'encounter' could not yield certainty that what we experience is indeed the presence of God. Also, since experience cannot be adequate to the idea of God that we have in our reason, it cannot directly relate us to the divine; rather, it can at most trigger in us a process of reflection on the nature of what we 'encounter', mediated by the rational concept of God. Thus, it seems that, according to Kant, there is no way in which we could 'access' the divine other than through reason, yet unless we locate the capacity to 'encounter' the divine 'in' our reason, we seem to be left without prospects for an '*immediate* and *personal* religious experience'. However, to claim that God makes himself present to us through our own reason might take us to the kind of position that Kant featured as enthusiastic and which he attributed to Spinoza (as the doctrine of 'seeing in God'). As said at the beginning of this section, Kant's attitude to enthusiasm was marked by ambiguity.

4

The primacy of the practical in Kant and Spinoza

4.1. Preliminaries

In Chapter 3 I suggested that the reason why Kant does not judge it at least notionally impossible to be an unbeliever and yet a moral person – whether of the sceptical type, a fatalist like Schulz or a theoretical atheist like Spinoza – is that he rejects the idea that action should be guided by knowledge. Thus, one's knowledge of the existence of God is not a prerequisite of being able to act morally; but nor does belief or faith in divine existence – in the Kantian sense of '*Glaube*' – constitute such a prerequisite. Since acting morally does not presuppose subscribing to any specific metaphysical tenets, the 'moral atheist', just like Kant, could prioritize the practical over the theoretical. Yet, given the well-established reading of Spinoza as a thinker who elevated knowledge to the rank of religion,[1] and one for whom 'true religion' would consist in the scientific cognition of nature, the claim about the 'moral atheist''s prioritizing the practical may come out as far from obvious.

According to Jonathan Israel, the radical Enlightenment originating in the ideas of Spinoza aimed to spark social and political changes by setting in motion a 'revolution of the mind'. The radical thought would sprout on 'a Spinozist tendency, combining one-substance doctrine or philosophical monism with democracy and a purely secular moral philosophy based on equality'.[2] Radical thinkers, such as Paul-Henri Thiry, Baron d'Holbach, promoted the idea that only by combating ignorance would prospects open for changes towards a more equal and just society.[3] The radical Enlightenment 'package' of ideas – mentioned in Chapter 1 – was meant 'one day to carry through a successful revolution of fact, leading to an entirely new kind of society'.[4] Keen as it was on shaping new patterns of action through a profound transformation of human beliefs, the radical 'fringe' animated by the thought of Spinoza appears to be far from endorsing the primacy of the practical.

Accordingly, the righteous unbeliever might not be modelled on the 'real' Spinoza, but rather on a figure like Friedrich Heinrich Jacobi. One of the few in his times who studied Spinoza's works first-hand, Jacobi discovered that 'this was the very position to which any attempt at a universal philosophical explanation or foundation must inevitably lead'.[5] But since he thought that Spinozism further leads to fatalism and atheism, that is, to positions he held to be untenable in practice, he recommended 'a "*salto mortale*" of faith in an intelligent, personal cause of the world'.[6] Therefore, the predecessor of the 'moral atheist' rejecting the idea that action should be guided by knowledge would rather be fideist Jacobi, whose '*salto mortale*', although spurred by the recognition of Spinozism as 'the only possible rational philosophy',[7] does not seem to represent the attitude of the 'real' Spinoza.

However, there might be a sense in which Spinoza can be claimed to assign primary importance to practical rationality – and which does not imply the need to attribute to him a lapse into fideism of the Jacobian breed. The argument would draw on Spinoza's account of human nature as marked by finitude and ineluctable cognitive limitations. Though in the *Ethics* Spinoza builds on the Cartesian project of a comprehensive system of knowledge, one of the ramifications of his ontology is that as a finite mode of infinite substance, the human being is likely unable to accomplish the kind of cognition that would equip him with the full mastery of nature. Accordingly, the human mind cannot be freed from inadequate ideas and the propensity to generate what we shall call 'metaphysical illusions'. Critical thinking is required to recognize this propensity but explaining why the mind would have the capacity to think critically poses a challenge. To address this challenge, we shall turn to Spinoza's idea of the unity of action and cognition and compare it with Kant's idea of the primacy of practical reason.

Before proceeding to the details of the argument, a caveat will be in order. Clearly, it is Kant, not Spinoza, who introduces the distinction between practical and theoretical *reason*. According to Kant, reason is the faculty that sets up laws (e.g. KrV, A 701/B 729, A 819/B 847, A 840/B 868) or principles (e.g. KrV, A 11/B 24, B 359, A 405). The legislation of reason manifests itself in two separate domains, nature and freedom, which he characterizes as follows:

> Our cognitive faculty as a whole has two domains, that of the concepts of nature and that of the concept of freedom; for it is a priori legislative through both. Philosophy is also divided accordingly into the theoretical and the practical....

Legislation through concepts of nature takes place through the understanding, and is theoretical. Legislation through the concept of freedom takes place through reason, and is merely practical.

(KU, 5:174)

Spinoza does not ascribe the legislative function to *human* reason. This is because he maintains that human cognitive capacities, and the human mind as such, cannot be singled out from nature, which is governed by uniform laws. He articulates this tenet in the Preface to Part Three of the *Ethics*, stating that 'the laws and rules of Nature according to which all things happen... are everywhere and always the same. So our approach to the understanding of the nature of things of every kind should likewise be one and the same; namely, through the universal laws and rules of Nature.'[8] The distinction between practical and theoretical reason belongs to Kant's philosophical idiom, not Spinoza's. To be able to compare the two thinkers with each other, then, let us assume that Kant's distinction between practical and theoretical reason can be applied more broadly and that it corresponds to the distinction between action and cognition in Spinoza.

4.2. The Cartesian project

According to Edwin Curley, Spinoza shares with Descartes the 'general notion' of philosophy, which 'determines the structure of the works they wrote' and manifests itself as 'the ideal of the unity of science', understood as a system that 'begins with metaphysics and ends in moral philosophy, after having considered the nature of man'.[9] With regard to its structure, Spinoza's *Ethics* can be viewed as an attempt at realizing Descartes's project of a deductive system of knowledge, adumbrated in the Preface to the *Principles of Philosophy*. Descartes introduces there a metaphor of a tree the roots of which represent metaphysics, the trunk – physics, and particular branches stand for special sciences: medicine, mechanics and ethics.[10] The whole tree represents philosophy – 'the study of Wisdom', that is, 'not only prudence in our affairs, but also a perfect knowledge of all the things which man can know for the conduct of his life, the preservation of his health, and the discovery of all the arts'.[11]

Descartes's conception of philosophy highlights the practical consequences of knowledge. Since the connections between parts of the tree symbolize deductive relations between different branches of the system, ethics – the discipline that crowns the tree – must be deducible from metaphysics (which is the most fundamental), comprising knowledge of God and the soul, and physics, which comprises knowledge of the material world. This means that unless both metaphysics and physics are complete, also ethics, the knowledge needed to regulate our conduct, cannot be accomplished. Thus, if we lack a full account of the material world, as indeed seems to be the case, we will also face uncertainty regarding what we should do to act well. As a remedy, Descartes devises a provisional moral code (*la morale par provision*) consisting of common-sense prescriptions, such as the recommendation that we adhere to the rules and customs followed in our country.[12] Underlying the idea of provisional morality, there is the assumption that actions can be motivated by beliefs based on non-epistemic grounds (cf. 3.4). Moreover, since the rules of conduct do not describe any reality, they are neither true nor false; rather, their validity lies in the usefulness or other non-cognitive merits that they may bring forth.

To some extent, Spinoza's *Ethics* reflects the structure of Descartes's tree: Part One covers the subject matter of metaphysics – God; Part Two focuses on the human mind and the nature of bodies, as well as the mind-body relation, that is, topics in psychology, physics and/or mechanics; and in Parts Three, Four and Five Spinoza addresses the main problem his work aims to solve, namely how to gain control over the emotions or affects (*affectus*) which make human life unhappy. Judging by its structure, it may seem that Spinoza's work shows the way to reach the ideal of 'the highest and most perfect Ethics',[13] yet the contents of the work do not exactly warrant such a conclusion.

Given Spinoza's account of the cognitive capacities of the human mind, the complete system of knowledge is anything but feasible. For, according to Spinoza, the human mind is a finite mode (*modus*) of substance considered under the attribute of thought, which means that it is an idea – or, to be more specific, a congeries of ideas.[14] Spinoza defines the mode as 'that which is in something else', meaning that it has its cause outside itself, and 'is conceived through something else',[15] that is, its existence and nature are not self-evident but, to be explained, require the existence of a different thing. Hence, the existence and nature of the human mind are not self-evident, a fact that affects the possibility of self-knowledge and which betrays the anti-Cartesian thrust of Spinoza's thought. As an idea, the mind represents an actually existing particular body.[16] This particular body itself has the status of a mode of substance considered under the attribute of extension. As a finite mode, this particular body has a cause outside itself, and neither its existence nor its nature is self-evident. The existence and nature of the body can only be explained by tracking the causal connections it enters into with other bodies, though not with the mind, because Spinoza holds that the attributes remain mutually independent with regard to the explanation of phenomena that occur within them.[17] If the causal connections, which a particular body associated with the mind enters into, are infinite, then it seems that the complete cognition of a particular human mind would be possible but from the viewpoint of a mind capable of representing infinite causal chains, that is, a mind whose corresponding object would itself be infinite. Yet there is only one such object in the universe as construed by Spinoza, and this is God or Nature. It follows that I could attain the comprehensive knowledge of my mind, or self-knowledge, only if my cognition approximated the cognition pertaining to the divine mind.

Thus, insofar as 'the most perfect Ethics' crowning the Cartesian system presupposes knowledge of the human soul, it is not possible for any human being to achieve this ideal. Hence, Spinoza's *Ethics* does not purport to realize the Cartesian ideal, but rather to address the consequences of the cognitive deficiencies which the kind of beings we are inevitably suffer. These consequences amount to what Spinoza calls 'bondage', which he defines as 'man's lack of power to control and check the emotions' that are based on inadequate ideas and as a result of which the man 'is not his own master but is subject to fortune'.[18] The remedy offered by Spinoza can be likened to a cognitive therapy, which would be effected by studying the causes of one's emotions or properly directing them – to the things we can know and understand, rather than to those which remain unfathomable to us.[19]

Turning to Kant now: his departure from the Cartesian ideal is marked not only by his distinction between theoretical and practical reason, but also by his denial of the very idea that ethics should build on knowledge. Attaining the kind of comprehensive knowledge that would be embodied by the Cartesian system is not only impossible for finite rational beings, according to Kant, but would also be detrimental from the moral-practical point of view because it would thwart the possibility of moral action. In the *Danzig Theology* notes, one can read: 'Outside of opining and believing (*Glauben*), apodictic knowing (*Wissen*) is the third degree of taking-to-be-true. Would it not be better if we had this? No, for thereby all morality would fall away' (V-Th/Baumbach, 28:1292). A parallel statement can be found in the Pölitz lecture notes on religion:

> Hence our faith is not knowledge, and thank heaven it is not!... For suppose we could attain to knowledge of God's existence through our experience or in some other way... suppose further that we could really reach as much certainty through this knowledge as we do in intuition; then all morality would break

down. In his every action the human being would represent God to himself as a rewarder or avenger; this image would force itself involuntarily on his soul, and his hope for reward and fear of punishment would take the place of the moral motives; the human being would be virtuous from sensible impulses.

(V-Phil-Th/Pölitz, 28:1084)

Why does knowledge, particularly of God's existence, drive out morality in Kant's view? One of the reasons why Kant thinks so is that since knowledge would replace faith which he regards as the only means of reinforcing the pull of the moral incentives in us, as we have seen in 3.3, knowledge would weaken our moral motivation. This implies that the knowledge of God's existence would equip us with additional non-moral incentives for our conduct that would compete with morality: the fear of punishment and the expectation of reward. We would then be even more vulnerable to reversing the order of priority in the incentives motivating our will, so that obedience to the moral law would be subordinated to the fear of punishment or hope for reward. Thereby, we would give in more easily to the propensity Kant identifies, in the *Religion*, as radical evil in our heart (cf. 5.3.2).

Kant's contention about knowledge of God undermining morality presupposes a conception of God that turns away from the rationalism of Descartes and Spinoza. Note that Kant associates knowledge of the divine existence with the imagery of God as distributing rewards and punishments, which appeals to our natural desires, especially the desire for happiness (cf. RGV, 6:6n.). It is far from obvious why knowledge of God, should it be possible, would have to imply such a conception of God. Spinoza, for example, would regard the conception as characteristic of the superstitious kind of faith (cf. 5.4.1), yet for Kant knowledge relates to sensibility by default. Thus, he may assume that if we *knew* that God existed, we would *represent* God as a rewarder and avenger because this is the way we could imagine God to be. Thus read, however, Kant's argument seems to beg the question.

4.3. The boundaries of knowledge

As I have argued in the last section, neither Spinoza's nor Kant's philosophical theory makes it possible for us to approximate the realization of the Cartesian ideal of a comprehensive system of knowledge, the corollary of a recognition of the limits of human cognitive capacities. Clearly, there is nothing novel in this recognition; but the point here is rather that emphasizing human finitude allows adopting a perspective from which arguments for the primacy of practical reason can be advanced. There is a noteworthy difference between Kant and Spinoza, though: for while Spinoza's theory of finite beings forms part of a theory of the infinite substance – *Deus sive Natura*, Kant's focus on human cognitive limitations rules out the possibility of making judgements about objects which go beyond the scope of these capacities. The doctrine which precludes the possibility of our acquiring knowledge of God, the immortality of the soul and freedom of the will – three objects providing the subject matter of dogmatic metaphysics (KrV, B 7) – is called transcendental idealism. In this doctrine, human cognition is constrained to 'appearances', the spatio-temporal objects of empirical cognition, and does not extend over 'things in themselves' (cf. KrV, A 369), that is, such objects which do not bear any temporal and/or spatial characteristics.

According to Stephen Palmquist, Kant's recognition of the intrinsically limited nature of human knowledge has led him to dislodging the anthropocentric stance in favour of a theocentric position. Kant's 'seminal doctrine of the *primacy of practical reason*', says Palmquist, 'represents the culmination of this line of thinking: an anthropocentric System would give primacy to theoretical reason, treating human knowledge as its central feature; Kant denies such knowledge only in the sense of rejecting its *centrality*, because his System puts the theocentric faith of practical reason in its place'.[20] Though the claim about Kant's position being theocentric remains far from obvious, the point here is that safeguarding the rationality of belief based on practical, hence non-epistemic, grounds hinges on denying the privileged status to human cognition and acknowledging the possibility of other perspectives from which the objects of our cognition could also be considered.

But neither is Spinoza's system anthropocentric, albeit for somewhat different reasons, for he ventures to assess human cognition against the standard of 'a given idea of the most perfect Being'.[21] It is because we have the 'standard' of cognition provided by the divine mind that we can become aware of the deficiencies of cognition peculiar for human beings. Accordingly, Spinoza notices that our minds produce 'inadequate ideas' – 'fragmentary and confused' representations of reality which do not convey truth.[22] In the *Treatise on the Emendation of the Intellect*, he justifies this claim by appealing to the ontological status of human beings: 'if it is in the nature of a thinking being... to form true or adequate thoughts, it is certain that inadequate ideas arise in us from this, that we are part of some thinking being, some of whose thoughts constitute our mind in their entirety, and some only in part'.[23] The human forms but a fragment of the divine knowledge, that is, of all possible knowledge in general. There is therefore for us no way to escape the fact that some of the ideas we have will be inadequate, other than changing our ontological status, *per impossibile*. Since we are humans, divine cognition remains outside our reach.

Recall the problem of the possibility of self-knowledge given Spinoza's views on the human mind, outlined in the previous section. According to Spinoza, since minds are complex ideas representing complex physical objects, that is, bodies,[24] for a mind to know itself would mean for it to represent the infinitely complex chains of causes that the body with which it is associated forms part of. Yet such an accomplishment requires an infinite understanding. Commenting on this part of Spinoza's doctrine, Gilles Deleuze pointed out that, on this account, it is not only the case that our 'body surpasses the knowledge that we have of it' – a truism one easily realizes, for example, when struck with a difficult-to-cure medical condition – but *'thought likewise surpasses the consciousness that we have of it'*. Our minds originate thus in the *'unconscious of thought'*, because some of the ideas that explain them fall outside our cognitive grasp, as do some of the causes affecting our bodies.[25] The result is that all our ideas are tainted by the ineradicable mark of inadequacy: 'the conditions under which we know things and are conscious of ourselves', says Deleuze, 'condemn us *to have only inadequate ideas*, ideas that are confused and mutilated, effects separated from their real causes.'[26] From this viewpoint, knowledge should be seen as an ideal that human beings aspire to, rather than any actual accomplishment of the human mind.

Against this background, Spinoza identifies a propensity evinced by the human mind seeking to satisfy its desire for knowledge without being able to overcome its built-in ignorance. This propensity consists in replacing rational explanations, that is, such explanations that provide us with the cognition of the causes of occurrences, with ideas that originate in the imagination and that, without being causally related to the occurrences under consideration, remain inadequate, hence false. The imagination, says Spinoza, nurtures itself on 'certain sensations that are (so to speak) fortuitous and unconnected, arising not from the power of the mind but from external causes, in accordance as the body, dreaming or waking, receives various motions.'[27] The imagination harbours misrepresentations of reality, including those raised to the rank of metaphysical truths. For example, it represents extension as finite, divisible and made of parts, whereas the intellect cognizes it as infinite, indivisible and one.[28] The figments of imagination, contends Spinoza, comprise also final causes,[29] the good and the bad, imperfections in nature and its beauty.[30] Since due to these figments 'we regard things, both in respect of the past and the future, as contingent', also time 'is a product of the imagination'.[31] In the *Theological-Political Treatise* Spinoza identifies the imagination as the underlying cause of superstition.[32] He claims, for example, that the prophets of the Old Covenant were endowed 'with a more vivid power of imagination', instead of extraordinary intellectual capacities, and because prophecies are based on imagination, we cannot be certain of their truth.[33]

Whereas Spinoza charges the imagination with bringing distortions into human cognition, Kant regards it as an 'indispensable function of the soul, without which we would have no cognition at all', though he calls this function 'blind', adding that we hardly ever become aware of its operations (KrV, A 78). In the A-edition version of the first *Critique*, the imagination performs one kind of the synthesis of the manifold data delivered by intuition, namely 'the synthesis of reproduction' (KrV, A 100–2), whereby the representational manifold is subsumed under a rule which guides its organization. Moreover, the imagination partakes of the process Kant calls 'schematism of the pure concepts of the understanding' (KrV, A 137/B 177f.), which consists in 'producing' intermediary representations connecting the categories of the understanding with the *a priori* intuition of time, and which is to guarantee the possibility of the application of the pure concepts to the objects of sensible intuition. Given the role of the imagination in Kant's theory of empirical cognition, some interpreters suggested that it may provide the 'common but to us unknown root' of the 'two stems of human cognition': sensibility and understanding (KrV, A 15/B 29).[34] Its constitutive function notwithstanding, the imagination, according to Kant, does not take us any closer to the divine perspective on the domain of cognition – the kind of perspective Spinoza would describe using the phrase '*sub specie aeternitatis*'[35] – but leaves us constrained to appearances.

Yet again a difference between Spinoza's and Kant's conceptions of human cognition may emerge, which would consist in this that whereas for Spinoza cognition comes in degrees and can be divided into separate kinds – a residue of the Platonic epistemological tradition – for Kant cognition seems to capture one kind of objects: spatio-temporal particulars. Accordingly, Spinoza distinguishes: (1) knowledge of the first kind (based on opinion and imagination), related to objects manifest to us in sensible experience or through symbols (linguistic signs such as words); (2) knowledge of the second kind (based on reason), derived from common notions and adequate ideas; (3) knowledge of the third kind, that is, *scientia intuitiva*. 'This kind of knowledge', he avers, 'proceeds from an adequate idea of the formal essence of certain attributes of God to an adequate knowledge of the essence of things.'³⁶ The possibility of *scientia intuitiva* relies on the assumption of unity between God and finite beings, so that the cognition of the one implies the cognition of the other: when it comes to their object, theology and physics prove to be compatible.

Clearly, Kant denies intuitive cognition insofar as it presupposes the involvement of intellectual intuition, a capacity which he claims that we do not have (cf. KrV, B 308; see also HN, 23:36). However, although knowledge in the proper sense of the term is for him restricted to empirical objects, including the laws and principles that govern them, Christopher Firestone and Nathan Jacobs have argued that Kant does indeed recognize different kinds of *cognition*: empirical and pure. Pure cognition, which can also be termed 'the cognition of reason', pertains to 'the proper objects of rational faith',³⁷ such as God and future life. We are able to cognize (*erkennen*) supersensible objects, though we cannot know (*wissen*) anything about them, since for one to have a cognition (*Erkenntnis*) it suffices that one be 'able to get something in mind' without it being necessary for the representational content of such a cognitive state to be accompanied by a sensible intuition, which is a necessary requirement for knowledge (*Wissen*).³⁸ And, importantly, empirical cognition does not provide the highest degree of cognition also for Kant, as he locates the end of our intellectual pursuits in the 'doctrine of wisdom', that is, in philosophy understood as a science of the unity of moral and natural ends in the ideal of the highest good (cf. V-Phil-Th/Pölitz, 28:1057; OP, 22:489; cf. chapter 6).

4.4. Metaphysical illusions

In the last section of Chapter 3, I discussed Kant's conception of a way of thinking which he describes as instantiating 'enthusiasm' (*Schwärmerei*). This way of thinking has been shown to parallel the one found in dogmatic metaphysics, on the one hand, and religious fanaticism, on the other. It is generated by a certain attitude of the mind, identified by Kant as 'persuasion' (*Überredung*), in which one conflates subjective with objective reasons for one's assent to a proposition. Yet also Spinoza would come close to identifying the kind of phenomenon that Kant's '*Schwärmerei*' is supposed to capture. To illustrate the point, we shall analyse Spinoza's rendering of two concepts forming the core of early modern metaphysical theories: 'mind' and 'freedom'.

Let us start from the mind. Spinoza's definition, adduced in sections 4.2 and 4.3, confirms his commitment to representationalism – the idea that the main function of the mind lies in generating representational content nomologically related to physical realities. But this conception of the mind should be read as a corollary of Spinoza's view on the relation between the mental and the physical, spelled out in Proposition 7 of Part Two of the *Ethics*: 'The order and connection of ideas is the same as the order and connection of things.'[39] This proposition implies that for any congeries of ideas, there is an array of 'things', physical objects corresponding to the congeries – and vice versa: physical objects, bodies, are paralleled by arrangements of ideas that represent the objects. Since the mind is a congeries of ideas associated with a particular body, given Spinoza's thesis cited above, it seems legitimate to conclude that everything that exists has a mind, thus it is not possible to distinguish a 'thing' that has a mind from a 'thing' that does not. As Michael Della Rocca has put it, 'mentality, for Spinoza, extends everywhere'[40] – a claim that expresses the basic tenet of panpsychism. Thus, defined in terms of Spinoza's metaphysics, 'mind' comes out as denoting no unique property that would distinguish a certain class of objects.

These counterintuitive panpsychist consequences may result from Spinoza's conflation of two properties, namely the property of having a mind (mentality) with the property of being poised for being represented by a mind (intelligibility or representability). For an idea that corresponds, say, to the table I am writing this book on does not have to be understood as the table's mind, but rather as the way in which my (or anyone else's) mind relates to this object. We may conjecture that the conflation would motivate an objection Kant raised against Spinoza in the Orientation essay, which says that Spinoza introduced 'thoughts which themselves think' (WDO, 8:144n.), that is, he confused thinkable contents with the acts of thought. Kant's remark, although cryptic, conveys an apt observation that for Spinoza the reality of thought, one of the infinitely many attributes of substance, is more fundamental than the distinction between the thinking subject and the object of thought. In Spinoza's view, thought cannot be explained in any more basic terms such as subjectivity.

According to one of Descartes's pivotal arguments, subjectivity constitutes an essential feature of the mind: there being a thought or an act of thinking necessitates the existence of the subject, the thinking 'I'. The argument, which revolutionized philosophy after Descartes, can be suspected to rest on the peculiarities of our language (or Descartes's languages, for that matter: Latin and French) and inner experience. The subject's experience is also supposed to warrant Descartes's claim concerning freedom of the will. For in the *Meditations*, he says: 'it is only the will, or freedom of choice, which I *experience* within me to be so great that the idea of any greater faculty is beyond my grasp.'[41] Yet, from

Spinoza's perspective, by introducing the 'I' or 'free will' Descartes toys with empty abstractions – inadequate ideas without a corresponding object on the side of the 'order of things'. As we have seen, there is nothing subjective about the 'mind' for Spinoza. The same might be said about freedom.

In the *Ethics*, Spinoza defines freedom as follows: 'That thing is said to be free [*liber*] which exists solely from the necessity of its own nature, and is determined to action by itself alone.'[42] A given thing is free if its existence can be explained by properties which determine its nature, rather than by the properties of a different thing, and if it acts unhindered by any external causes, exercising its own causal power and thus originating new chains of causes from itself. In this sense, only God can be free, according to Spinoza, because only God's nature implies existence and only God is a '*causa sui*'.

But in Spinoza's ontology whatever is, is either self-caused (substance) or has a cause outside itself (modes). Since for a thing to have a cause outside itself means to be caused either by God or by other modes,[43] not only God but also the modes, including finite modes, exercise causal power. Thus, although absolute freedom can be predicated of God alone, some degree of freedom, that is, causal power derivative of the nature of a thing, can be attributed to any mode inhering in Spinoza's substance. Construed in this way, freedom would be a property that pertains to any existing thing, hence a property that would not distinguish the human being from other things furnishing the 'order of nature'. Against this background, the kind of freedom that Descartes envisaged his inner experience to give him access to emerges as a metaphysical illusion.

Given the foregoing, Spinoza can be read as offering a deflationary account of subject-related concepts, such as 'mind' and 'freedom'. These concepts, building the backbone of Cartesian metaphysics, prove to designate no realities and can eventually be dismissed as redundant. This conclusion might be too hasty, though, at least with regard to the concept of freedom, for there are also alternative accounts of it to be found in Spinoza's writings. Accordingly, in the *Short Treatise on God, Man and His Well-Being*, Spinoza connects freedom to the activity of thinking and describes it as 'a firm reality which our understanding acquires through direct union with God, so that it can bring forth ideas in itself, and effects outside itself, in complete harmony with its nature; without, however, its effects being subjected to any external causes, so as to be capable of being changed or transformed by them.'[44] In the *Theological-Political Treatise*, he contends that freedom constitutes an intrinsic and inalienable feature of thought and judgement: 'no man', avers Spinoza, 'can give up his freedom to judge and think as he pleases, and everyone is by absolute natural right the master of his own thoughts.'⁴⁵ Hence, as Stuart Hampshire has argued, Spinoza would make room for the emancipation of the mind from causal-deterministic relations in nature by means of intellectual activity. For Spinoza, 'the detachment from causes in the common order of nature... lasts while self-critical thinking lasts'.⁴⁶

Nonetheless, also these alternative accounts fail to establish that freedom is a non-trivial property distinguishing a certain class of beings, such as the Cartesian 'thinking subjects'. For according to Spinoza particular attributes of substance, hence also things conceived under these attributes, enjoy explanatory independence: each attribute 'must be conceived through itself'.⁴⁷ Therefore, occurrences within the attribute of thought, or what can be called mental events, cannot be explained by reference to occurrences within the attribute of extension, or what can be called physical events. This means that there can be no causal relations between occurrences considered under different attributes: no idea can affect a physical event or object and no physical event or object can have a causal impact on an idea. Hence, thought is free from causal impacts by default, as it were, and being free in this sense amounts to existing in the mode of an idea. Thought is free because it is not governed by causal relations, but only by such relations as are proper to it, namely the logical ones. Given Spinoza's panpsychism, all beings are free in this way, which renders freedom an inspecific, and so trivial property of beings.

In one of the senses spelled out above, whatever exercises its causal power is free. Yet this sense of freedom does not preclude the idea that a thing which exercises its causal power itself has a cause. Thus, being free is compatible with being subject to causal efficacy and is a property that comes in degrees. On the variety of the compatibilist account of freedom that Spinoza seems to espouse, it is not the case that a thing can be free only if it is exempt from causal determinations. But this, according to Spinoza, is how many people think when they take themselves to be free whereas in fact they do not know the causes of their actions. (Mark that he does not equate the apparent lack of determining causes with self-determination, characteristic of the divine being: the former can be deemed a metaphysical illusion, not the latter.) In the *Ethics*, Spinoza explains this popular misconception as follows:

> Men are deceived of thinking themselves free, a belief that consists only in this, that they are conscious of their actions and ignorant of the causes by which they are determined. Therefore, the idea of their freedom is simply the ignorance of the cause of their actions. As to their saying that human actions depend on the will, these are mere words without any corresponding idea.⁴⁸

Spinoza traces the metaphysical illusion of freedom to the ignorance of the causes of one's actions. A person who holds herself to be free in this sense seems to be incapable of providing any explanation for her actions. But, somewhat counter-intuitively, in light of an axiom which says that 'the knowledge of an effect depends on, and involves, the knowledge of the cause',[49] this means that the person does not even have proper knowledge of her actions as such. Or, she may have inadequate ideas related to what has brought her actions about, in particular, she may regard herself to be the sole and sufficient cause of her actions, thus putting herself in the position of a being whose actions follow from its nature alone, such as God. In this latter case, not being able to track the entire chain of causes leading up to her actions, the person would locate the origin of the chain in herself, creating thereby the illusion of her own exclusive efficacy.

There are noteworthy similarities between Spinoza's account of the idea of freedom as grafted on the ignorance of the causes of one's actions, developed in the *Ethics*, and his account of belief in miracles, put forward in chapter 6 of the *Theological-Political Treatise*. Spinoza explains there that 'common people'[50] conceive any event as miraculous which they 'cannot explain by comparison with any other normal event'.[51] This way of thinking of the 'common man' would be reflected in the Cartesian metaphysics generating empty abstractions instead of causal explanations of events. Metaphysical illusions produced by the mind which seeks explanations but does not realize the scope of its cognitive constraints would therefore parallel superstitions characteristic of a *'religio vana'*.[52] The analogy between philosophical *'Schwärmerei'*, built on dogmatic metaphysical notions (HN, 18:434–8), and the spurious forms of religious belief – 'superstition' and 'enthusiasm' (RGV, 6:174–5) – can also be found in Kant.

Thus, what the 'common man' would share with the Cartesian metaphysician would be a propensity to posit realities that work as 'fillers' of the explanatory gaps arising as a result of the intrinsic limitations of human knowledge. Arguably, to recognize what we have called metaphysical illusions, one needs to inquire into the nature of cognition particular for finite rational beings, its limits and scope – and this is what critical reflection, or a critique of reason, amounts to. But can critical thought be accounted for within the naturalist framework of Spinoza's philosophy? Is there space for critical reflection within the confines of a system that considers subjectivity 'metaphysically quite groundless',[53] as Leszek Kołakowski once put it?

There are two ways of addressing this question: one leading directly through textual evidence and the other more speculative, requiring that we put together different strands of Spinoza's thought. We shall consider the second option in the subsequent section of this chapter. Regarding the first one: in the *Ethics*, Spinoza says that accompanying the idea which he calls the mind, there must also be an idea 'united to the mind'. Spinoza calls it 'the idea of an idea' and explains its presence appealing to the reflexivity of cognitive states. 'For as soon as anyone knows something', he avers, 'by that very fact he knows that he knows, and at the same time he knows that he knows that he knows, and so on ad infinitum.'[54]

Yet the reflexivity of cognitive states does not explain the capacity for self-critical thought, for we can continue to demand an explanation of the reflexive nature of knowledge, and so of thought, a feature absent from the modes of extension. Should Spinoza ground his claim about the self-reflexive nature of thought in inner experience, he would fall back on the Cartesian positions and lapse into inconsistency. To circumvent this corollary, I shall offer an alternative explanation of the capacity for critical thought, grounding the capacity in Spinoza's conception of the interdependency between thought and action.

4.5. The primacy of the practical

I have highlighted some common points between Kant and Spinoza, which pertain to the limits of human knowledge and the critique of the kind of metaphysics that takes the finite subject as its point of departure, yet without properly recognizing the corollaries of its finitude. According to Yirmiyahu Yovel, the notion of finitude furnishes the very foundations of Kant's critical philosophy: 'we cannot be rational except through reason's finitude, just as this finitude must be attributed to us as creatures of reason.'[55] The aim of this chapter has been to suggest that also Spinoza's philosophy can be investigated through the lens of human finitude. The suggestion concurs with Nancy Levene's proposal that 'what structures Spinoza's thought... is not just nature but human nature',[56] and this is marked by the fact of finitude. It is this fact that shall motivate prioritizing the practical by both Spinoza and Kant.

4.5.1. Spinoza

Given Spinoza's claim about the uniformity of the laws and principles which govern nature, adduced in section 4.1, one may suggest, in somewhat metaphorical terms, that modes exist in the way that imitates the existence of substance – God or Nature. For example, both God and finite beings are free in that they manifest causal efficacy, the difference being that the latter can afford it to a limited degree, and that they are subject to the causal efficacy of other beings. Likewise, as much as God exists from the necessity of its nature, the divine essence comprising existence,[57] so too finite beings are necessitated to persevere in existence by their nature alone. Spinoza terms this feature '*conatus*', or striving, and equates it with 'the actual essence of the thing itself'.[58] Because of the striving that constitutes the very being of a *particular* thing, the human being included, no thing can cease to exist of its own nature, but only once its perseverance in being has been thwarted by an external adversity that diminishes the thing's power.[59]

If freedom amounts to being causally efficacious, then the outcome of the diminishing of one's causal efficacy will be one's limitation of freedom. Since the Spinozean world is governed by the principle of causality – or its rationalist counterpart: the principle of sufficient reason[60] – those things whose causal efficacy can be diminished must be such things that are subject to the causal efficacy of other beings. Accordingly, for beings other than God that remains absolutely free, being causally efficacious, or active, goes together with enduring states of passivity. This means not only that finite beings like us are sometimes acted upon by other beings, both of the same and different kinds, but also that when we act on other beings, we enjoy the reciprocal effects of these beings' acting upon us.

Now, Spinoza establishes an intrinsic relation between activity, expressing itself in causal efficacy, and adequate ideas: for such states or occurrences of which I am the cause, the explanation – and so the idea of what has brought them about – is in me. Thus, one's causal efficacy entails one's entertaining an adequate idea, hence knowledge. In the *Ethics*, Spinoza says:

> Insofar as a man is determined to action from the fact that he has inadequate ideas, to that extent... he is passive; that is... he does something that cannot be perceived solely in terms of his own essence, that is... something that does not follow from his own virtue. But insofar as he is determined to an action from the fact that he understands, to that extent he is active... that is... he does something that is perceived solely in terms of his own essence, that is... which follows adequately from his own virtue.[61]

Thus, cognitive states cannot be isolated from the context of action, not just in the sense that they guide our actions – they could not insofar as they belong to the 'order of ideas' whereas actions belong to the 'order of things' – but rather because they form unity with actions. Since only active states, that is, such states in which we exercise our causal efficacy, are accompanied by adequate ideas, hence knowledge, it must be due to such states that one can escape the illusions of the Cartesian metaphysician on the one hand and the ignorance of the 'common man' on the other. Knowledge, reflection and critical thought, therefore, come along with action. (Mark that the question whether knowledge which accompanies the exercise of one's causal efficacy is *consciously* possessed by the subject bears little relevance for Spinoza.) Spinoza's unifying action with cognition warrants an observation, made by Etienne Balibar, that 'from the very beginning his metaphysics is a philosophy of praxis, of activity'. The practical orientation of Spinoza's metaphysics would also have political consequences, issuing in a plea for the 'liberation' of human nature.[62]

The primacy of the practical comes to the fore in Spinoza's conception of a 'universal religion' (*religio catholica*). The core of this religion, which we shall deal with in more detail in Chapter 5, lies in the basic precept which says that 'worship of God and obedience to him consists solely in justice and charity, or love towards one's neighbour'.[63] The universal religion, accessible as the 'Word of God' in one's heart or in the Christian and Jewish Scriptures (purified from irrelevant doctrines, or just read critically), dispenses with theological knowledge and encourages moral life conduct as a sufficient condition of having a religion. This would be the kind of religion that Kant was prone to attribute to the 'righteous unbeliever' considered in Chapter 3. Denying the relevance of theological doctrines for faith, Spinoza says:

> [A]s to the question of what God, the exemplar of true life, really is, whether he is fire, or spirit, or light, or thought, or something else, this is irrelevant to faith. And so likewise is the question as to why he is the exemplar of true life, whether this is because he has a just and merciful disposition, or because all things exist and act through him and consequently we, too, understand through him, and through him we see what is true, just, and good. On these questions it matters not what beliefs a man holds... The view one takes on these and similar questions has no bearing on faith.[64]

If morally good actions were such actions that could be attributed to the agent's causal efficacy, then given the doctrine of the unity of action and cognition which derives from the *Ethics*, morally good actions would have to be accompanied by adequate ideas, because the agent would figure at the origin of these actions. Given the involvement of adequate ideas in action thus conceived, obeying God by acting morally, living by the precepts of the universal faith, may then turn out to lead to the cognition of God – or to an adequate conception of the divine. We might presume that, based on universal moral precepts, acceptable to everyone regardless of their theological beliefs, the practice of *religio catholica* could not only give rise to an adequate conception of God, but also prompt extinguishing the confessional strife witnessed by Spinoza and his contemporaries in abundance.[65]

4.5.2. Kant

Kant's concept of transcendental freedom approximates Spinoza's account of freedom in one of the senses of the word, namely as the agent's causality. Yet, unlike Spinoza, Kant thinks that an action can be attributed to an agent only if the agent is the sole and ultimate cause of the action. He describes this kind of freedom as 'a causality' which 'must be assumed' and 'through which something happens without its cause being further determined by another previous cause, i.e., an absolute causal spontaneity beginning from itself a series of appearances that runs according to natural laws' (KrV, A 446/B 474). Transcendental freedom provides the condition of the imputability of actions (and thoughts, as Colin McLear has recently argued[66]) to the subject,[67] yet though we can consistently think of our actions being free in this way, we cannot *know* that we are thus free, that is, we cannot establish the reality (or even real possibility) of freedom (cf. KrV, A 558/B 586). Kant makes it clear that we can think of ourselves as agents only if we think of our actions as guided by the operations of a faculty that follows its own set of laws, in the *Groundwork of the Metaphysics of Morals*, where one can read:

> As a rational being... the human being can never think of the causality of his own will otherwise than under the idea of freedom; for independence from the determining causes of the world of sense (which reason must always ascribe to itself) is freedom. With the idea of freedom the concept of *autonomy* is now inseparably combined, and with the concept of autonomy the universal principle of morality, which in idea is the ground of all actions of *rational beings*, just as the law of nature is the ground of all appearances.
>
> (GMS, 4:452–3)

But again, though Kant stipulates that the moral law, legislated by pure practical reason, can 'ground' the actions of rational beings provided that the agent is capable of extricating himself from the impact of competing causes, such as sensible drives or even the divine will understood as agency external to the subject's will, this stipulation allows no more than the claim that we can act only 'under the *idea* of freedom'. From this it does not follow that we can indeed act as free or that we do so in reality. The logical possibility of freedom does not entail its real possibility, let alone its actuality.

In the *Critique of Practical Reason*, Kant seeks to address this concern in that he appeals to the 'fact of reason' – consciousness of the moral law that can motivate the subject's actions. Thus, in the words of Ralph Walker, 'Kant holds that our awareness of the moral law enables us to establish the reality of freedom, which is something that theoretical reason could never do.'[68] The reality of freedom would be derived from the moral consciousness rather than being given directly to reason: 'Consciousness of this fundamental law', says Kant, 'may be called a fact of reason because one cannot reason it out from antecedent data of reason, for example, from consciousness of freedom' (KpV, 5:31). If the moral law 'in' our reason compels us to act in a certain way, we must be able to follow the moral law, hence resist non-moral incentives, in particular sensible inclinations, that come from outside our reason. This in turn means that in order to be able to act morally, we must be free.

Yet could we not acknowledge the compelling force of the moral law without being able actually to follow it, because our resolution to follow the law would always be overpowered by non-moral incentives? Like the incontinent (acratic) person in Book VII of Aristotle's *Nicomachean Ethics* (see line 22 and further at 1145b), one would then be aware of one's moral duties, but mere awareness would not suffice for one to overcome sensible inclinations, as a matter of fact. If it is possible to conceive of such a scenario, is it not too optimistic, *pace* Walker, to claim that the 'fact of reason' allows establishing the reality of freedom? The awareness of the moral law would then be a necessary but not a sufficient condition of the reality of freedom.

However, there are more considerations in the second *Critique* that can help establish the sought-for conclusion. These considerations appeal to the distinction between practical and theoretical reason and warrant the supposition that the interest of practical reason trumps the deficiencies which pertain to reason in its theoretical or speculative use, and which result from the limited nature of human cognition. Whereas the interest of theoretical reason 'consists in the *cognition* of the object up to the highest a priori principles', that of practical reason 'consists in the determination of the *will* [*Wille*]' (KpV, 5:120), that is, in reason's self-determination, given that Kant equates the will with practical reason (cf. GMS, 4:412). The primacy of the practical implies that insofar as freedom constitutes a prerequisite of the interest of reason in its practical use, we are entitled to endorse the reality of freedom – to believe that we are free despite the lack of evidence corroborating this claim that would be apt from the theoretical point of view and that could be furnished by a specific kind of experience. This way, practical reason provides an 'extension' of reason onto the objects of metaphysical cognition, such as God, freedom and the immortality of the soul, which Kant held reason to be naturally interested in (cf. KrV, B7, B 31–2). This extension, Kant hastens to add, does not widen the scope of truths cognized by theoretical reason, though:

> if pure reason of itself can be and really is practical… it is still only one and the same reason which, whether from a theoretical or a practical perspective, judges according to a priori principles; and… even if from the first perspective its capacity does not extend to establishing certain propositions affirmatively, although they do not contradict it, *as soon as these same propositions belong inseparably to the practical interest* of pure reason, it must accept them… being mindful, however, that these are not its insights but are yet extensions of its use from another, namely a practical perspective.
>
> (KpV, 5:121)

The need to exercise moral self-legislation necessitates endorsing the reality, and not just possibility, of freedom. Thus, to deny the latter, we would have to resign from attributing to ourselves the status of moral agents. Endorsing the reality of freedom, reason 'constructs' or establishes the 'space' for moral agency. In this function, reason could be likened to a legislator for a political community who passes laws with a view to safeguarding individuals' agency – acting on the assumption that all members of the community are equally capable of exercising their political rights. We can find an illustration of this idea in a remark Kant makes in passing in a note of Part Four of the *Religion*:

> I admit that I am not comfortable with this way of speaking, which even clever men are wont to use: 'A certain people (intent on establishing civil freedom) is not ripe for freedom'; 'The bondmen of a landed proprietor are not yet ripe for freedom'; and so too, 'People are in general not yet ripe for freedom of belief'. For on this assumption freedom will never come, since we cannot *ripen* to it if we are not already established in it (we must be free in order to be able to make use of our powers purposively in freedom). To be sure, the first attempts will be crude… yet we do not ripen to freedom otherwise than through our *own* attempts (and we must be free to be allowed to make them).
>
> (RGV, 6:188n.)

The reality of freedom for Kant is not something that needs to be corroborated by theoretical considerations, or by experience furnishing us with proper instantiations of our exercise of freedom. As much as there can be no political freedom without the actual possibility for every citizen to exercise it, a possibility that builds on the presupposition that all citizens are free, so too the realization of moral autonomy requires that we acknowledge that agents are in fact capable of rational self-determination. The end of creating a civil society based on laws legitimates the otherwise ungrounded supposition that all citizens are free. Likewise, the interest of practical reason legitimates the conditions of exercising moral agency.

4.5.3. The radical Enlightenment

In the opening paragraphs of this chapter, some concerns were raised as to the plausibility of attributing to Spinoza, and hence to the radical Enlightenment, the tendency to prioritize practical over theoretical rationality. Yet, as the above considerations show, Spinoza conceives of thought and action as forming unity. In opposition to the Platonic philosophical tradition, thought for Spinoza does not direct itself, in an act of contemplation, towards a pre-existing reality, but rather, as the 'other side' of the causal activity of its bearer, is meant to affect reality and even, in a sense, to construct it. The tendency to give priority to the practical does not therefore defy the radical Enlightenment, but, on the contrary, pervades its foundational tenets. In thinkers considered radical, such as Spinoza, Diderot and d'Holbach, Israel has claimed that 'we encounter that absolute, uncompromising linkage of reason, knowledge, and philosophy with morality (and politics)',[69] stripped of the vestiges of theological dogma and religious tradition and poised for comprehensively reshaping the social and political realities. Spinoza's merger of action and cognition also has important consequences for validating our knowledge claims. For, on this account, truth does not need an external warrant or criterion, but becomes confirmed by praxis, if one may so put it. Thus construed, actions generate adequate ideas, that is, truth – and truth is no longer an abstract concept but a notion expressing our dynamic relation to and our engagement with reality. True or adequate ideas are practically significant.

This pragmatic thread also surfaces in Kant's doctrine of the primacy of practical reason, which submits reason's theoretical pursuits to an 'interest' which can only be satisfied within the practical dimension of this faculty. As we have seen in Chapter 3, epistemic grounds, which promote reason's theoretical pursuits, do not suffice to motivate certain modes of assent that we need to exercise in virtue of our rationality. Reason in its practical function not only enables the realization of the interest of reason as such – in that it legitimates cognitions that could not be accepted within the theoretical field, yet remain crucial from the viewpoint of our rationality. Reason in its practical function also confirms its capacity for self-legislation, that is, the fact that it not only escapes causal determinations by external objects, but primarily that it provides the source of the principles in accordance with which it operates. Kant's practical reason reveals the nature of human rationality as constitutive of itself. Demonstrating reason's capacity to legitimate its self-determination in the practical domain, Kant departs from the Cartesian ideal of ethics built on theistic foundations and approximates the 'separation of morality from theology that became fundamental to all Radical Enlightenment'.[70]

5

Kant's religious rationalism and Spinoza

5.1. Religious rationalism

In 1794 Kant received an injunction not to publish on religious matters, expressed in a letter from Frederick William II, the conservative successor of Frederick the Great, in which the king levelled an accusation against Kant of 'misusing his philosophy to distort and disparage many of the cardinal and basic teachings of the Holy Scriptures and of Christianity' (SF, 7:6). Although some have found this assessment exaggerated,[1] Enlightenment scholars like Ian Hunter, Michael Sauter and James Schmidt have argued that the king's decision and the 1788 edicts of Johann Christoph von Wöllner on which it was based, could be justified, given the historical context of their issuance.[2] According to Hunter, what the Prussian authorities found particularly troubling was the promotion of religious rationalism in which Kant would also be involved, his 'religious philosophy' constituting 'a characteristic expression of North German religious rationalism'.[3] The religious rationalists, who by no means created a uniform category of preachers and theological writers, would 'proselytize' a religion in its own right, potentially threatening the status quo by 'undermining the confessional balance'[4] between Christian denominations: Lutheran, Reformed and Catholic. In Hunter's picture:

> Deeply indebted to the anthropology and perfectionism of Leibnizian-Wolffian metaphysics, religious rationalism covered a wide cultural spectrum in a variety of forms. It reached all the way from the secret societies, where this metaphysics was taught as an esoteric knowledge to the *illuminati*, across radical rationalists like Carl Friedrich Bahrdt, to the 'liberal' Protestant theology of the neologians, who used it to transform sacramental religion into perfectionist moral anthropology.[5]

A brief overview of early modern works on 'rational religion' suffices to acknowledge the heterogeneity of this movement (see the endnote).[6] Accordingly, 'religious rationalism' can be understood as a network of related phenomena, spanning the late seventeenth century and the Enlightenment era. These phenomena include an attempt to specify which and in what way religious creeds can be compatible with reason and to rationally explicate revealed doctrines, but also a glorification of the powers of reason as God's gift.[7] According to Leszek Kołakowski, 'within Christian culture' religious rationalism can be construed as 'a principle according to which canonical writings should be interpreted in such a way that their contents are adjusted to the requirements of natural reason'.[8]

Hunter claims that religious rationalism was perceived as a threat to the constitutionally established balance between confessions – to which Wöllner's edict on religion added recognition and protection of such 'sects' as the Jews, the Herrnhutter, the Mennonites and the Bohemian Brethren[9] – because it formed a religion sui generis. Yet, if eighteenth-century Prussia sought to safeguard peaceful coexistence of different confessions, why would the occurrence of a competitive 'confession' have to distort that peace? Hunter's appeal to proselytizing practices of the rationalist preachers does not suffice to address this question: after all, proselytism can also mark religious orthodoxies. The narrative of secularization – bringing to the fore the parallel processes of the rationalization of faith and religious critique – could be employed to explain conservative reactions to religious rationalism, yet Hunter rejects it as a product of nineteenth-century philosophical history, unfitting to account for the processes underway a century before.[10]

Alternatively, if religious rationalism was considered a threat, this might not so much be due to its hostility to the confessional balance as to its affinity with the critique of revealed religion traceable to Spinoza's *Theological-Political Treatise*, widely accused of championing an anti-Christian agenda.[11] Frederick Beiser makes a related point, drawing a connection between radical reform movements in Germany and Spinozism. According to Beiser:

> Almost all the early Spinozists in Germany were the unhappy children of the Protestant Counter-Reformation. Most of them had been, or still were, pietists, and all of them had become bitterly disillusioned with the course of the Reformation. They were fiercely loyal to its original ideals: the universal priesthood of believers, freedom of conscience, the necessity for an immediate relationship to God. But in their eyes the Reformation had gone astray and betrayed its own principles.[12]

The reason of the disillusionment experienced by the German religious radicals inspired by Spinoza was the alliance between church and state that the Lutheran clergy, no less than the Catholic, had turned out to foster. The key aim of the religious rationalists being to adjust scriptural revelation to the requirements of natural reason, they must have assumed that the use of one's natural capacities suffices to unravel the intricacies of the biblical text. Accordingly, the skills of a rational thinker should replace the authority of an ecclesiastic when it comes to the interpretation of the Bible. The skills could be possessed by anyone, though paradigmatically by philosophers, as suggested in the title of an essay by Lodewijk Meijer, a Dutch member of Spinoza's circle – *Philosophia S. Scripturae interpres* (1673).[13] Questioning the monopoly of the churches for scriptural exegesis, religious rationalists would challenge the privileged status of the clergy and shake the foundations of institutional Christianity, encouraging secularization, even if *avant la lettre*.

In this chapter, the junctures at which religious rationalism and the Spinozist critique of revealed religion intersect will be traced in Kant's philosophical theology. Reading some key texts of Kant's philosophy of religion, such as the metaphor of two concentric circles, his 'definition' of religion and the doctrine of the 'prototype' of morally perfect humanity, I shall also set his views against those represented by heterodox thinkers: Carl Friedrich Bahrdt (5.2) and Johann Christian Edelmann (5.3), and finally by Spinoza (5.4). Unlike the early modern clandestine authors influenced by Epicureanism and/or representing *libertinage érudit*,[14] these thinkers did not work towards uprooting religion, but they sought to establish a tight bond between reason and religion (5.4). Thus construed, religious rationalism encouraged the emancipation of reason from ecclesiastical authority, though not a wholesale abandonment of religion.

5.2. Kant's rational religion

In line with Heinrich Heine's terse description, Kant could be perceived as an archenemy of deism.[15] Indeed, having undermined the key arguments of rational theology, Kant put an end to attempts at seeking knowledge of God by means of reason, characteristic of the deist position. Thus, if he proposed a variety of rational religion, his proposal should be distinguished from deism, or such a version of it that allows the possibility of the rational knowledge of God. Kant himself explicitly rejects the deist stance, which he describes as a position that 'accepts only transcendental theology' – the claim that 'there is a cause of the world' – but does not determine 'whether this cause is a freely acting being' (V-Phil-Th/Pölitz, 28:1001). In contrast, a theist endorses the view that there is 'a *living* God who has produced the world through knowledge and by means of free will'. Kant in turn subscribes to '*theismus moralis*' – 'the kind of theology in which God is thought of as the *summum bonum*, as the highest moral good' (V-Phil-Th/Pölitz, 28:1001–2, cf. V-Phil-Th/Pölitz, 28:1011).

Yet, as Allen Wood once argued, if we define deism as 'the opinion of those that acknowledge one God, without the reception of any revealed religion' – a definition to be found in John Dryden's poem titled *Religio laici* (1682)[16] – then Kant's attitude to rational religion thus conceived may seem more ambiguous. Kant does not reject revelation; for denying the intention to come up with a 'religion *from* mere reason', he admits that revelation may contain doctrines that can be 'recognized *by mere reason*' (SF, 7:6n.; cf. VARGV, 23:93). However, Kant's is a rational religion precisely in the sense that it amounts to an attempt to establish compatibility between reason and revealed doctrines. Also, as will be clear from his 'definition' of religion (cf., e.g., RGV, 6:154), he urges that what is *essential* to religion must be of rational provenance. Eventually, trying to separate the rational 'core' of religion from its non-rational 'shell' or 'husk',[17] Kant bestows upon reason the role of the 'judge' of revelation, eligible to carry out the separation.

The aim of this section is to explain in what sense Kant represents religious rationalism without being committed to the deist stance, or at least the variety of it that considers God to be cognizable by reason. To do so, we will take a closer look at several places in Kant's text, such as the metaphor of concentric circles (5.2.1) and his account of religion as a set of duties commanded by God (5.2.2). Subsequently, Kant's account of religion will be compared with an account by Carl Friedrich Bahrdt, a radical freethinker purportedly influenced by Spinoza (5.2.3). Finally, the concern will be addressed whether reading Kant as a religious rationalist relies on the assumption that he reduces religion to ethics (5.2.4).

5.2.1. The metaphor of two concentric circles

In the second Preface to *Religion within the Boundaries of Mere Reason*, Kant enjoins the reader to consider a revealed religion, such as Christianity, as bared of its empirical components – such as are acquired in the course of history and the justification of which requires that we turn to particular experiences at determinate places and times. This should get us to an 'inner circle' containing 'the pure religion of reason' and enclosed within a broader circle which represents historical faith. Then, he encourages that we make an opposite move whereby the rational components would be separated from the revealed religion understood as 'a historical system'. The aim of this procedure would be to see whether some of the 'empirical' parts of the religion do not 'lead back to the same pure rational system of religion' when considered in light of 'moral concepts' (RGV, 6:12). Kant contends that if a pure rational core can be distilled from revealed religion and if at least some parts of the latter can be 'adjusted' to the 'rational system', then 'we shall be able to say that between reason and Scripture there is, not only compatibility but also unity, so that whoever follows the one (under the guidance of moral concepts) will not fail to come across the other as well' (RGV, 6:13). The question thus is what would account for the rational and revealed religion being compatible.

This question could be approached in two ways. First, we could explain the sought-for compatibility appealing to historical contingencies and admitting that it is simply the case that some forms of revealed religion are intrinsically (more or less) rational. This explanation, though, fails to tackle the problem that the question confronts us with and risks coming dangerously close to betraying a bias towards a particular form (or particular forms) of historical faith. The second approach seems to be more fruitful and more Kantian in spirit, namely: the compatibility of rational and revealed religion could be established by acknowledging that reason may contain, so to say, the transcendental conditions of religious faith (this is not Kant's own term, to be clear). This approach could be aligned with those readings that emphasize the continuity between Kant's account of religion and the whole critical project. Adina Davidovich and Stephen Palmquist, for example, associate the aim of the *Religion* with that of the third *Critique* and identify it as related to the question 'What may I hope?', addressing both the practical and the theoretical interests of reason (cf. KrV, A 805/B 833). According to Palmquist, the *Religion*, just like the *Critique of the Power of Judgment*, represents a 'judicial standpoint' and 'given its more systematic organization' could be thought of as replacing the third *Critique*.[18] Firestone and Jacobs discuss even the interpretation of Kant's *Religion* as a 'fourth' *Critique* and 'a transcendental *Critique of Religion*'.[19]

One could object against this approach pointing out that, according to Kant, 'only common morality is needed to understand the essentials of this text, without venturing into the critique of practical reason, still less into that of theoretical reason' (RGV, 6:14). Indeed, countering a reviewer's accusation, Kant stresses that his work targets a wide audience and does not require any knowledge of the arcanes of his philosophical system. Kant's retort can be an understatement, though, because the bulk of the *Religion*'s argument rests on the conception of the highest good (starting at RGV, 6:5–6), which itself draws on the doctrine of postulates developed in the three *Critiques*. Alternatively, then, Kant may suggest that when it comes to the *application* of his account, introduced in the *Religion*, to particular ecclesiastical faiths, no acquaintance with the critical philosophy is needed. But the application of Kant's conceptions should not be conflated with the justification of the method he used to arrive at them, and this can derive from the critical philosophy.

Still, we can no more than draw an analogy between Kant's approach in the *Religion* – aiming to determine under what conditions faith and reason can be mutually compatible – and the transcendental enterprise developed in the *Critique of Pure Reason*, investigating the conditions under which experience can be considered apt for producing knowledge claims. The analogy would say that as much as the conditions of the possibility of scientific cognition are to be sought in the cognitive faculties of the subject, so is the rational core of religious faith to be sought in human reason. Accordingly, it cannot be the specific character of historical revelation that would account for the rational character of a religion. Therefore, what this 'transcendental' approach to Kant's conception of religion adumbrated in the metaphor of two concentric circles would imply is that considered in itself and without being adjusted to or interpreted by reason, revealed religion as such cannot be rational. In other words, we can think of religious faith being compatible with reason only if we 'ground' it in reason.

5.2.2. Kant's 'definition' of religion

In light of the foregoing, Kant could be read as 'projecting' the conditions of the rationality of faith on revealed religion. This 'projecting' approach can also be detected in his 'definition' of religion as 'the sum of all our duties regarded as divine *commands*' (SF, 7:36; cf. SF, 7:74, RGV, 6:84, 154, MS, 6:440, 443, 487, KpV, 5:129).[20] The 'definition' combines elements traceable to philosophical tradition. Like the account of Cicero, in which *religio* is taken to proceed from *relegere* meaning 'to recollect' or 'to go through something meticulously', it evokes the attitude of conscientiously attending to one's duties. Following Lactantius, for whom *religio* derives from *religare* which means 'to bind (back)', Kant's 'definition' highlights obedience to the commands of a lawgiver.[21] Yet Kant makes it clear that the duties we ought to follow as God's commands do not comprise duties *to God*. This is because, he contends, 'a human being has duties only to human beings (himself and others)', that is, to such agents that are persons *and* 'given as an object of experience' (MS, 6:442), which cannot be the case with God. Kant's 'definition' narrows thus the subject matter of religion to actions we can perform towards other human beings and ourselves, thereby excluding those forms of theism in which the crucial element of faith is conceived in terms of believers' relation to the 'living' God. In a vein reminiscent of deism, Kant comments on his account of religion:

> [T]his definition of a religion in general obviates the erroneous representation of religion as an aggregate of *particular* duties immediately relating to God, and thereby prevents that we take on... *works of courtly service* over and above the ethico-civil duties of humanity (of human beings to human beings)... There are no particular duties toward God in a universal religion; for God cannot receive anything from us; we cannot act on him or for him.
>
> (RGV, 6:154n.)

Two aspects of religion are encapsulated in Kant's 'definition': one formal and the other material. When it comes to its material aspect, 'religion does not differ in any point from morality' (SF, 7:36): fulfilling one's duties is what religion is all about. The formal (subjective) aspect pertains to the way in which the duties are considered, namely as (*tanquam, instar*) (cf. Refl, 19:646; MS, 6:443, 487) commanded by God. Accordingly, religion amounts to a mode of consideration of our duties in which the idea of God is 'added' to our awareness of the duties. Kant denies the need for any 'assertoric knowledge' of the existence of God in religion. Instead, he claims, 'an assertoric faith' relying on 'the minimum cognition' of the *possibility* of divine existence should suffice (RGV, 6:154n.).

The modality of the 'assertoric faith' seems to make room for attributing religion even to someone who does not endorse belief in the existence of God, but rather suspends his judgement on the matter. Kant's remarks on faith in RGV, 6:154n. coincide thus with his idea, adduced in chapter 3, that a sceptical atheist could have religion. Yet since the condition specified in this passage bears on theoretical cognition, one should not too hastily conclude that religion, according to Kant, can do without the practical cognition of divine existence, hence without the doctrine of postulates. Given his numerous references to the moral argument based on the notion of the highest good (cf., e.g., RGV, 6:5–6, 8n., 97, 134, 182), this cannot really be the case. As we shall see in Chapter 7, the late Kant would consider alternative ways of grounding religion in reason, which would allow bypassing the moral argument. But at the time of drafting the *Religion*, he holds that there is an irreducible feature which makes religion different from morality. This is the idea of God as 'a moral ruler of the world' who legislates the moral laws and attends to their observance as 'one who knows the heart' (*Herzenskündiger*)

(RGV, 6:99). The idea, accompanying our awareness of duties, is meant to 'strengthen the moral incentive in our own lawgiving reason' (MS, 6:487).

Yet the account of religious faith as intended to strengthen our moral motivation is not entirely free from tensions. First, since we should abide by the moral law and fulfil our duties simply by virtue of being aware of them, no additional motivation apart from respect for the moral law (cf. KpV, 5:73–5, 78) is required. To address this concern, it suffices to recall Kant's anthropological considerations regarding the factors, ingrained in our nature, that systematically undermine our commitment to morality. These factors, which incapacitate our consistent exercise of morality in the course of life, comprise our innate propensity to evil (for more on 'radical evil', see 5.3.2) and cognitive limitations: both the moral dispositions of others and our own character being 'opaque' to us,[22] we need an additional reason to hope that we can continue on the moral path – and this additional reason is provided by belief in an omniscient God overseeing our attempts at moral progress (cf., e.g., RGV, 6:67).

The second concern is the following: if morality leads to religion (cf. RGV, 6:6, 8n.), we should think of God's commanding our duties to us in a way that does not contradict reason's autonomy, that is, the principle that reason is bound by the law which it legislates for itself (cf. GMS, 4:440, 452; KpV, 5:32, 63). Should divine legislation compromise the autonomy of practical reason, religion would lose its moral foundations. Since Kant does not reject the doctrine of autonomy and autonomy rules out the scenario in which we should follow laws originating from a different legislator than our reason, he cannot mean that, literally, our duties are commanded by God. Rather, adding the idea of God as a moral lawgiver does not amount to more than a way in which we can present our duties to ourselves. Yet if religion differs from morality solely with regard to the mode of presenting its subject matter, thus ultimately with regard to the vocabulary it employs, can religion genuinely reinforce our moral motivation? If religion constitutes a mode of presentation of morality, there is not much in Kant's 'definition' that would go beyond mere 'deification' of practical reason. On the other hand, given the critical doctrine of the postulates of pure practical reason, as well as the arguments developed in those parts of the *Religion* that precede the 'definition', it might be somewhat misleading to claim that he reduces religion to obedience to the moral law, the idea of a divine legislator adding only a compelling force and absolute character to the law. Kant's point may instead be that morality, legislated by practical reason, forms the essential part – the *sine qua non* – of religion.

5.2.3. A digression on Carl Friedrich Bahrdt

Kant was certainly not alone in defining religion in moral terms; indeed, he seems to have followed a trend widespread among religious rationalists and the Enlightenment reformers of religion. Taking as an example Carl Friedrich Bahrdt (1741-92), one can show that Kant's understanding of religion corresponds to ideas expressed in the writings of some radical authors of the epoch.

Bahrdt – a freemason whom Israel describes as 'a pre-eminent figure of German radical thought' and an ardent advocate of freedom of the press[23] – features a religious person, in his *Catechismus der natürlichen Religion*, as one who follows her duties 'because she is convinced that it is God's will, and out of respect for the highest holiness of God'.[24] In the spirit akin to Kant's, Bahrdt defines religion as 'practical cognition of God, that is, such cognition of God's properties and our relations with him that influences our actions'.[25] He encourages his readers to 'pray with [their] deeds', for 'God speaks to [us] through deeds, hence he wants to be worshipped also by deeds'.[26] Though, in the spirit of Spinoza, he claims that one arrives at the cognition of God, 'his existence, his wisdom, his infinite love, and his truthfulness' through the cognition of nature,[27] like Kant he contends that it is by 'the moral laws of reason' that one is necessitated to believe in God,[28] whom he then presents as 'distribut[ing] happiness according to merit'.[29] Bahrdt considers rational religion (*vernünftige Religion*) beneficial to the moral improvement of humankind, hampered by greedy and power-thirsty 'priests and despots'. He urges that 'it should be the first concern of all good people to work as much as possible towards the moral improvement of humankind in general and towards the eradication of all superstition and all that disturbs the free use of reason, and to promote rational religion as much as one can'.[30] Moving between ideas that one can find in Spinoza, Kant and Christian theology, Bahrdt advocates a rational religion in which 'genuine service to God, the only pleasing prayer, the most noble way of revering our Creator are deeds (*Thaten*),'[31] but these deeds must be accompanied by the cognition of God and moral laws as his will.[32] A good person unaware of the existence of God or lacking the idea of the divine entity would not thereby be a religious person.

In a work titled *Neues Christenthum, oder letztes Vermächtniß an Freund und Feinde*, Bahrdt enumerates what he considers the defining traits of a true Christian. They comprise, first, the denial of faith (*Glauben*), imposed by way of 'brainless discontented chatter',[33] in favour of the cognition of nature. He does not use the term 'faith' in this pejorative sense throughout all of his writings, though, as in *Würdigung der natürlichen Religion* he defines natural religion as 'a rational cognition or ... *faith* in God which arises as a consequence of reasoning'.³⁴ Second, a true Christian, according to Bahrdt, follows the commandment to 'love God through one's neighbours'.³⁵ To this – third – Bahrdt adds the claim that God does not speak to us by means of signs (*Zeichen*), likely implying the letter of Scripture, but through works (*Werken*). Fourth, those who stand for the religion based on external ceremonies should be 'allowed to die out' (*aussterben lassen*), though one should treat them with compassion since they have been misguided by 'age-old legends and childish prejudices'.³⁶ Fifth, a true Christian should manifest her religiosity in acting well towards others and not in pointless prayers: 'All the puppetry which you count as religion is a play of kids (*Kinderspiel*) that God does not find pleasing.'³⁷

Despite several key differences, Bahrdt and Kant share an important tenet: they both think that true religion should have a moral core and consist in acting well – or, as Spinoza put it, exercising justice and charity to our neighbours.³⁸ Also, none of them rejects the idea of God as a necessary constituent of religion, though Bahrdt suggests that this idea be derived from the cognition of God available through nature, whereas for Kant the idea of God originates from moral-practical faith (*Glaube*) and not from empirical cognition or knowledge (*Wissen*) (cf. KrV, A 820/B 848–A 831/B 859). Clearly, in one of the senses of the word, Bahrdt associates faith with superstition and does not consider anything close to Kant's proposal to explain faith as a mode of assent to reasons (cf. chapter 3). He also speaks more openly against the institutional church and does not advocate an ethical community existing in such a form. Kant's view of human nature as tainted at its roots by the propensity to evil (cf. RGV, 6:29f.) finds no equivalent in Bahrdt, for whom evil is a consequence of imperfections which an individual comes to be aware of and which are grafted on moral corruption occurring when we let 'alleged revelations' enslave our reason and fall into superstition instead of searching the truth.³⁹

Discussing Kant's 'definition' of religion above, I pointed out that it can be read as featuring religion as a way to present morality so that its motivational force would increase. On such an account, religion would equate morality, albeit 'deified'. For Bahrdt, the 'deification' of morality rests on the presupposition that acting well requires that we cognize God through nature. Thus, true religion, which manifests itself in good deeds, must be based on the cognition of nature, that is, on science. Yet is there anything genuinely 'religious' in religion thus construed? Does not Bahrdt's use of terms such as 'God' and 'religion' mask an entirely secular doctrine targeted at religious institutions? If we refuse to read his text literally, we may have to admit that, under theological vocabulary, he smuggles a religiously indifferent naturalist ethical theory. Alternatively, taking his claims at face value, we may recognize a 'revisionist' intent behind his account of religion. This takes us to the problem of reductionism – a corollary of defining religion in moral terms. The problem, surely, concerns Kant as well.

5.2.4. Does Kant reduce religion to morality? A note on Palmquist

The claim that Kant reduces religion to morality provides part and parcel of what Firestone labels 'traditional interpretation' of Kant's rational religion. The interpretation would assume that the 'theoretical strictures' imposed on the knowledge of God by the critical philosophy are 'inescapable'. According to Firestone, 'traditional interpreters judge that Kant's effort to establish a foundation for theology in his moral philosophy is a failure, or at least a failure in ways that might matter to the adherents of most religions.' The attempts to provide a doctrine of religion based on morality 'are thought to be inadequate – either hopelessly convoluted or reducible to his moral philosophy in a way that eliminates their positive contribution to Kant's thought'.[40]

Throughout his work on Kant, Stephen Palmquist has consistently argued against the 'traditional interpretation' and the reductionist stance it promotes. Palmquist reads '*bloß*' in the title of Kant's work on religion as an ambiguous term and thus renders it as 'bare' which means both 'naked' or 'unclothed' and 'mere'.[41] Accordingly, religion 'within the boundaries of *bare* reason' would refer to religion considered in abstraction from its external 'clothing' – those empirical components of a religion that fall within the 'outer circle', to recall the metaphor adumbrated in 5.2.1, that is, the historical faith based on scriptural revelation. Kant's project would then consist in investigating, in light of the system of pure reason, what is left from religion after it has been stripped of its external 'husk', rather than in devising a religion out of the resources of reason alone. This blocks the reduction of religion to an *a priori* moral doctrine because such a doctrine, although necessary, or even essential, does not suffice to constitute a religious creed.

In Palmquist's view, religion occupies a different place in Kant's critical system than morality: as already stated, it represents the judicial standpoint of reason from which Kant addresses the question 'What may I hope?', whereas his ethical theory deals with the question 'What ought I to do?', assigned to the practical standpoint.[42] Religion offers a reflective outlook on nature, considered from a teleological perspective, hence as harmonized with moral ends. It opens the possibility of a world in which the order of nature does not conflict with the moral order, as is the case in the empirical world in which ills and rewards are distributed randomly, regardless of moral desert or the lack thereof. Since the world in which happiness is distributed proportionately to virtue – in which nature harmonizes with the moral law – is the end of morality, we need the 'pure faith of religion' (cf. RGV, 6:106, 115, 118, 121, 153) as a source of hope for the fulfilment of this end. Therefore, without religion morality would be 'teleologically incomplete'.[43]

However, Palmquist does not reject reductionism in one of the senses of the term; namely he admits that for Kant 'morality enables us to *explain* religion'.[44] Thus, he recognizes the fact that Kant reduces religion to morality in the explanatory, though not in the eliminative sense.[45] He admits, too, that Kant raises morality 'to the status of religion'.[46] Yet such a contention takes us back to the 'radically rationalist' and revisionist account of religion attributable for example to Bahrdt (see 5.2.3 above). Interestingly, Yirmiyahu Yovel, who advocates a 'secular' and reductionist reading of Kant's religion, partly concurs with Palmquist, for he contends that by '"reducing" religion to morality' Kant 'at the same time attributes the supreme features of religion to morality'.[47]

We can agree with Palmquist's points, spelled out thus far, both with regard to Kant's rational religion as an irreducible 'perspective' within the critical system and with regard to the explanatory dependence of religion on morality. This notwithstanding, given Kant's idea of morality as the foundation and the end of religion, Palmquist, or any other interpreter for that matter, is not able to counter the claim that Kant indeed refuses to consider the non-moral aspects of religion to be as essential as the moral ones. Let us illustrate this observation with a fact related to Kant's method of scriptural exegesis. It is of course the case that, as Otfried Höffe has emphasized, 'since the Church Fathers: Origen, Ambrose, and Augustine, Christian theology has known the doctrine of multiple senses of the Scripture'.[48] But Kant's enterprise to unify the rational with the revealed religion, introduced with the metaphor of two concentric circles, rests on the assumption that all these senses can be reduced to the moral one. The irreducibly mystical aspects of revelation, such as the Trinity, become 'irrelevant' – all the more so if they 'transcend all our concepts' – unless 'we read a moral meaning into them' (SF, 7:39). Collins's lecture notes on moral philosophy aptly summarize Kant's position on morality as the *raison d'être* of religion:

> Religion is not the origin of morality, but consists in this, that the moral laws are applied to the knowledge of God.... All religion presupposes morality... All religion gives force, beauty and reality to morality, for in itself the latter is an

ideal thing.... Religion gives weight to morality, it should be the motive thereof. Here we recognize that he who has so conducted himself as to be worthy of happiness may also hope to achieve this, since there is a being who can make him so. And this is the first origin of religion, which is possible even without any theology. It is a natural progression from morality into religion.... Religion is the condition for conceiving the binding force of laws.

(V-Mo/Collins, 27:307–8)

5.3. Salvation through reason? Kant and the Christian dogma

As we have seen, opening the *Religion*, Kant outlines a project of vindicating the compatibility of revealed religion with a moral faith based on reason. If this aim is to be achieved, the revealed doctrines that surpass the capacities of human reason, such as the Incarnation, and even those that at least *prima facie* contradict reason, such as the Trinity, should be reinterpreted to conform to the strictures of our rationality. For a trinitarian Christian, for example, doctrines such as God's Incarnation in the historical figure of Jesus, a fundamental article of the Christian creed, fall on the side of mysteries that cannot be rationally explained and comprehended. Hence, an attempt to adjust them to reason will result in removing the mystical aspects of faith. A doctrine which escapes 'rationalization' – translation into the conceptual framework of the moral religion – will then be dislodged onto the peripheries of 'true religion' and judged to be irrelevant to rational faith. Since doctrines such as the Incarnation constitute the centrepiece of Christianity, the unity between rational and revealed religion cannot be achieved without a significant revision of the revealed contents. To say that Kant's project succeeds in adjusting *parts* of revealed religion to its rational counterpart means thus to admit a partial defeat of the enterprise at issue, especially if the parts originally considered crucial are moved to the peripheries.

This section will argue that Kant's project of establishing the unity fails to integrate some key components of the revealed with the rational religion. Kant launches a critique of revelation (5.3.1) which suggests that, without being interpreted along the lines of the moral faith, revelation does not render a source of 'true religion'. Furthermore, what has been read as Kant's translation of some Christian doctrines into the language of rational religion – such as the doctrine of original sin into that of radical evil (5.3.2) and the salvific mission of Christ into the doctrine of the 'prototype' of a morally perfect humanity (5.3.3) – imports tenets foreign to (at least the orthodox version of) Christianity and possibly unfit for being translated back into its language. Kant's conception of the prototype, besides, can be shown to have Platonic underpinnings, akin to those underlying the account of Λόγος by Johann Christian Edelmann, a German freethinker (5.3.4).

5.3.1. The critique of revelation: Kant's correspondence with Lavater

In a letter dated 8 April 1774, Johann Caspar Lavater (1741–1801), a Swiss theologian, asked Kant for an opinion about his *Miscellaneous Writings*, and in particular 'whether or not you think that my actual view of scriptural faith and prayer agrees essentially with the teaching of Scripture'. Then he went on to explain his own position, writing that for him the biblical teaching 'is not cold dogma. It is the most ultimate matter of the heart' (Br, 10:166). Kant responded to Lavater's queries in a letter from 28 April 1775. He emphasized there that we should distinguish between 'the *teachings* of Christ' and 'the *report* we have of those teachings' (Br, 10:176). The former, as 'moral teachings', constitute 'the fundamental doctrine of the Gospels', whereas 'the dogmas of the New Testament' should be regarded as 'auxiliary' (Br, 10:176). A reason for this recommendation is that 'considered as history, our New Testament writings can never be so esteemed as to make us dare to have unlimited trust in every word of them' (Br, 10:178).

Kant's enunciations to Lavater corroborate the conjecture that he is prone to express doubts about the status of the Scriptures as the 'Word of God'. Hence, like Spinoza in the *Theological-Political Treatise* (see 5.4.1), he would not take the divine origin of the Scriptures for granted. I shall consider four ways of justifying this position.

First, in the 'silent decade' preceding the formation of the critical project – the period in which he wrote to Lavater – Kant may have held the view that God, being an intelligible object, cannot be cognized with certainty through historical reports, but only by means of reason, and even then we cannot predicate of him much more than that he exists and remains related to finite beings as a cause to effects. These tenets could be established on the basis of Kant's 'possibility proof' (see Chapter 2) and in his Inaugural Dissertation (1770), titled *De mundi sensibilis atque intelligibilis forma ac principiis*. In the critical period, Kant of course precludes the possibility of acquiring knowledge of God both from reasoning and from experience. Thus, no historical reports would be fit for mediating cognition of the nature of God, let alone his will or plans regarding human beings. Insofar as reports contained in the Scriptures are to refer to the supernatural, their truth cannot be confirmed as such a confirmation would demand the possibility of experiencing the supernatural (e.g., SF, 7:63; WDO, 8:142–3).

Second, it can be doubted whether Scripture stands for the 'Word of God' because, containing 'reports of the evangelists and apostles' to whose times we are 'not close enough' (Br, 10:177), it only mediates what Kant calls 'historical faith'. This kind of faith, as he avers in the *Religion*, is 'merely based on facts' (RGV, 6:103), and thus has no universal validity. 'Based upon revelation as experience', historical faith bears 'only particular validity, namely for those in contact with the history on which the faith rests' and 'carries... the consciousness of its contingency' (RGV, 6:115). Considered as a historical account, the Scriptures do not have the kind of universal validity that we would expect the 'Word of God' to have. One may surmise, therefore, that Kant entertains the idea that God does not 'speak' to us, if one may so put it, through Scripture.

Third, given its limited validity, it cannot be through Scripture that we are supposed to enter into an immediate relation with the divine. Rather, such a relation should be sought through conscience: 'no book', contends Kant, 'whatever its authority might be... can substitute for the religion of conscience'. And he continues: 'For although statutes may bring about the performance of rituals, they cannot beget inner convictions. Because of this presupposition, I seek in the Gospels not the ground of my faith but its fortification' (Br, 10:179). This suggests that Kant endorses the view on which the 'Word of God' is accessible to us immediately in our conscience, or, as we can read in the *Religionslehre*, 'through our own reason', a mode he calls 'inner divine revelation' (V-Phil-Th/Pölitz, 28:1117; cf. RGV, 6:122).

Finally, Kant could have been aware of the arguments undermining the divine origin of the Scriptures before he came up with his critical account of rational religion, because such arguments were aired at the time and were mediated by the authors he read, for example, Hermann Samuel Reimarus.[49] One of the sources of the arguments in question was also Spinoza's *Theological-Political Treatise*, challenging both the authorship of some books of the Scriptures[50] and the availability of the original of the Gospels to us – due to the fact that the Gospels were not written in the language spoken by Jesus, so the Bible in the vernacular would be a translation of a translation into Greek of a *report* of the words of Jesus.[51] Despite Kant's likely lack of acquaintance with Spinoza's *Treatise*, he betrays an awareness of this fact since he notices that the moral message of 'the teacher of the Gospels' is deposited in 'human reports which we must eventually trace back to very ancient times, and in languages now dead', which makes it difficult, if not impossible, 'to evaluate their historical credibility' (RGV, 6:112). Thus, although the Scriptures 'must be the object of the highest respect, for this is what human need requires in order to be certain of the duty to divine service' (RGV, 6:107) – that is, as a 'vehicle' of pure moral faith – in light of his exchange with Lavater, already the early Kant would hold the Scriptures to be an imperfect work written by the human author, and not the primary source of the 'Word of God'.

5.3.2. Radical evil and original sin

Kant's critical approach to Scripture may motivate scepticism regarding the truth-value of the biblical narrative as a historical account, and thus invite the rejection of the literal interpretations of the text. Yet it does not rule out the plausibility of reinterpreting the Holy Writ along the rationalist lines – in terms of Kant's moral faith. According to Otfried Höffe, 'the content [of the *Religion* – A.T.] deals with the four building blocks of Christianity: original sin, Christ, judgment day, and the Church,'[52] these key doctrines being 'translated' into the idiom of Kant's rational religion. Firestone and Jacobs have dubbed this a '"*Religion*–as–Translation" thesis'. According to this thesis, the *Religion* is to be regarded 'not as an extension of Kant's arguments in the critical philosophy, but as a translation of the Christian faith.'[53] A similar approach can be found in a commentary by Lawrence Pasternack who claims that 'the experiment of *Religion* moves through four central issues in Christianity', in particular: the nature of sin (Part One), redemption (Part Two), ecclesiology – 'the Universal Church of the Pure Rational System of Religion, the history of Christianity, Providence and eschatology' (Part Three), and our attitude to religious rituals and doctrines (Part Four).[54]

Other scholars also read Part One of the *Religion* as Kant's engagement with the Christian doctrine of original sin. For example, Höffe notices that 'in the first part of the *Religion*, the Christian dogma of original sin, the substantive understanding of evil as an inherited characteristic of the human race, is transformed into the propensity to evil.'[55] Similarly, Allen Wood contends that 'Kant's project in Part One of the *Religion* is... to articulate the Christian doctrine of original sin in terms of rational morality, so that the religion of reason can also be seen as a saving response to it.'[56] Leslie Stevenson concurs with the foregoing and points out that 'unlike so many other Enlightenment thinkers, Kant has a strong sense of human sinfulness, for... Part One of the *Religion* offers an elaborate analysis of what he calls the "radical evil" in human nature, thereby giving his interpretation of the doctrine of original sin.'[57]

The term 'radical evil' may be of biblical provenance – the Vulgate translation speaks of *'cupiditas'* as *'radix malorum'* at 1 Tim 6.10 – yet Kant endows it with his own meaning and, unlike the biblical author, he does not locate the root cause of evil in greed, covetousness or any other desire that human beings can experience. Still, the following analogy can be drawn between original sin and radical evil: whereas original sin consists in disobedience to the divine will, radical evil manifests itself in disobeying God by failing to follow the moral law.[58] Thus, both doctrines – the Christian and the Kantian one – trace the source of evil in us to an original act of disobedience attributable to the finite rational agent. However, unlike the Christian doctrine of sin, Kant's account of evil rules out the conception that corruption is transmitted 'by way of inheritance from our first parents' (RGV, 6:40), not only because this conception locates the origin of evil in time, but primarily because it does not enable imputing responsibility for evil's origin to each single agent (cf. RGV, 6:43).

Human beings, claims Kant, are by nature endowed with predispositions to the good, of which he distinguishes three: to animality, humanity and personality (RGV, 6:26). Although vices can be 'grafted' onto the first two predispositions – for example, developing humanity, we are likely to acquire 'vices of culture', such as jealousy or rivalry, when we excessively strive to become better than others (RGV, 6:26–7) – there is no vice corresponding to the predisposition to personality, that is, to 'the susceptibility to respect for the moral law as of itself the sufficient incentive to the power of choice' (RGV, 6:27). Moral evil cannot derive from the use we make of our feeling of awe towards the moral law, hence, to explain this kind of evil, an additional factor should be introduced which will trump this feeling. Kant finds this factor in the 'propensity to evil' which he explicates as 'the subjective ground of the possibility of an inclination' to base one's principles of action (maxims) on non-moral incentives (RGV, 6:29). This propensity, he says, is acquired and not contained in the concept of human nature; otherwise, it would be necessary for us to have it and we could not be held accountable for succumbing to evil (RGV, 6:32). Kant traces the acquisition of the propensity to evil back to an 'intelligible deed' – 'the use of freedom through which the supreme maxim... is adopted in the power of choice' (RGV, 6:31). In this intelligible, thus non-temporal, act one chooses the maxim which allows prioritizing non-moral incentives over the moral law as the ground of the determination of one's will (RGV, 6:32). Though acquired, radical evil – the corruption of 'the ground of all maxims' (RGV, 6:37) – is innate in the sense that only by virtue of being human can we develop the urge to subordinate morality to self-love (cf. RGV, 6:21, 25, 32).[59] Thus, evil lies outside the purview of an entity whose will remains unsusceptible to non-moral incentives, as does the divine will.[60]

Kant emphasizes that the propensity to evil 'must... always come through one's own fault' and that unlike a natural predisposition it is 'something that a human being can be held accountable for' (RGV, 6:32). Thus, importantly, in contradistinction to the genetic narrative of the Bible, suggesting that evil is transmitted from generation to generation, Kant's account attributes moral depravity to the foundational choice of 'the supreme maxim' which every human being makes on her own. Radical evil is not an evil act of the 'first man', commencing the divine history of salvation, but the root of moral depravity traceable to an individual's choice. Accordingly, whereas the Christian endorses the view that we are prone to evil as a corollary of a contingent deed at the beginning of human history, the Kantian locates the cause of evil outside the temporal order – in human freedom, thus making evil an indelible, though also contingent, aspect of human agency.

Kant's rejection of the hereditary nature of evil has other weighty consequences. As much as there are no external forces that would determine our evil proclivities, also turning away from evil – which Kant calls a 'revolution' and a 'change of heart' (RGV, 6:47) – must be accounted for in terms of the agent's inner disposition. As Manfred Kuehn has noticed, Kant holds that 'we need to save ourselves' and we can attain this in that we 'perfect ourselves morally'.[61] This rules out the Augustinian stance on which 'without divine grace man will always do evil'.[62] Though Kant does not deny that we may need to resort to God's grace, he trims down the role of grace to the empowerment of our capacities. In the 'General remark' concluding Part One of the *Religion*, he says:

> Granted that some supernatural cooperation is also needed to his becoming good or better, whether this cooperation only consist in the diminution of obstacles or be also a positive assistance, the human being must nonetheless make himself antecedently worthy of receiving it; and he must *accept* this help... i.e. he must incorporate this positive increase of force into his maxim: in this way alone is it possible that the good be imputed to him, and that he be acknowledged a good human being.
>
> (RGV, 6:44)

Later in the text Kant adds that only if one 'has made use of the original predisposition to the good in order to become a better human being, can he hope that what does not lie in his power will be made good by cooperation from above' (RGV, 6:51–2). Clearly, Kant conditions the hope for grace upon one's being able to deserve it by acting morally. This implies that acting morally itself does not hinge on grace. Neither does turning away from evil depend on grace insofar as we construe it simply in terms of acting morally. But does the 'change of heart' amount merely to being able to act morally or does it also involve something beyond this capacity, for example, perseverance in moral action or pursuing the 'highest good' as the actions' corollary? Only if we understand the conversion as more than a restoration of one's capacity for acting well, space can be spared for the divine succour. In a nutshell, God would be needed for us to maintain our orientation towards the good, but not to make us able to do good as such.

5.3.3. The prototype and Jesus

The core of the 'orthodox' Christianity, whether Catholic, Lutheran or Reformed, is formed by the belief that Jesus of Nazareth is the Christ – the long-awaited messiah presaged by the prophets of the Old Testament and the Son of God who came to redeem humanity from sin after the fall of the 'first man'. And as much as Kant's doctrine of radical evil has been read as an interpretation of original sin, so likewise his conception of 'the prototype of a humanity well-pleasing to God' (RGV, 6:119, 129), expounded in Part Two of the *Religion*, has been deemed to provide a rendition of the biblical story of Jesus 'within the boundaries of mere reason'.[63]

Kant's idiom encourages such a reading despite his avoidance to mention the name of Jesus throughout his work, which abounds in expressions derived from the Gospel of John and the Nicene Creed, such as 'God's only-begotten Son' who 'came down... from heaven', '"the Word"... through which all other things are', in whom 'God loved the world', etc. These expressions refer both to Christ in the Bible and to the prototype in the *Religion*. Accordingly, the following analogy emerges between Jesus and the prototype: while the former came to deliver us from sin, the latter is to 'give us force' (RGV, 6:60–1) to overcome the evil propensity into which we have lapsed perverting our original commitment to the moral law. Thus, both Jesus and the prototype have a 'salvific' function. According to Palmquist, for the prototype to have its due motivational power, Kant 'must appeal to some historical tradition'.[64] Christianity provides such tradition; so, the prototype should be identified with Jesus to play its motivational role.

Yet while Kant describes the prototype as having divine origin – calling it an idea that 'has come down to us from heaven' – he also presents us with arguments against identifying the *historical* Jesus with the 'ideal of moral perfection' and 'the prototype of moral disposition in its entire purity' (RGV, 6:61). For he denies that the figure he refers to as the 'teacher of the Gospel' (many places, e.g., RGV, 6:128, 134, 162, 195, 201) and the 'teacher of the one and only religion' (RGV, 6:85) should be thought of as having divine nature. Thus, though he uses the biblical expressions to designate the prototype – an idea of morally perfect humanity that 'resides in our morally-legislative reason' (RGV, 6:62) – he does not refer to the historical Jesus in this way. Kant's interpretation of Scripture along the lines of pure moral faith shall result, accordingly, in sidelining or even dismissing the central tenet of Christianity – the Incarnation. From the viewpoint of rational religion, it is legitimate to depict the biblical Jesus as an idea insofar as we do not ascribe empirical reality to Jesus thus conceived. Jesus considered as an idea cannot be a historical figure and considered as a historical figure, he cannot be attributed divine nature.[65]

Kant argues against attributing divinity to the Jesus of scriptural revelation in the following way: First, if to acknowledge the objective reality of the prototype, we had to proffer an example of a human being embodying moral perfection, the moral law itself would turn out to have no determining force. Since the moral law commands unconditionally, regardless of whether anyone has ever existed who fulfilled its commands, also the prototype in our reason remains in power even if no empirical instantiation of it could be found. If one requires that such an instantiation be provided, as an illustration of the possibility of a morally flawless life, one manifests 'moral unbelief' (RGV, 6:63).

Second, we cannot be certain that any human person encountered in experience embodies the ideal of moral perfection, because 'outer experience yields no example adequate to the idea' (RGV, 6:63). Due to the problem of epistemic opacity, moreover, an inference from a report on a person's deeds to his moral disposition cannot yield a reliable, let alone an infallible conclusion.

Third, the presence of the prototype in us being incomprehensible enough, its hypostatization in an empirically real human being would only contribute to mounting 'mysteries'.

Finally, if the teacher of morality had divine nature, he 'could *not* be presented to us *as an example to be emulated*' (RGV, 6:64). This is because of the disparity between human nature, mired in evil, and the morally flawless nature of the divine being: if having divine nature were required for us to perfect ourselves morally – an end Kant claims everyone has a duty to pursue – moral betterment would fall beyond human capacities. Thus, equating the biblical Jesus as a historical figure with God would imply undermining the possibility for human beings to improve themselves by merely following the moral law.

Yet Kant does not claim that Jesus did not exist, nor that it is *impossible* that he had been divine; rather, he considers the Christian dogma of God's Incarnation meaningless from the practical perspective. 'Not that we would thereby absolutely deny that he might indeed also be a supernaturally begotten human being,' avers Kant. 'But, from a practical point of view any such presupposition is of no benefit to us, since the prototype which we see embedded in this apparition must be sought in us as well (though natural human beings)' (RGV, 6:63–4).

Kant's conception of Jesus bifurcates thus into an account of the teacher of morality described in the Bible and an account of the ideal of a morally perfect human being, ingrained in our morally practical reason. Kant secures the objective reality of the ideal precisely by tracing its origin back to reason (RGV, 6:62f.). As such, the 'prototype of a humanity well-pleasing to God' can be compared to the 'transcendental ideal (*prototypon transcendentale*)' (KrV, A 571/B 599) of the first *Critique*, embodying the totality of reality and containing the ground of all possible determinations of objects, which Kant calls an '*ens realissimum*' (KrV, A 575/B 603). Both the prototype in the *Religion* and the prototype in the first *Critique* constitute ideal objects: the maximum of moral goodness and the maximum of reality, respectively. As such, they cannot be given in empirical cognition, and we cannot know whether any objects exist which would correspond to them.

It is noteworthy that Kant's failure to accommodate the Incarnation in its 'orthodox' version within his variety of rational religion does not entail that the historical Jesus of the Christian revelation can be dispensed with as of no value to rational religion. For due to 'a peculiar weakness of human nature' (RGV, 6:103), the ideas vital for the religion of reason require sensible representations – or symbols – to be grasped and so to play their motivational role. Allen Wood, for example, contends that in Kant's religion symbols make the contents of ideas cognitively accessible to us. A symbol, says Wood, 'gives us experiential access to what it symbolizes'.[66] This contention notwithstanding, thinking of Jesus as a symbol of a morally perfect humanity is of course not equivalent to recognizing in the Nazarene the moral ideal itself, let alone a divine entity.

5.3.4. Christ as a Platonic idea: Kant *vs.* Johann Christian Edelmann

Kant's borrowing the biblical idiom from the Gospel of John, as well as his references to the Gospel's Prologue, are not accidental. Scholars emphasize that the Gospel of John differs from the three remaining synoptic gospels in that it represents a stage of advanced theology, rather than just offering an account of *res gestae*.⁶⁷ This is because the Gospel of John imports philosophical content from sources foreign to the biblical story of Jesus. Kant himself might be drawing on these sources. Firestone and Jacobs, for example, suggest that Kant develops a version of 'transcendental Platonism' according to which the prototype embodies 'an ideal *human* within God',⁶⁸ the 'ideal humanity implicit in God's own being'.⁶⁹ The prototype manifests some features of a Platonic idea, such as transcendence to a particular human mind (for 'we are not its authors' [RGV, 6:61]) and non-temporality. As an 'uncreated exemplar of perfect humanity',⁷⁰ the prototype should be distinguished from the human species, which is an object of experience and that needs to struggle with radical evil. Kant describes our awareness of this moral ideal in biblical terms: as 'a state of abasement of the Son of God' (RGV, 6:61) which, incomprehensible to us as it is, can be appreciated as an act of divine grace.⁷¹

Relatedly, Christopher Insole suggests that Kant's philosophy of religion be read as a version of 'Christianised', though not Christian Platonism. Kant's version of Platonism cannot be Christian, according to Insole, because of 'his denial, neglect, or ignorance about core dimensions of the Christian tradition', such as the Incarnation and the Trinity.⁷² More recently, Insole has argued that Kant's conception of the prototype of a morally perfect human being originates in the Platonic conception of divinity in which 'the only proper object of divine thought, or willing, is itself. In a long tradition of reflection... we find the idea that the self-conception of the divine, the *logos*, or the wisdom of God, is the image of its source'.⁷³ Insole notes that in the *Religion* 'Kant translates into the "pure religion of reason" the notion of the Incarnation, in terms that evoke a divine self-conception'.⁷⁴ On this account, the ideal of morally perfect humanity would 'proceed' from the divine mind – recall the metaphor of the prototype having come down to us from heaven – as God's own idea of himself as legislator of the moral law who instantiates moral perfection.

The foregoing interpretations achieve at least two aims. First, they cast light on what it means for the prototype to play a motivational role reinforcing the agent's attempts at overcoming her propensity to evil. When we act morally, following the example of the morally perfect human being, we strive to become like God. The idea maintains its motivational power by adding more dignity and significance to our efforts to become better human beings. Second, the above interpretations allow situating Kant's thought in a broader historical context of religious rationalism, in the proximity of such thinkers as Johann Christian Edelmann (1698–1767) whom Leo Bäck, in a short book on Spinoza's early influence on theology in Germany, described as 'the most radical and open Spinozist from the period before Lessing'.⁷⁵

Edelmann wrote a work, titled *Die Göttlichkeit der Vernunft* (1742), in which he argued that the word 'Λόγος', used in the Prologue to the Gospel of John, should be translated as 'reason' (*Vernunft*), and not as 'word' (*Wort*).[76] To support his claim, Edelmann refers to the authority of early Christian and Neoplatonic authors: Amelius, Justin Martyr, Athenagoras, Clement of Alexandria, Gregory of Nyssa, Origen, John Damascene, Dionysius the Areopagite and Ignatius of Antioch; their translators and compilers such as Ambrosius Ferrarius and Isaac Casaubon; and the Renaissance humanist Marsilio Ficino. Unlike reason, Edelmann explains, word is not a substance but an accident dependent on the person who utters it, therefore it has an external cause; nor is it eternal or everlasting, but transient and without an essence.[77] In his book Edelmann develops a doctrine of Christ as divine reason that revealed itself in Jesus of Nazareth. There is no other Son of God, he contends, 'than divine reason inhering permanently in God and proceeding from him, which has shown and from time to time revealed itself, filled with grace and truth, not only in Christ, the firstborn of all creatures, but also in all of his brothers'.[78] According to Edelmann, reason makes the human being what she is and endows her with an eternal essence (*Wesen*) without which she would cease to be human.[79] Furthermore, the reason which dwelt in Jesus, 'our brother',[80] is the same as the reason which forms the essence of human beings, thus humans participate in the divine reason.[81] Since divine reason constitutes our nature and God is this reason, God is closer to us than we would ever think: for He is *in us*.[82] Hence, drawing on an idea that he finds in Origen,[83] Edelmann concludes that our reason makes us 'deified' – it makes us into God, as the penultimate line of the treatise reads.[84] Since a true Christian lives according to the guidance of reason and recognizes obedience to reason as her duty,[85] those heathens who lived in a rational way, like Pythagoras and Plato,[86] were true Christians despite not knowing Jesus: 'Christians did not begin to emerge in the world from today or yesterday onwards, but from the very beginning they have been everywhere and in all times.'[87] To live a rational and thus sinless life,[88] says Edelmann – betraying strict Platonic dualism of soul and body – one should resist sensuous incentives, reject the guidance of the 'external eyes'[89] and turn away from 'the darkness of the flesh'.[90]

Edelmann's treatise has a polemical edge and, its copious references to ancient and early Christian authors notwithstanding, it targets primarily his contemporaries. Appealing to the early Church Fathers, Edelmann accuses modern Christians, especially the Lutherans, of having abandoned their roots. For, he contends, modern Christians mistakenly claim that reason and faith stand in mutual opposition and that reason should be subjugated, 'held captive (*gefangen nehmen*).'[91] Edelmann's work strikes a critical note, depicting church officials as 'blind guides (*blinden Leiter*)'[92] who have forged an erratic notion of God to mislead believers and impose on them their own authority instead. Several remarks on the nature of God echo Spinozist tenets. For example, arguing for 'reason' as the right translation of '*Λόγος*', Edelmann points out that word does not exist on its own and, unlike God, it does not have its 'origin from and in itself (*von und aus sich selber*)',[93] an idea reminiscent of Spinoza's notion of God as *causa sui*.[94] Equating God with reason, Edelmann compares God with 'the light that enlightens all people' and, using a pantheist metaphor, says that God 'fills all in all'.[95] Also the claim that since we have the concept of God, we are able to cognize him, calls to mind Spinoza's tenet that we can deduce truths about God from the idea of God which we have due to the fact that we think.[96]

Running through *Die Göttlichkeit der Vernunft*, besides, there is an anti-Trinitarian tendency which can also be tracked down in Kant's writings. Comparing the Trinity to a deity of the ancient Pomeranians, Edelmann notices that Scripture does not say anything about 'three persons in a unique and undivided divine entity', and calls the Trinity 'a three-headed beast' and 'a meaningless monstrosity of the priests'.[97] As a mystery surpassing our rational capacities, thus prior to its reinterpretation along the lines of moral faith, also Kant downplays the conception of a triune God. He contends that 'the doctrine of the Trinity, taken literally, has *no practical relevance at all*... – Whether we are to worship three or ten persons in the Deity makes no difference' (SF, 7:39) – although he points out that the concept of 'three divine persons', modelled after the idea of 'world governance', has been instantiated in many religions, including those of the ancient peoples, such as Zoroastrianism, Hinduism, the religion of the Egyptians and the Goths. 'Even the Jews', Kant adds, 'seem to have pursued those ideas in the final period of their hierarchical constitution' (RGV, 6:140–1n.). This suggests that, given the universality of the conception, the trinitarian dogma must be poised for 'rationalization', which rules out its literal interpretation. A rationalized version of the dogma is encapsulated in Kant's 'moral concept of God' as legislator, ruler and judge (e.g. MpVT, 8:257; V-Phil-Th/Pölitz, 28:1073–4).

This non- or anti-Trinitarian tendency is not the only similarity between Kant and Edelmann. Another similarity between the two thinkers comes down to the claim that the divine is accessible to us through our own reason – and that in fact reason suffices to maintain a relation with the divine, conceived as *Λόγος* by Edelmann and as the prototype of morally perfect humanity symbolized by the 'Son of God' on Kant's account. Accordingly, since the prototype has its source in our reason (Kant), and since our reason is a manifestation of the divine Λόγος (Edelmann), scriptural revelation is not essential in mediating the relation between God and human beings. Thus, rational religion thrives on ideas that do not belong to any historical context and the purport of which is universal. Moreover, for Edelmann, human beings are equal with one another and with Jesus in whom the divine reason or wisdom revealed itself, as it does in other humans – although Jesus, as Edelmann claims in his later *Glaubens-Bekentniß* (1746), received exceptional gifts and virtues from God, which is why he earned the name of Christ, and his disciples used this name to emphasize Jesus's excellence.[98] According to Kant, humans are equal with God in being bound by the self-legislated moral law: whether it is 'the prototype of a humanity well-pleasing to God', 'the teacher of the Gospel' or actual human beings, they differ in the degree of realizing the morally good disposition, but stand as equal under the moral law.

Yet there is an important difference between Kant and Edelmann which pertains to their conception of the relation of finite rational beings to God. According to Kant, the ideal humanity exemplified by the 'Son of God' is not marred by radical evil, unlike the nature of actually existing humans. Thus, insofar as humans are tainted by the evil propensity, 'the prototype of moral disposition in its entire purity', to which 'it is our universal human duty to *elevate* ourselves' (RGV, 6:61), remains a *transcendent telos* of our efforts to morally better ourselves. For due to their innate propensity to evil, human beings face obstacles in realizing their full moral potential, obstacles which they have a duty to strive to overcome. In contrast, Edelmann does not recognize any obstacles on our way to become divine, save a superstitious religion placing more weight on external rituals than on one's direct relation to God, and advocating the 'subjugation' of reason to the senses ('the flesh'). Absent external contingencies, no intrinsic feature of humanity could thwart its 'participation' in the divine. Kant, in turn, envisages this participation as a projected endstage of our moral development and the much-desired outcome of our propensity to evil being overcome.

5.4. Biblical criticism: Reading Kant in Spinoza's lights

Spinoza's *Theological-Political Treatise* might have earned the reputation of a 'book forged in hell'[99] but, as Jacob Freudenthal put it, within two centuries from his death the philosopher's name has become 'the shibboleth of contending theories of the universe, and ever as the one or the other gains the upper hand, the highest admiration for his system alternates with the most scornful contempt for it'.[100] Leo Bäck meticulously enumerated different guises under which Spinoza appeared to his descendants, both admirers and opponents: thus, for example, Friedrich Rappolt cloaked him in the naturalist garb, Leibniz – in that of a mystic, Christian Korholt, in a book titled *De tribus impostoribus magnis*, ascribed atheism to Spinoza, to be shared with Herbert of Cherbury and Thomas Hobbes.[101] The reading of Spinoza as an atheist, materialist and naturalist became widespread after the publication of a lengthy article by Pierre Bayle in his *Dictionnaire historique et critique* (1697), resulting in what Freudenthal and more recently Beth Lord have assessed as misconstrual.[102]

These controversies notwithstanding, Spinoza's ideas continuously influenced philosophy and theology in Germany, the Low Countries and throughout Western Europe. In the preceding sections, examples were given of mingling Spinoza's ideas with Christian theological conceptions in the works of Carl Friedrich Bahrdt and Johann Christian Edelmann. But Spinozism, transmitted by preachers, such as Pontian van Hattem, Jacob Bril and Johann Heinrich 'Ponytail' Schulz, also known under the name of 'Spinozists on the pulpit',[103] affected wider circles, too. According to Freudenthal, 'the spirit of his Pantheism seized hold of numerous men who moved and laboured in the midst of the people: clergymen of the reformed church and simple handicrafts men'.[104] It inspired bolder attempts at a critical reading of Scripture, already underway among the English deists, Hobbes and the Socinians. For instance, Matthias Knutzen noticed inconsistencies, ambiguities and disorderliness in the biblical text, and urged that reason or conscience, planted in us by nature, rather than any particular book, be identified as 'the true holy Scriptures'.[105] Friedrich Wilhelm Stosch, who authored *Concordia rationis et fidei sive harmonia philosophiae moralis et religionis Christianae* (1692), insisted that Scripture be explained so as to reject those claims which contradict reason, for the 'light' of reason comes before that of revelation. It is unwise, he observed, to believe that every single word of the book was dictated by God; at any rate, the main purpose of the Bible is to teach 'the simplest moral truths' to the people.[106]

As we have seen (in 5.2.3 and 5.3.4), this critical approach to revelation – manifested by granting to reason the role of the ultimate warrant of 'revealed' truths – mostly targeted the institutional church, rather than constituting an attack on religion as such. The critics of revealed religion had a reformatory intent. To illustrate this intent, the distinction between a true religion and its spurious – or superstitious – forms would be introduced. Accordingly, Theodor Ludwig Lau, the author of *Meditationes philosophicae de Deo, mundo et homine* (1717), equated true religion with the 'inner cult whose sanctuaries are heart and the understanding', by contrast to the 'religion of the society, a political religion', propagated by the churches.[107] To replace the discredited forms of faith, Spinozism offered a universal religion, based on a theological minimum: 'the doctrine of one God operating in all', which would inspire 'pure love of God and fellow humans'. Georg Lichtenberg prophesied that 'purified Spinozism' would become the religion of the future.[108]

The critical reading of Scripture, together with the quest for a universal religion, provided the cornerstone of religious rationalism thriving in the period from the late seventeenth century until at least the *Pantheismusstreit* between Jacobi and Mendelssohn. A great spiritual transformation was about to ensue. Freudenthal described this transformation enthusiastically: 'The claims of universal conformity to reason were asserted in opposition to religious dogmas, and Rationalism raised its head in the midst of a theology hitherto regarded as unassailable: one stone after another gave way in the firm fabric of ecclesiastical doctrines.'[109]

Kant, like Spinoza, would offer an account of a universal religion and deliver a critical reading of revelation in that he separated the rational core of religion from its non- or extra-rational husk. It is thus sensible to look for affinities between his account and Spinoza's, Kant's ideas on revealed religion being cognate with Spinoza-inspired religious rationalism. In this section, we shall bring these affinities to the fore, presenting both Spinoza (5.4.1) and Kant (5.4.2) as critics of revealed religion. As we shall see, though, it is not only Kant who recognizes in revelation a 'vehicle' of rational faith; arguably, also for Spinoza revealed religion can be construed as a stage in the development of human rationality, rather than merely a form of superstition which his critical account would aim at uprooting.[110]

5.4.1. Spinoza's critique of revelation

A vast part of Spinoza's main work engaging with the problem of the relation between religion and politics, the *Theological-Political Treatise*, presents the application of a new method of scriptural exegesis. Spinoza's method of reading the Scriptures parallels the Cartesian method of truth-seeking in science because it also starts from a recommendation that we suspend our conviction – which presupposes the authority of religious and political institutions and has likely been acquired from them – concerning the truth and divine origin of Scripture. It is not justified, contends Spinoza, to 'assume as a basic principle for the understanding of Scripture and for extracting its true meaning that it is throughout truthful and divine – a conclusion which ought to be the end result of study and strict examination'.[111] Criticizing Maimonides's approach to scriptural exegesis, in which all apparent contradictions and inadequacies found in the biblical text should be explained away with the help of philosophical or metaphysical assumptions,[112] Spinoza appeals to what looks like a version of the Protestant principle of *sola Scriptura*, and stipulates that 'all our understanding of Scripture and of matters spiritual must be sought from Scripture alone'.[113] Spinoza's hermeneutics resembles also the scientific method of Francis Bacon, for it encourages a careful assembling and analysis of data to construct definitions on their basis,[114] yet it rules out importing scientific presuppositions into the explanation of the text of Scripture. If the method of scriptural exegesis proposed by Spinoza can be deemed radical, it is so for two reasons: first, because it encourages an inquiry into the origins (or roots – *radices*) of religious belief; and second, because it motivates a thoroughgoing revision of the significance of religion.

In what follows three narratives on religion running through the *Treatise* will be distinguished in line with Yirmiyahu Yovel's recognition of the following kinds of religion in Spinoza: spurious religion based on observances and rituals (*religio vana*); universal religion teaching obedience to moral principles without grounding these principles in metaphysical truths (*religio catholica*); and true religion based on the cognition of 'God or Nature' and culminating in the 'intellectual love of God'[115] (*vera religio*).

The first narrative, related to spurious religion, appeals to the affects that inexorably accompany human life, especially hope and fear. Uncertain of the future, says Spinoza, human beings seek to remedy their anxiety, turning to dreams and delusions of imagination only to drive away one kind of affects with another kind thereof. Amidst existential instability, superstition sprouts together with disregard for reason:

> Reason they call blind, because it cannot reveal a sure way to the vanities they covet, and human wisdom they call vain, while the delusions of the imagination, dreams and other childish absurdities are taken to be the oracles of God. Indeed, they think that God, spurning the wise, has written his decrees not in man's mind but in the entrails of beasts, or that by divine inspiration and instigation these decrees are foretold by fools, madmen or birds. To such madness are men driven by their fears.[116]

Superstition is thus deeply entrenched in human nature and serves to cater for our crucial needs and desires, in particular the desire to maintain oneself in existence despite adversities and threats from the outside world which we are not able to control. Drawing upon the superstitious mindset as a source of religion in one of its forms, Spinoza uncovers that underlying the emergence of religious belief and weaved through the scriptural imagery, especially in those fragments that contain prophecies, is a play of human affects.[117]

Though the superstitious forms of religion have non-rational underpinnings, they reveal that religion has the capacity for channelling human emotions (affects) and as such can be employed to inculcate moral norms in society. Here comes the second narrative, related to the universal religion. On this account, Scripture is no longer read as compiled of products of the imagination fuelled by passions, but as a guidebook which helps instil obedience to basic moral principles, yet without this implying the need for the knowledge of God. As an instrument of moral instruction, Scripture conveys 'simple doctrines easily comprehensible by all', which Spinoza encapsulates in the injunction, 'to obey God with all one's heart by practicing justice and charity'.[118] This moral precept does not hinge on the accuracy of the descriptions of events contained in the Bible, and the natural light of reason alone suffices to recognize its rightfulness. It thus expresses the 'Word of God', which is not only contained in the Scriptures, but also inscribed in our hearts or minds, and which epitomizes 'religion universal to the entire human race, or catholic religion'.[119] The Scriptures can therefore serve as a vehicle of the 'Divine Law' which is not contained exclusively in holy books and revealed doctrines.

Containing a rational core, the Scriptures provide a bridge to the 'true religion', subject matter of the third narrative. According to this narrative, religion amounts to knowledge of 'God or Nature' – the 'supreme good' for the human being[120] – whereas the second narrative omits the cognitive component of religion and focuses on the attitude of obedience, motivated by its precepts. What could justify the role of Scripture as a 'bridge' connecting the two kinds of religion? The answer we shall tender is a bit speculative and it is to be sought in Spinoza's account of Christ.

Christ plays a key role in Spinoza's conception of universal religion (*religio catholica*); he is even called 'the way of salvation', understood as beatitude or happiness, since he instantiates morally flawless conduct.[121] According to Spinoza, in Christ 'the Wisdom of God... took on human nature'[122] and Christ was the most excellent among 'men of outstanding wisdom', such as King Solomon.[123] What makes Jesus unique is that he enjoyed immediate cognition of God, though Scripture does not make this cognition explicit: 'To him God's ordinances leading men to salvation were revealed not by words or by visions, but directly, so that God manifested himself to the Apostles through the mind of Christ.'[124] Spinoza avers that Christ 'communed with God mind to mind'[125] and 'perceived things truly and adequately'; he was thus 'the mouthpiece of God'.[126] The capacities Jesus was endowed with, though natural, must have been rare, which is why he would legitimately earn the name of a 'divinely sent teacher' and a moral exemplar.[127]

Spinoza's remarks on Christ are cryptic and metaphorical enough to cast doubt on the genuine character of his intentions. Steven Nadler, for example, suggested that by significantly toning down his critique of Christianity, Spinoza drew a strategic alliance with heterodox Christians among whom he had friends.[128] Yet one could also surmise that Spinoza's attribution of the immediate cognition of God to Christ would have much weightier purport than pleasing his Christian colleagues. For one could suppose that by attributing to Christ the knowledge of the divine mind, Spinoza draws, albeit indirectly, on his doctrine of '*scientia intuitiva*' – what he features as the highest degree of knowledge culminating in the 'intellectual love of God', an idea introduced in the *Ethics*.[129] If Christ's immediate cognition of the divine mind could be read as an analogue of '*scientia intuitiva*', then the kind of morality that Christ embodies as an exemplar and which forms the core of the universal religion could be regarded as a practical consequence of the adequate cognition of 'God or Nature'. In other words, if we link Christ's knowledge with the ideal of knowledge furthered in the *Ethics*, we will arrive at the conclusion that Spinoza holds the ethics instantiated in the figure of Jesus to be compatible, or even identical, with the kind of morality that a person entertaining the comprehensive knowledge of nature would exercise.[130]

Thus, insofar as Christianity promotes a universal moral teaching, it could transform into a religion based on knowledge if the moral principles it commends could be grounded in the rational cognition of God or Nature. Christianity would thereby become eligible to form a variety of natural religion. To endorse scriptural revelation means, in light of the foregoing, to take a step towards a true religion. If Scripture teaches the same universal morality that is accessible to a person who derives prescriptions for conduct from her cognition of nature, from the practical – though not theoretical – point of view, revelation could work as a substitute of the rational cognition of nature. Spinoza's critique of revealed religion leads to the recognition that 'faith' and 'reason', while being independent, do not contradict each other.

5.4.2. Revealed *vs.* rational religion

We have seen that Spinoza's critique of revealed religion can be read as a proposal to recognize in revelation an incipient form of a rational religion (5.4.1). Moreover, by linking it to a religion based on reason, Spinoza unveils the universalist tendency inherent in Christianity – an enterprise which also Edelmann embarked on (5.3.4). The idea of Christianity as a natural religion – or a religion containing a rational core – was not foreign to Bahrdt (5.2.3). It is also not unfamiliar to Kant who, as we have shown, shares some key tenets with Spinoza: the view that the backbone of religious faith must be rational (5.2.1) and that Scripture does not aim at truth but at moral instruction (5.3.1). Spinoza and Kant approximate thereby what Graeme Hunter describes as 'radical Protestantism', which he attributes to Spinoza.[131]

Having provided a 'definition' of religion in RGV, 6:154 (see 5.2.2), Kant distinguishes between revealed and natural religion. One prioritizes the revealed over the natural religion if one needs first to establish what God demands from us in order to know one's duties. To start from duties as divine commands, in turn, means to give priority to natural religion over its revealed counterpart. Within the position that claims that natural religion is 'alone morally necessary', Kant distinguishes two stances: rationalism, which denies neither the possibility nor 'the necessity of a revelation as divine means for the introduction of true religion', and naturalism, which refuses 'the reality of any supernatural divine revelation' (RGV, 6:154). Rationalism is then divided into pure rationalism, that is, the claim that supernatural revelation is not necessary for religion, and supernaturalism that claims the opposite.

There is some controversy among commentators as to which of these positions is Kant's own. Lawrence Pasternack thinks that Kant sticks to pure rationalism.[132] According to Firestone and Jacobs, Kant remains agnostic between pure rationalism and supernaturalism.[133] Palmquist, who largely follows their diagnosis, admits that Kant inclines towards pure rationalism.[134] Allen Wood used to opt for rationalism and consider *pure* rationalism inconsistent because the position would entail that we should fulfil some God-given duties while denying moral significance to them, but recently he has revised his earlier view and endorsed pure rationalism.[135] Peter Byrne is clear that Kant rejects supernaturalism, and suggests that despite siding with pure rationalism, Kant 'casts doubt on the viability' of this position.[136]

Concerning divine revelation, Kant succinctly expresses his agnosticism: 'no human being', he says, 'can determine anything through reason regarding these matters' (RGV, 6:155). Since naturalism denies reality to divine revelation, it surpasses the bounds of what reason can legitimately determine about 'these matters', thus it cannot represent Kant's position. Yet, as to the necessity of divine revelation as a means of introducing 'true religion', Kant's stance is rather nuanced.

By way of illustration, let us consider his treatment of miracles. Although, claims Kant, appeal to miracles was a useful tool for introducing a new religion in ancient times, once the religion has been established, there is no need to resort to them anymore (RGV, 6:84–6). Miracles are contrary to reason; hence they cannot figure at the foundation of a rational religion. Encountering putative 'theistic miracles', says Kant, 'reason is as paralyzed, for it is held back in its affairs according to recognized laws while not being instructed in a new one' (RGV, 6:86–7). Yet, unlike in the case of 'demonic' miracles – instances of a subject undergoing the experience of being possessed, so to say – which are 'most irreconcilable with the employment of our reason' (RGV, 6:87), we have at least a negative criterion of what *cannot* count as a divine miracle for sure: this will be an occurrence which 'is directly in conflict with morality', such as the injunction that 'a father... kill his son who, so far as he knows, is totally innocent' (RGV, 6:87). Thus, if they require subverting the moral law, miracles are incompatible with the religion of reason. Moreover, since we have no idea how to incorporate faith in miracles into our maxims, such faith cannot have any practical relevance (RGV, 6:88n.). Kant emphasizes, also, that claims concerning miracles betray 'presumptuousness and immodesty', because they undermine the principle that events in nature should be interpreted as 'effects of nature' (RGV, 6:89n.), hence in accordance with its laws. Therefore, belief in miracles does not accord with Kant's rational religion as it might require removing the cognitive constraints determined by the critical philosophy.

On the other hand, Kant holds scriptural revelation to be requisite to ground the authority of the visible church – the form of an ethical community needed for the propagation of rational faith (cf. RGV, 6:103; for more on Kant's views on church, see Chapter 6). As he avers, 'the authority of Scripture... establishes the ecclesiastical faith which, as popular faith, cannot be ignored, since no doctrine exclusively based on reason would seem to the people to make an unalterable norm; they demand a divine revelation' (RGV, 6:112). Thus, although 'true religion' originates in reason, revelation serves as a means by which rational faith is made accessible to believers. It might therefore precede pure moral faith in the order of cognition while being, so to say, constitutively dependent upon it. This dependence would consist in the fact that moral faith provides the principles for the interpretation of Scripture, the key to its reading (RGV, 6:109f.) – and only as a result of such an interpretation can the unity between reason and religious belief be asserted. For Scripture to make the moral faith accessible to us, moral senses have to be attributed to it in advance.

Getting back to the distinction between pure rationalism and supernaturalism, within the position that endorses natural religion as 'alone morally necessary', one can notice that Kant's stance – on which revelation needs to be harnessed to the realization of the ends of reason – engenders an amalgam of pure rationalism and supernaturalism. To the extent that revelation serves as a means of propagating rational faith, it is necessary for 'true religion', yet this implies its instrumentalization. To see that Kant instrumentalizes revelation, it suffices to show that he recommends imposing moral senses on revealed doctrines and assigns the role of the 'supreme interpreter' of Scripture to the critical-philosophical reason (RGV, 6:109). For, according to Kant, an interpretation guided by the principles of pure moral faith, 'may appear to us as forced, in view of the text (of the revelation), and be often forced in fact; yet, if the text can at all bear it, it must be preferred to a literal interpretation that either contains absolutely nothing for morality, or even works counter to its incentives' (RGV, 6:110).

Kant's biblical hermeneutics may thus bear a resemblance to the method advanced by Maimonides but criticized by Spinoza: to read the Scriptures with philosophical or scientific assumptions involved whenever this can ensure a coherent rendition of the text. But Kant's goal diverges from the goal of Maimonides in that it does not amount to understanding Scripture as such or making it coherent with reason's principles. Also, unlike Spinoza, Kant does not seek to establish that the kernel of scriptural revelation is fit for the natural light of reason, but rather moulds the revealed contents to accord with his rational religion. Against this background, Yovel has argued that, as a means of promoting rational faith, Kant's biblical exegesis 'is an aggressive activity, offering the mode of *engagement* in the social and cultural processes of his time'.[137] These processes have been labelled as 'enlightenment' and Yovel construes them as geared towards secularization. Given that the indispensability of revelation would be premised on recognizing its expediency in introducing 'true religion', there might be more than a grain of truth in Yovel's assessment. Kant's project to employ revelation in propagating rational religion echoes Spinoza's idea from chapter 19 of the *Theological-Political Treatise* of religion as the state's instrument of reinforcing public morals. Thus construed, there is a secularizing strand in both Kant and Spinoza.

6

The enlightened church: Kant's contribution to debates on secularization

6.1. The radical critique of the church

According to Jonathan Israel, the demand for a 'total separation of morality and theology was indeed the very cornerstone of the radical Enlightenment'.[1] To support this claim, examples of individuals and societies can be adduced that instantiate this separation. Bayle propagated the picture of Spinoza as a 'righteous atheist' and praised the Chinese for having created a well-organized society of heathens. If people and societies can be moral without religion, Bayle would argue, morality and political order do not have to be grounded in revealed religion but can be established on secular foundations. If religion turns out to be irrelevant for moral and political matters, its actual presence in social life and in the public sphere stands in need of justification.

The critique of religious authorities seems to be the default position adopted by the enlightened authors. Israel recounts that 'even those most implacably opposed to radical ideas had to ask whether there really is... some clearly demonstrable, rational test proving revelation, faith, and ecclesiastical authority indispensable or at least incontestably beneficial to society's well-being'.[2] As a recurring critical mantra would go, the church would foster superstition to manipulate uneducated masses, so that the clergy could maintain political influence and enjoy a socially privileged status. The anti-clerical rage motivated John Toland, an Irish freethinker, to accuse the clergy of forging mysteries and contaminating the originally rational Christian faith. In *Christianity Not Mysterious* Toland diagnosed: 'Now their own Advantage being the Motive that put the Primitive Clergy upon reviving Mystery, they quickly erected themselves by its Assistance into a separate and politick Body.'[3] On the other side of the Channel baron d'Holbach wrote about the contrivances of the ecclesiastics who would employ the doctrine of the afterlife to advance their dominion over society and civil authorities. In *The System of Nature*, d'Holbach wrote:

> It must indeed be allowed, that this doctrine [of the future life – A.T.] has been of the greatest utility to those who have given religion to nations and made themselves its ministers: it was the foundation of their power; the source of their wealth; the permanent cause of that blindness, the solid basis of those terrors, which it was their interest to nourish in the human race.[4]

Kant shares this anti-clerical posture to a degree. For, as we have seen in Chapter 1, he joins in the epistemic, moral and political critique of revealed religion. Identifying a form of religiosity which he dubs 'counterfeit service' (*Afterdienst*) and features in terms of following observances and rituals that does not contribute to one's 'becoming well-pleasing to God' in the way of 'a good life-conduct' (RGV, 6:170–1), he makes it clear that religion potentially encourages moral corruption. Yet, unlike d'Holbach, he does not interpret the doctrine of the afterlife as a device in the hands of power-thirsty priests, but rather invites it as a corollary of the postulate of immortality (KpV, 5:122–4).[5] Also, unlike Toland, Kant does not see a useful tool of manipulating the ignorant many in the mysteries of faith, which he reads as largely irrelevant from the viewpoint of the moral faith and in need of a rational interpretation (cf. RGV, 6:142, SF, 7:39).

Still, his assessment of the institutional Christianity is predominantly negative. The Christian faith, according to Kant, is the only ecclesiastical faith which can be compared with the pure moral faith that the 'founder' of Christianity aimed to teach (RGV, 6:124f.). Kant complains, though, that from the times it 'developed a learned public of its own', there is nothing in the history of Christianity that would 'recommend' this faith 'so far as the beneficial effect which we rightly expect from a moral religion is concerned' (RGV, 6:130). Subsequently, he enumerates various kinds of folly and iniquity committed by the Christian church, in both the East and the West: from the 'mystical enthusiasm' of monks and hermits, and celibate 'useless to the world', through 'a blind superstition' incited by belief in miracles, wars and the Crusades waged by the 'spiritual leader' of Western Christianity, inspiring church members to 'bloodthirsty hatred against their otherwise-minded confreres' (RGV, 6:130–1). Recognizing a despotic bent in ecclesiastical faith, Kant concludes that history shows that the church has abandoned its original foundations:

> This history of Christianity (which, so far as it was to be erected on a historical faith, could not have turned out otherwise), when beheld in a single glance, like a painting, could indeed justify the outcry, *tantum religio potuit suadere*

malorum!, did not the fact still clearly enough shine forth from its founding that Christianity's true first purpose was none other than the introduction of a pure religious faith, over which there can be no dissension of opinions.

(RGV, 6:131)

Appealing to the original purpose of ecclesiastical faith, Kant does not recommend a departure from institutional religion provided that it can be employed as a means of 'awakening and sustaining our attention to the true service of God' (RGV, 6:193) expressible in a morally upright life. Nor does he deliver reasons to relegate religion from the public sphere. Rather, on the basis of Kant's account of the 'visible church', the following argument for the public presence of religion could be made: Insofar as the church represents an ethical community within the political (juridico-civil) one, it can serve as a means by which morality would be brought to and realized within the political community; briefly, religion can help 'insert' morality into politics.[6]

However, given Kant's critique of both the historical and the existing religious institutions, the kind of 'church' which he makes space for in the public sphere can be no more than a project that matches the requirements of the critical philosophy. Thus, far from defending ecclesiastical authority, Kant would offer a revisionist account of the church. Arguably, he may even subscribe to a position approximating that of the radical enlighteners, namely that unless the church's reform is carried out, institutional religion should be dispensed with. This chapter offers a discussion of Kant's position concerning the 'ecclesiastical faith' along the adumbrated lines.

6.2. Kant's enlightened church

Let us consider the following argument:

(1) To strengthen their struggle against radical evil, human beings should join an ethical community (RGV, 6:96–7). (2) For us human beings, the ethical community can exist in the form of a 'visible church' (RGV, 6:100–1, 103). (3) Hence, to strengthen their struggle against radical evil, human beings should join the visible church (from 1 and 2). (4) Since the autonomy of practical reason is the foundational principle of all moral actions, acting morally means exercising autonomy (GMS, 4:440). (5) The struggle against radical evil is the same as striving for one's moral improvement (an analytic truth). (6) By reinforcing the struggle against radical evil, the church promotes the moral

improvement of human beings (from 3 and 5). (7) By promoting the moral improvement of human beings, the church promotes their autonomy (from 4 and 6). (8) Exercising moral autonomy provides an instance of using one's rational capacities autonomously (an analytic truth). (9) Enlightenment consists in maturing to use one's rational capacities autonomously – to exercise one's rational autonomy (WA, 8:35). (10) Thus, by promoting the moral improvement of human beings, the church furthers enlightenment (from 7, 8 and 9).

The overall purport of the argument can be encapsulated by the claim that the church as construed by Kant aims to promote enlightenment. But this claim is contentious. For example, one may inquire, why would not the church's end come down to working towards individuals' salvation or mediating their relationship with God? Whereas enlightenment has an immanent goal, we may think of the church's goal as transcendent.

Before we can deal with this overall purport of Kant's argument, which shall affect our perception of Kant's contribution to debates on secularization, two interpretive problems will be considered subsequently. First, given that Kant characterizes enlightenment as the subject's ripening to use her rational faculties without the tutelage of others, how can we associate it with the kind of communal enterprise that reinforcing our moral pursuits by the church is supposed to bring? Should the church inculcate shared patterns of conduct, as it apparently does as a *community*, how can this add to the agent's autonomy as such? Second, given Kant's distinction between practical and theoretical reason, one could inquire whether moral autonomy, to be reinforced by an ethical community, is indeed the kind of autonomy that the process of enlightenment is supposed to promote. For enlightenment may promote autonomy of a different breed – intellectual, scientific or that which consists in freedom to express one's opinions in public. What would make it plausible to think of the ends of enlightenment as ethical?

6.2.1. Two perspectives on moral agency: personal and communal

We can think that the church as an ethical community can help us overcome our propensity to evil and work towards transition from bad to better provided that the struggle against evil and the striving for perfecting oneself morally are not treated solely as tasks that an individual is to undertake on her own and for which she retains full responsibility. Yet, given that moral conversion – which Kant refers to as a 'change of heart' (RGV, 6:47, 67, 88, 197n.)[7] and which is the first step in one's turning away from the evil propensity – relies on an agent's resolution, there can be no role to play for the ethical community at least in the initiation of the struggle against evil. The change of heart cannot be replaced or even enhanced by religious activities, manifestations of belief or the endorsement of religious convictions as a way of removing the evil propensity and acquiring a moral disposition: 'no expiations, be they of the penitential or the ceremonial sort, no invocations or exaltations (even those of the vicarious ideal of God's Son) can make up for the lack of this change of heart or, if the change is there, in the least increase its validity before the heavenly tribunal' (RGV, 6:76). Transition from bad to better can thus be explained without appealing to a community in the form of a church, or indeed in any other form. The moral quality of an action hinges on the agent's motivation alone. This motivation can be strengthened by an ideal which our reason presents to us as the 'prototype of a humanity well-pleasing to God' (RGV, 6:119). Our fight with the evil propensity in us cannot implicate other agents, though, because each of us is solely responsible for undertaking it – as well as for having incurred the propensity (cf. RGV, 6:35). How could then our struggle be reinforced by participation in an ethical community?

A viable way of addressing this concern is to say that the role of the ethical community is not to strengthen our moral endeavours by adding extra incentives to those that the moral requirements themselves furnish us with, but rather by counteracting the pull of the non-moral incentives that make it more difficult for us to strive for moral betterment. This proposal would follow Courtney Fugate's compelling account of the highest good as Kant's way to 'neutralize' happiness as a ground of heteronomous moral motivation by subordinating it to virtue within the ideal of the highest good.[8] That we need a community which will guard us against the pull of non-moral incentives becomes clear once we realize that the kind of society human beings form by nature only reinforces the impact such incentives have on individuals. In a vein reminiscent of Rousseau, Kant describes the detrimental impact of social interactions on the agent's morality:

> It is not the instigation of nature that arouses what should properly be called the *passions*, which wreak such great devastation in his originally good predisposition. His needs are but limited, and his state of mind in providing for them moderate and tranquil. He is poor (or considers himself so) only to the extent that he is anxious that other human beings will consider him poor and will despise him for it. Envy, addiction to power, avarice, and the malignant inclinations associated with these, assail his nature, which on its own is undemanding, *as soon as he is among human beings*. Nor is it necessary to assume that these are sunk into evil and are examples that lead him astray: it suffices that they are there, that they

surround him, and that they are human beings, and they will mutually corrupt each other's moral disposition and make one another evil.

(RGV, 6:93–4)

According to Lawrence Pasternack, Kant's depiction of the dynamic of the generation of vices as a result of social interaction captures a phenomenon which he refers to in an earlier essay, titled *Idea for a Universal History with a Cosmopolitan Aim* (1784), as 'unsociable sociability' and which he describes as boosting civilizational progress by spurring permanent rivalry and competition between individuals.[9] Pasternack notices that at the time of drafting the essay Kant believed that the results of agents' prioritizing self-interest over morality could be contained by juridical means, but in the *Religion* he shifted to the view that 'no human juridical solution is sufficient' to achieve this end,[10] which is why he would turn to the ethical community construed as a church. Pasternack restates his claim about the insufficiency of merely political means to channel the morally corrupting impact of human society on its members in a commentary on Philip Rossi's *The Ethical Commonwealth in History*.[11]

In a recent symposium on Kant on relations between church and state, Gordon Michalson advocates an alternative reading of Kant's turn to community in the *Religion*. Michalson claims that Kant's idea of the visible church 'finds its starting point in his account of the "kingdom of ends"' introduced in the *Groundwork*.[12] Kant defines the 'kingdom of ends' as 'a systematic union of various rational beings through common laws' (GMS, 4:433) and 'a world of rational beings (*mundus intelligibilis*)... through the giving of their own laws by all persons as members' (GMS, 4:438). The idea here is that the very act of moral legislation makes the agent into a member of the community of rational legislators. The form of the moral law, which is universal, necessitates this outcome. To legislate the moral law for oneself means to legislate the law for each and every rational being, hence for a community of rational agents. The ethical community derives therefore from the fact of rational moral agency – from the autonomy of moral agents. On Michalson's account, Kant's 'visible church' would constitute an empirical representation – a 'schema' (RGV, 6:132) – of an ethical community construed as the 'kingdom of ends'. Against this background, it seems that what justifies the appearance of the ethical community in the form of a church are no more than historical contingencies.

However, consulting textual evidence, we can realize that the ethical community construed as the 'kingdom of ends' does not correspond exactly to the ethical community in the form of a church. The pivotal difference between these two kinds of ethical community lies in the form of sovereignty over the members of each of them: whereas the kingdom of ends has an egalitarian structure, every member of it wielding the power of the sovereign, the church, both visible and invisible, forms 'a people of God' subsumed 'under divine moral legislation' (RGV, 6:100–1). What explains the difference between Kant's accounts of the ethical community in the *Religion* and in his earlier critical works is the emergence of anthropological considerations: whereas the *Groundwork* and the second *Critique* feature agents guided by practical reason, the *Religion* pictures an ethical community as aspired to by finite rational beings mired in evil and afflicted by the weaknesses and limitations of human nature. Apart from susceptibility to the corrupting influence of others, these limitations are reflected in the 'opacity' of our own moral character and of the moral characters of other people. Since we cannot know whether any member of the human society has a good will, to be able to hope for a moral community, we have to posit a divine being – an omniscient being 'who knows the heart' (*Herzenskündiger*; RGV, 6:99) – and 'a people of God' in which everyone strives to develop a morally good disposition. It seems, thus, that underlying the replacement of the kingdom of ends by church in the *Religion* is Kant's overall pessimistic conviction that it would be unreasonable or naïve to envisage that by their own efforts human beings could form a community of agents purged of vicious motives: for 'how could one expect to construct something completely straight from such crooked wood?' (RGV, 6:100).

Kant thinks of the ethical community *in the form of a church* as requisite to reinforce moral agency because only a community construed as an association of good-willed individuals united in their moral pursuits can help keep selfish inclinations and the mechanism of rivalry at bay; it is also requisite because of the insufficiency of a mere union of rational beings, given the deficiencies of human nature. There is, however, also a positive reason for claiming that moral agency requires a community for its full development and that the community should adopt the form of a church. Incumbent on 'the human race towards itself', says Kant, there is 'a duty *sui generis*' to abandon the 'ethical state of nature' (RGV, 6:96–7), in which only the juridico-civil but not the moral laws could apply, and to enter an ethical community. For only as a member of an ethical community can an individual engage in 'the promotion of the highest good as a good common to all'. Since to be able to hope for the objective reality of the highest good, we need to postulate 'a higher moral being through whose universal organization the forces of single individuals, insufficient on their own, are united for a common effect' (RGV, 6:97–8), promoting the highest good necessitates building a church – an ethical community recognizing the divine sovereign.[13]

6.2.2. Enlightenment

We have seen that Kant justifies the need for the church as a community aimed to protect us from the corrupting impact of human society, which we are exposed to just because we are part of it. The church would further our struggle against radical evil and hence promote our efforts towards moral improvement by making us less vulnerable to the vices of social life. We shall now proceed to the second problem signalled at the end of section 6.2 and related to the argument proposed therein, namely, what justifies the claim that enlightenment has a moral end, being poised for promoting moral autonomy.

Kant defines enlightenment as a process whereby the human being emerges 'from his self-incurred minority [*Unmündigkeit*]' (WA, 8:35). By minority he understands the condition of being under the tutelage of others when it comes to the use of one's understanding. Competitive accounts of enlightenment define it as a pursuit of knowledge, education and culture that shall prove practically beneficial to mankind. For example, for Moses Mendelssohn, enlightenment (*Aufklärung*) consists in the formation (*Bildung*) of man and citizen in the theoretical respect and comprises rational cognition (*vernünftige Erkenntnis*), being complemented by culture (*Kultur*) which covers the practical aspects of *Bildung*.[14] According to Andreas Riem, 'enlightenment' designates 'the effort of the human spirit to cast light (*ins Licht... setzen*) on all objects of the world of ideas, all human views (*Meinungen*) and their consequences, and on all that has influence on humankind, according to the principles of a pure doctrine of reason, with a view to promoting that which is useful'.[15] That he brings to the fore the *way* in which we use our rational capacities, instead of rational cognition as such, is evident from Kant's recognizing in freedom of thought – that is, 'freedom to make *public use* of one's reason in all matters' (WA, 8:36) – a necessary condition of enlightenment. In the Orientation essay (1786), he articulates freedom of thought as 'the subjection of reason to no laws except *those which it gives itself*' (WDO, 8:145), hence as rational autonomy. It is essential for freedom of thought that the censorship of publications ('*civil compulsion*') and coercive practices within religious institutions ('*compulsion over conscience*') be removed (WDO, 8:144–5).

Yet, reading a bit further, we shall see that Kant's definition of enlightenment in terms of rational autonomy makes up a prelude to a more comprehensive account which includes the moral dimension of the process. This dimension is encapsulated in the motto he thinks epitomizes the enlightenment's agenda and which is expressed by Horace's maxim *'Sapere aude!'* (WA, 8:35). The maxim exhorts us to have the courage, thus to overcome the vices of cowardice and laziness, and so it calls for adopting a moral posture of a certain kind. What we need the courage for is to be wise, to have wisdom – *sapientia*.

Dispersed throughout Kant's writings, one can find a handful of remarks on wisdom. Accordingly, he claims that as 'perfection of cognition in the derivation of every end from the system of all ends', wisdom pertains to God alone, though 'insofar as our cognition of human action is derived from the principle of a possible system of all ends, it can be called human wisdom' (V-Phil-Th/Pölitz, 28:1057; cf. EAD, 8:336). The ends of human reason are divided into 'technical-practical' and 'moral-practical'. Philosophy, as 'the science of the *final end* of human reason', is 'a doctrine of wisdom' (OP, 22:489; cf. KpV, 5:108–9) and is 'directed towards something founded on God himself' (OP, 21:7; cf. PKR, 8:44). The human being can acquire wisdom by relating her actions to the system of ends, both physical, that is, provided by nature, and practical – the connection of all rational beings under the moral law. The ends of nature and the moral ends are united in the ideal of the highest good for which Kant postulates the existence of God as the condition of its realization. He even equates 'a first *original being*' with the highest good (WDO, 8:137) – 'a supreme intelligence as the highest *independent* good' (WDO, 8:139) – the morally perfect agent in whom there are no incentives competing with morality. Since, as Kant says, 'moral teleology makes good the defect of physical teleology, and first establishes a theology' (KU, 5:444), nature can be thought of as purposeful, that is, manifesting moral order, only within the idea of the highest good which presupposes the existence of God. Given that wisdom pertains primarily to God and that God instantiates the ideal of the highest good, the courage to be wise in the case of finite rational agents would consist in what these agents are able and bound by duty to do, which is to *promote* the highest good (cf. KU, 450–1). Briefly, enlightenment implies for Kant the furtherance of the highest good.

One of the reasons adduced in 6.2.1 for the ethical community to adopt the form of a church – a commonwealth under God's sovereign rule – was that only in such a community would it be possible for us to hope that the moral ideal of the highest good can be realized (cf. RGV, 6:97). Since enlightenment for Kant involves essentially pursuing the moral ideal, the church is requisite to realize the goal of enlightenment. Enlightenment is precisely the goal of the church as construed by Kant, so that not only do the ends of the two converge but they are indeed identical.

6.2.3. Religious or secular? The highest good and the Kantian church

On the reading sketched above, Kant could be identified as a 'religious enlightener' (cf. 1.1 for more on the 'religious Enlightenment'), furthering the view that religion is not only compatible with enlightenment but indispensable for the realization of its pursuits. Such a reading would imply dismissing the 'secular' interpretations of the highest good, called forth in 3.3. However, it may not suffice to suppress the secularizing tendency inherent in Kant's account of the ethical community.

Conceived in secular terms, the highest good would be 'a state of affairs to be achieved in *this* world, through *human* activity', as Andrews Reath has put it.[16] This condition 'would be realized through a system of social institutions which supports the realization of certain moral ends'.[17] Similarly, Yovel contends that in the *Religion* Kant does not envisage the highest good as a transcendent reality, but rather as 'the consummate state of *this* world, to be realized through a concrete development in time';[18] it is then 'our own world brought to perfection' in which nature is supposed to serve as 'the empirical substratum for a new world that will be a copy or a manifestation of the moral idea'.[19] Against this backdrop, the church would be construed as one of the institutions requisite to bring about the immanent end of humanity – to construct a moral world in the course of historical progress. Onora O'Neill, in turn, would see in the church one of many possible ethical communities which could contribute to attaining the goals of enlightenment.[20]

All these proposals require flouting those parts of textual evidence which clearly speak for the theological or religious account of the highest good, which, for example, Fugate and Pasternack have argued for (cf. 6.2.1). They also entail overlooking the overall pessimistic tenor of Kant's views on human nature. Nonetheless, it seems that at least Yovel correctly identifies a secular thread in Kant's account of church. For whether we read the highest good as a secular or a religious ideal, its function can be regarded as having thoroughly immanent purport: to enhance our responsiveness to the demands of the moral law.

Even if we cannot stay on the morally right track without an ethical community represented by a church, and without belief in God, still these may provide but props for our moral life, without having any intrinsic significance. In other words, the reason why we should enter the church, according to Kant, can be expressed in 'this-worldly' categories: to lead a morally better life, rather than to work towards our salvation in the world to come – even if we should believe in the world to come to make sense of our moral efforts in this world. That is to say, the religious reading of the highest good does not suffice to dislodge the secularizing tendency from Kant's conception. Thus, in its Kantian version, the 'religious Enlightenment' would inspire a radical refashioning of the meaning and purpose of religion – and attaching it to what Charles Taylor has featured as an 'immanent frame'.[21]

6.3. The church as a project

Kant's treatment of the church as an instrument of the moral transformation of human society can be anchored to the imagery of ecclesiastical faith as a 'vehicle' of pure moral religion, present throughout his writings on religion and rational theology (see, e.g., RGV, 6:106, 115, 117–118, 123n., 136n., SF, 7:37, 42, 52). Yet this does not amount to flatly admitting that, according to Kant, the existing religious institutions can be employed in carrying out social reform guided by 'enlightened values'. Kant's approach is not based on a factual or descriptive claim, unlike the approaches of contemporary intellectual historians acknowledging the contribution of religion to the making of the Enlightenment era.[22] Rather, given his characterization of 'the true (visible) church' – a church which 'displays the (moral) kingdom of God on earth inasmuch as the latter can be realized through human beings' (RGV, 6:101) – we can surmise that Kant *projects* an ethical community under God's sovereign rule which would best fit for the role of the said vehicle. Such a community should satisfy four criteria corresponding to the four types of the pure concepts of the understanding in the first *Critique*: (1) universality [quantity],[23] (2) purity[24] [quality], (3) freedom [relation] and (4) unchangeableness [modality]. These features define what could be regarded as (the empirical manifestation of) a rational church, that is, a church based on moral-practical principles.

Universality implies that there can be only one true visible church. This condition can be satisfied due to the church being founded on principles valid for any ethical community, that is, on the moral law (or the 'laws of virtue' (RGV, 6:95)), rather than on dogmas established in relation to historical revelation, which given the contingency of historical revelation could be diverse. Since only rational principles can guarantee universality to the true visible church, only rational principles can provide the backbone of the ecclesiastical faith which aspires to universality.

Purity means that the main motivation underlying the act of entering the church by each of its members should be moral. The church must be 'cleansed of the nonsense of superstition and the madness of enthusiasm' (RGV, 6:102), that is, it cannot promote 'counterfeit service' (RGV, 6:172), whereby morally irrelevant practices would replace 'pure dispositions of the heart' (RGV, 6:115), and cannot encourage belief in the possibility of experiencing supersensible realities (cf. RGV, 6:174).

Further, the relations between the church members and between the church and political authority should be based on *freedom*. This condition seems to reiterate Kant's point that, unlike the political commonwealth, the ethical one should be established on the 'laws of virtue' which are not coercive in contradistinction to the 'public juridical laws' (RGV, 6:95). People are free to join the church thus construed, or to abandon it, without being motivated to act by non-moral incentives, such as the fear of punishment. Kant compares the constitution of the church to that of a household or family in that its members should relate to the sovereign of the community as 'a common though invisible moral father' and build their mutual relations on love, conducive to a 'free, universal and enduring union of hearts' (RGV, 6:102). This condition precludes the kind of hierarchy that involves one human being exercising power or being an authority unto another.

The fourth feature of the true visible church is the *unchangeableness* of its constitution. Kant points out that this condition does not comprise the administrative regulations in a church which can be adjusted to social and historical circumstances. As the subsequent section's title adumbrates that 'the constitution of each and every church always proceeds from some historical (revealed) faith... and this is best founded on a holy scripture' (RGV, 6:102), it might seem that Kant blatantly contradicts himself, because there are many different faiths based on revelation and the true church is supposed to be one. Kant's appeal to historical revelation, though, intimates the mode in which he thinks we can access the church's unchangeable foundations, which are to be no more than mediated by scriptural revelation.

Since none of the existing religious institutions embodies all of the four principles taken jointly, Kant's project of the true visible church should rather be read as containing guidelines for reforming such institutions. Yet the true visible church itself bears a transitory character, rendering a waystage to 'a new order of things' in which 'the universal religion of reason' (RGV, 6:122) would take the reins. The reform of religious institutions is to lead eventually to their demise. This confirms the reading of Kant's church, suggested in 6.2.3, as a prop in our moral life, hence not an 'end in itself'. A rational community of moral agents, which Kant also calls the 'kingdom of God on earth' (e.g. RGV, 6:132–4, 176, SF,

7:68) and which is to constitute the endstage of the reform, would do without the institutional church – though clearly not without God. Kant illustrates this development, reminiscent of enlightenment as a process of ripening to use one's rational capacities without the guidance of others, with a metaphor of the human embryo:

> Thus at last the pure faith of religion will rule over all, 'so that God may be all in all'. – The integuments within which the embryo is first formed into a human being must be laid aside if the latter is to see the light of day. The leading-string of holy tradition, with its appendages, its statutes and observances, which in its time did good service, become bit by bit dispensable, yea, finally, when a human being enters upon his adolescence, turn into a fetter.... The degrading distinction between *laity* and *clergy* ceases, and equality springs from true freedom, yet without anarchy, for each indeed obeys the law (not the statutory one) which he has prescribed for himself, yet must regard it at the same time as the will of the world ruler as revealed to him through reason, and this ruler invisibly binds all together, under a common government, in a state inadequately represented and prepared for in the past through the visible church.
> (RGV, 6:121–2)

To summarize: Kant's considerations suggest that ecclesiastical faiths should be reformed in line with the precepts founding the true visible church, in order to approximate the universal faith of what we have called rational church (see above). The emergence of the rational church would then encourage the abandonment of the institutional scaffolding of ecclesiastical faiths. The church thus construed would eventually embody the moral community unifying all rational agents of good will under 'divine moral legislation' (RGV, 6:101).

However, given that Kant held that Christianity, at least in its original form, prior to its having developed a dogmatic core, is the sole ecclesiastical faith eligible for comparison with the tenets of pure moral faith (cf. 6.1), one could surmise that his idea of reform pertains to Christianity, first and foremost, and that like Edelmann, he would see in Christianity alone potential for transforming into a universal faith, based on rational principles. Relatedly, in a comparative essay on Kant and Thomas Morgan, Wojciech Kozyra has argued for Marcionian inspirations behind Kant's project of morally revolutionizing Christianity at the cost of discarding its Jewish heritage.[25] Yet Nicholas Tampio defends the inclusivity of the Kantian church, drawing on recent developments within Islam towards a more rational conception of faith which acknowledges pluralism and the need for a secular state to sustain it.[26] Still, from *The End of All Things* (1794), it seems to transpire quite evidently that Kant privileges Christianity as closest to the ideal of rational religion. He presents Christianity as 'supposedly *destined* to be the world religion', espousing a '*liberal* way of thinking' and inspiring love for the moral law (EAD, 8:339). Kant says:

> Christianity has the intention of furthering love out of concern for the observance of duty in general: and it produces it too, because its founder speaks not in the quality of a commander demanding obedience to his will, but in that of a friend of humanity who appeals to the hearts of his fellow human beings on behalf of their own well-understood will... Thus it is from the *liberal* way of thinking... that Christianity expects the *effect* of its doctrine, through which it may win over the hearts of human beings when their understanding has already been illuminated by the representation of their duty's law.
>
> (EAD, 8:338)

Given the secularizing thread in Kant's conception of church brought out above (cf. 6.2.3), and his apparent privileging Christianity as particularly fit for 'rationalization', the hermeneutically compelling idea could be attributed to him that it is Christianity that stands at the headwaters of the contemporary processes of secularization.[27] However, Kant's praise of Christianity in the above-cited essay can also be read against the background of the historical context in which the essay appeared. This context would be provided by the religious policy of Frederick William II and his minister Johann Christoph von Wöllner, imposing strict regulations on preaching and other forms of public speaking on religion (cf. 5.1 for more details on this issue). Accordingly, Kant's remarks in *The End of All Things* would not so much be meant to develop the idea of Christianity as a universal religion, as to support a case for separating religion from politics – the church from the state.

Kant's argument against conflating religion and politics draws on the distinction between two kinds of laws governing the ethical and the political communities (cf. RGV, 6:95f.). The laws of the ethical community merit love as they are based on freedom, whereas those of the political one, being coercive, are intended to elicit compliance and observance. The laws of the ethical community cannot be enforced on citizens without this leading to the erosion of the community's foundations. As Kant states emphatically: 'woe to the legislator who would want to bring about through coercion a polity directed to ethical ends! For he would thereby not only achieve the very opposite of ethical ends, but also undermine his political ends and render them insecure' (RGV, 6:96). Kant suggests that welding together religion and politics eventually compromises the ends of both; for by introducing coercive laws into religion, the state undermines the moral core of religion, which must be based on freedom. Given that the ethical community in the form of a church was to 'insert' morality into politics (cf. 6.1), by introducing coercive laws into the domain religious, the state frustrates the possibility to make politics more moral.

This is not to say, however, that Kant fails to recognize the need for the ethical and political community to work out a certain mode of coexistence. Their coexistence is indeed necessitated by the fact that both communities have a public (*öffentlich*) dimension (cf. RGV, 6:95–6). Therefore, as James DiCenso has argued, 'Kant does not disconnect moral community from existing institutions. Just as sub-communities can act as an ethical leaven in the larger public sphere... the capacity to realize moral laws requires appropriate political conditions. The ethical state is a composite regulative principle guiding our efforts to transform the public sphere toward greater autonomy and inclusivity.'[28] On DiCenso's reading, Kant thinks of the church and the state as deeply interrelated, so that an authoritarian government, for example, is not only unable to foster political freedom, but also creates conditions which perpetuate heteronomous forms of agency. According to DiCenso, the Kantian church is intended at promoting 'a true enlightenment described as an order of law originating in moral freedom,'[29] a condition both moral and political.

In what follows, we shall look again into Kant's idea of the church as a vehicle of enlightenment furthering moral autonomy – the conclusion of the argument outlined in section 6.2. The question which remains to be addressed with regard to this conclusion is how to reconcile human autonomy, requisite for moral agency, with divine legislation in the ethical community available to us through ecclesiastical institutions.

6.4. Divine legislation and human autonomy

The idea of the church's ends converging with those of enlightenment and consisting in the furtherance of moral autonomy presents the following difficulty: how can our moral autonomy be compatible with 'divine moral legislation' (RGV, 6:101)? For whereas the former amounts to our reason legislating the moral law to itself, the latter implies that all human duties are to be regarded as 'divine commands' (cf. RGV, 6:99, 110, 152, 154, 179n., 192; SF, 7:36, 64, 74). But surely being commanded by God and being commanded by one's own reason are two different qualifications of duties, unless these two kinds of legislation are somehow identified. Given this discrepancy, the question arises in what way moral autonomy can coexist with divine legislation.

We have already seen several intricate ways of putting these two together. These ways are all related to Kant's idea of the highest good as realizable through an ethical community in the form of a church. In this section, we shall go through some accounts of the highest good to inquire into the possibility of making moral autonomy and divine legislation mutually compatible. As a result of these considerations, the conclusion shall emerge that this task cannot be fully completed with the resources available within the critical philosophy; rather, its completion might necessitate rethinking the relation between human reason and the divine, perhaps of the kind as Kant adumbrates in the sketchy notes of his final unfinished work published as the *Opus postumum*.

Before discussing these accounts, let us restate that Kant's appeal to divine legislation appears in the context of the highest good understood as a unity of moral virtue and happiness adequately proportioned to it (cf., e.g., RGV, 6:5, 8n.; V-Phil-Th/Pölitz, 28:1074–7) or as a moral world in which agents' strivings to pursue the moral path are harmonized with the fulfilment of their natural desire for happiness (cf., e.g., KrV, A 808/B 836–A 811/B 839). The moral world, which need not be conceived as an empirical, causally structured order of phenomena – indeed, in the first *Critique*, drawing upon Leibniz, Kant calls this world a '*regnum gratiae*' (KrV, A 815/B 843) – is thus a world as would be governed by divine sovereign that would guarantee proportionate distribution of happiness in relation to moral worth or would harmonize agents' efforts with their pursuit of happiness.

The accounts of Kant's conception of the highest good can be divided into theological (or religious) and secular (or historical). The secular accounts of the highest good, represented by Reath, Yovel and DiCenso, describe the moral world as an ideal to be realized by us and in this world, without positing a transcendent realm: God and future life. On this account, the highest good constitutes a political project which we have a duty to promote and which we can promote, for example, by means of reforming the existing institutions, the church and other religious communities included, so that they would be more apt to support individual autonomy and other 'enlightened values'. Accordingly, the ethical community in the form of a church can further the realization of the moral world but is not indispensable for this purpose. Our moral autonomy does not conflict here with divine legislation simply because divine legislation is not requisite to bring about the moral ideal. Characterizing the church as an ethical community governed by God, Kant merely employs the symbolic language of religion which we can retranslate, without any loss of significant content, into the language of morality. As Michalson has argued, the ethical community would originate from the idea of the 'kingdom of ends' in which each rational legislator sets the law for herself and all other rational beings.

The secular accounts of the highest good solve the apparent conflict between human autonomy and divine moral legislation by 'diluting' the latter in the former, thus by denying any save metaphorical or symbolic significance to Kant's talk about God. In other words, they safeguard human autonomy at the cost of divine sovereignty in the moral world. Clearly, such readings are revisionist and necessitate a thoroughgoing redaction of Kant's texts. They gloss over our weaknesses, limitations and the realities of social life, all of which Kant takes into account in his conception of the highest good and the need for ethical community. They do not properly recognize our anthropological predicament: the quagmire of the radical evil which we have fallen into on our own, yet which may be impossible for us to overcome if we rely on our efforts alone, given the weaknesses at issue. Moreover, they overlook the fact that inherent in Kant's idea of the highest good, there is a notion of justice: the requirement that happiness be distributed in accordance with an agent's moral worth and that the moral worth of the agent be assessed against the standard of moral perfection and by an impartial judge who has an insight into the nature of our moral dispositions.

The theological interpretations make up for these deficiencies of the secular reading. Several kinds of such interpretations can be distinguished, depending on which aspect of the highest good is emphasized. First, some theological readings emphasize the motivational role of the highest good, and so of the ethical community that would serve to promote it. Stephen Palmquist, for example, points out that if they are treated as a means by which 'the human being... seeks to work upon himself (to give life to his dispositions by means of the *idea of God*)' (RGV, 6:195n.), religious practices available within a church will result in our 'moral empowerment'.[30] Likewise, John E. Hare maintains that the 'divine supplement' provided by ecclesiastical faith is necessary to bridge the 'moral gap'[31] – the disparity between 'moral demand', which Kant puts on us very high, and 'natural human capacity' whereby we fall short of being able to live up to the demand.[32] Since morality confronts us with requirements that we cannot fulfil despite being obliged to do so, moral faith is requisite for the 'ought implies can' principle to remain in force.[33] Yet one may wonder in what way recourse to the 'divine supplement', apparently allowing some form of heteronomous motivation, is to strengthen the exercise of autonomy. How is the 'supplement' supposed to help us overcome the 'moral gap' if our use of the 'supplement' only confirms the existence of the 'gap'?

This problem – or, should we say, paradox – does not seem to affect the second kind of the theological reading, which can be found for instance in Fugate. On this reading, positing the highest good would be construed as a way to remove 'all hindrances to morality' (KrV, A 808/B 836). The moral world under divine legislation would be conceived as a world in which the obstacles to exercising moral autonomy have been lifted. The idea of such a world can motivate the agent to suppress non-moral incentives by subordinating them to morality. But does not this proposal stipulate too much by suggesting that moral faith provides as much as a condition of the possibility of the exercise of moral autonomy, at least full-fledged? By contrast, is not faith supposed to issue from moral action, as we have seen in Chapter 3?

The third variety of the theological reading, which could be attributed to Pasternack, avoids this problem by construing the highest good as a kind of fulfilment of morality. Distinguishing between the highest good as a duty and the highest good as an ideal,[34] Pasternack divides labour between God and us: while our share is to become worthy of happiness by acting morally, God would distribute happiness, making the ideal consummate. Unlike the other two kinds of the theological interpretation, Pasternack's does not involve mixing heteronomous motives into our exercise of morality or reversing the dependence relation between faith and morality. Yet, if we remove the motivational role of the highest good and do not think of it as an 'enabler' of moral action, the question arises about its role in Kant's system. Pasternack seems to suggest that we think of the moral world as a world in which divine justice would be executed by morality being rewarded with happiness. Thus, acting morally we would contribute to building a divine state, bringing about a 'kingdom of God on earth' (cf., e.g., RGV, 6:101, 132, 134, 176n.) understood as the eschatological completion of morality. In this picture, moral autonomy does not collide with divine legislation since God does not account for our exercise of autonomy but rather for the consequences of moral action.

However, if belief in God – and so the realization of the moral ideal in the ethical community – is not a prerequisite of moral action, or does not play a motivational role, can it have anything over and above an 'aesthetic' function, making morality more appealing to us without affecting our autonomy? Or, if our role in bringing about the highest good is reduced to following the moral law, should not our actions be perceived as a means to the construction of a divine plan, rendering our autonomy an instrument in the hands of God? While the secular readings of the highest good had the drawback that they would lead to denying God's share in the realization of the moral ideal, the theological readings may be regarded as jeopardizing human autonomy, challenging the idea of morality as intrinsically purposeful. In the last chapter, we shall reach out to the *Opus postumum* to see if autonomy can be made compatible with divine legislation without the need to compromise either.

7

The divinity of reason in the *Opus postumum*

7.1. 'A forest of contradictions': The theological content of fascicles 7 and 1

Kant's *Opus postumum* comprises preparatory drafts for a work that was initially intended to form, as he puts it in many passages, 'transition from the metaphysical foundations of natural science to physics', in which he aimed to show how it is possible that the pure concepts of the understanding apply to the objects studied by physics. However, some parts of the work do not fit into this natural-scientific scheme because they contain a doctrine of practical self-positing (*Selbstsetzungslehre*) and of transcendental philosophy as 'the absolute whole (system) of ideas… immediately directed towards objects… which, independently of experience, are postulated by pure reason as objects [for the sake of] its (experience's) possibility' (OP, 21:80). Hence, regarding the ultimate part of the work, which features a new project of transcendental philosophy, a hypothesis has been made that the collection of Kant's late notes incorporates drafts of two works.[1]

Though the hypothesis is nowadays largely dismissed,[2] the interpretative challenge remains, especially concerning the theological passages of Kant's 'final synthesis'. The first difficulty pertains to the relation between these passages and the rest of the *Opus postumum*, containing discussions of ether as the transcendental material condition of the possibility of experience and its objects.[3] Kant builds two theories: one related to the physical world and one – to the area of human action, so the question arises how these two theories can correspond to one another and what connection between their subject matter can be established. Kant's proposed solution is to introduce a principle connecting the two domains: 'man', 'I' or 'the rational subject' (e.g. OP, 21:22, 29).

The second difficulty, with which I deal in this chapter more thoroughly, poses a challenge to those who study Kant's theological views. The challenge consists in how to reconcile apparently inconsistent ideas of the divine that he develops in different passages of his late unfinished work. Reiner Wimmer has distinguished seven chains of theses about God in the *Opus postumum*: (A) God as an idea of reason; (B1) The concept of God as identical with that of the moral subject and (B2) the object of pure practical reason; (C1) God as lawgiver and (C2) judge; (D) God as a postulate of pure practical reason and (E) God as a being the existence of which is implied by its concept.[4] (Later on, a critical assessment of some of Wimmer's proposals will be provided.) These theses, when set against one another, manifest ambiguities in Kant's late conception of God and even prove to be mutually inconsistent, as is the case, for example, with D and E.

Here is some textual evidence of possible inconsistencies: whereas in a passage of fascicle 1, one can read about 'God, the world (*both outside me*) and the rational subject which connects both through freedom' (OP, 21:22; italics A.T.), an earlier fragment in fascicle 7 denies God's transcendence in relation to the finite subject. Kant says in it: 'There is a God in moral-practical reason, that is, in the idea of the relation of man to right and duty. But *not as a being outside man*' (OP, 22:60; italics A.T.). Marking this apparent inconsistency in Kant's theological considerations in the *Opus postumum*, Vittorio Mathieu described them metaphorically as a 'forest of contradictions'.[5] To illustrate the adequacy of this description, it suffices to adduce a few passages. Thus, on the one hand, Kant explicates the concept of God by means of the concept of substance, saying for instance: 'A universal, morally law-giving being, which, thus, has all power, is God. There exists a God, that is, one principle which, as substance, is morally law-giving' (OP, 22:122). And: 'The concept of God is the concept of an obligating subject outside myself' (OP, 21:15). On the other hand, he denies substantiality to God stating:

> The concept of such a being is not that of substance – that is, of a being which exists independent of my thought – but the idea (one's own creation, thought-object, *ens rationis*) of a reason which constitutes itself into a thought object, and establishes synthetic a priori propositions, according to principles of transcendental philosophy. It is an ideal. There is not and cannot be a question whether such an object exists, since the concept is transcendent.
>
> (OP, 21:27)

Attributing to God both transcendence and immanence to human reason does not have to make a theological conception internally inconsistent as such: suffice it to think about Augustine's God conceived of as transcendence in the immanence of the human mind or soul.[6] Yet Kant wavers between attributing to God a mind-independent status and reducing God to a mere idea of reason, and this is what creates an impression of inconsistency. The following pair of statements illustrates the point: 'A command, to which everyone must absolutely give obedience, is to be regarded by everyone as from a being which rules and governs over all. Such a being, as moral, however, is called God. So there is a God' (OP, 22:127). But: 'His name is *holy*, his honor is worship, and his will almighty, but he himself is idea' (OP, 21:52). On top of that, Kant identifies God with practical reason, entertaining the idea of religion without the presupposition of divine existence. He says:

> The concept of God is the idea of a moral being, which, as such, is judging [and] universally commanding. The latter is not a hypothetical thing but pure practical reason itself in its personality, with reason's moving forces in respect to world-beings and their forces. (OP, 22:118)

> The characteristic of a moral being which can command categorically over the nature of man is its divinity. His laws must be obeyed as divine commands. Whether religion is possible without the presupposition of the existence of God. *Est deus in nobis.* (OP, 22:130)

Yet these contradictions may be apparent or form part of an antinomy that Kant failed to fully develop and address. His reference to God 'outside me', the moral lawgiver and substance, could be read as marking the practical perspective from which the existence of God is postulated. God could be considered an idea of reason, and thus not an independently existing substance, from the theoretical point of view which entitles us to endorse the regulative status of the ideas of metaphysics without positing any objects corresponding to them. Thus, the existential claim would be made from within the practical stance but not from within the theoretical one. Such an explanation of the apparent inconsistencies remains in line with Kant's critical tenets. Likewise, the suggestion that religion does not have to presuppose the existence of God echoes his statement in Part Four of the *Religion* that 'no assertoric knowledge is required in religion (even of the existence of God)' (RGV, 6:154n.).

However, it is Kant's identification of God with practical reason in the *Opus postumum* that brings about important changes in his philosophical theology and philosophy of religion. First, leading to the denial of divine transcendence, it challenges Kant's moral theism (cf. V-Phil-Th/Pölitz, 28:1011); for if 'God in us' is practical reason or an aspect of it, he cannot exist as a substance bearing the properties that would be ascribed to him by theistic metaphysics, such as infinity, omniscience and omnipotence (see SF, 7:76 for infinity and KrV, A 815/B 843 for the other two features). Thus, Kant's new position could be seen as inviting atheistic consequences, a conclusion that matches an anecdotal report by Friedrich Abegg, summing up Kant's late convictions thus: 'Believe nothing, hope for nothing! Do your duty here.'[7] Second, identifying God with practical reason may undermine the critical doctrine of the postulates of pure practical reason[8] for it turns the claim about the existence of God into a self-evident truth that comes along with moral awareness. Finally, Kant's 'deification' of practical reason could result in what Adela Cortina labelled a 'dissolution' (*Auflösung*) of the theistic concept of God, rendering the concept entirely superfluous.[9]

Does Kant really *identify* God with practical reason in the *Opus postumum*? And are the above-listed consequences inevitable? An unqualifiedly positive answer to these questions would imply that the late Kant subverted the whole system of critical philosophy he would build over thirty years or so. To avoid this implication, we should follow Erich Adickes's recommendation to read particular statements made by Kant in the context of his other statements and against the background of all his philosophy, instead of considering them in isolation.[10] Accordingly, throughout the *Opus postumum* Kant keeps distinguishing God from finite rational beings and indeed endows God with features he never attributes to human reason, such as 'greatest perfection', omniscience, omnipotence and being the first cause of all things (OP, 21:50). Furthermore, he introduces the following 'division' of beings, according to which 'God' and 'man' belong to two different categories: 'A being who has only rights and no duties (moral-practical reason according to its laws and principles), *God*. (2) Who has rights and duties: *man*. (3) Beings which have neither rights nor duties, which have no desires at all (mere matter). (4) Those which have desires, but no will' (OP, 22:50). Also, Kant describes God as a 'moral being who would be thought as *obligating*, but as *obligated* by no other' (OP, 22:124). The description corresponds to the account of the '*holy* will', introduced in the *Groundwork*, which, unlike the will of finite rational beings, requires no imperatives, and so cannot be 'obligated', because it does not succumb to non-moral incentives (GMS, 4:414).

Moreover, even if Kant equates God with practical reason, this does not have to render the *idea* of God superfluous. First, Fregean considerations might be in play: two terms can refer to the same object while presenting the object in different ways. Thus, religion and rational theology can provide a language to convey the same contents as are conveyed by the language of morality. Second, identifying God with practical reason does not have to imply reducing the former to the latter; in fact, one can think of this identification as involving both the rationalization of the divine and the deification of the rational without prioritizing any side of the equation. Third, there are passages in which Kant identifies God not with practical reason but with its 'product', that is, the moral law. For example, in the Pölitz lecture notes one can read that God 'is the moral law itself, as it were, but thought as personified' (V-Phil-Th/Pölitz, 28:1076; cf. V-Phil-Th/Pölitz, 28:1091). Thus, in the end, God would be identified with the whole moral domain, rather than with practical reason alone as legislator of the moral law.[11]

The deification of morality, however, would entail a radicalization of Kant's conception of religion because it would encourage the idea that 'true religion' consists essentially in no more than moral conduct. This way we arrive at the notion of religion as a rational activity: as Kant contends in *The Conflict of the Faculties*, 'religion is a purely rational affair' (SF, 7:67). Yet this notion of religion is notoriously ambiguous: on the one hand, it corroborates the picture of Kant as a staunch opponent of atheism, established, for example, on the basis of the second-edition Preface to the *Critique of Pure Reason* (cf. KrV, B xxxiv). This picture presents Kant as claiming that belief in God provides an indispensable component of moral action, religion being an inevitable corollary of our practical rationality. On the other hand, furthering the idea of religion as a 'rational affair' can weaken the independence of religion from ethics to the point of 'diluting' the former in the latter, as it were. Accordingly, Kant's late conception of religion would oscillate between a (close-to-eliminative) reduction of religion to ethics and the idea of the finite rational being as an essentially religious being (something like a Kantian version of Mircea Eliade's *homo religiosus*). This chapter aims to bring these late developments in Kant's conception of religion to the fore.

7.2. Vaihinger and Adickes on Kant's late theology

The ambiguity which marks the notion of religion as a fully rational activity is reflected in the divergences among the interpreters of Kant's theological views in the *Opus postumum*. The main line of division can be illustrated by the positions of Hans Vaihinger, on the one side, and Erich Adickes, on the other. According to Vaihinger, Kant's idea of God is a 'heuristic fiction' which encourages an 'as-if mode of approach'.[12] Practical belief in God, in Vaihinger's view, means acting *as if* God were judging us, so it does not really require that we endorse belief in the existence of God (in the common sense of the term 'belief'). In fact, someone who acts *as if* God existed does not believe that God exists, but only displays conduct characteristic of those who endorse theistic belief. Thus, Vaihinger makes room for an account in which morality and belief in God are wholly independent of one another: the idea of God as a heuristic fiction may figure in the description of a person's action without belonging to her own beliefs. This account resonates with Kant's suggestion that religion need not presuppose the existence of God (cf. OP, 22:130): it is not belief, but action motivated by respect for the moral law that forms the core of religion. Adickes, in contrast, interprets Kant as a consistently theistic thinker. The main difference between Kant's moral theism of the critical period and the view represented in the *Opus postumum*, contends Adickes, consists in replacing the doctrine of the postulates of pure practical reason with a direct inference of divine existence from the moral law. This way, the existence of God emerges as 'absolutely self-evident'.[13]

There is some textual evidence that corroborates the reading along the lines of Adickes. Kant says, for example: 'There is a God: for there is in moral-practical reason a categorical imperative, which extends to all rational world-beings and through which all world-beings are united' (OP, 22:105). And: 'The mere (*bloße*) idea of God is at the same time a postulate of his existence. To think of him and to believe [in him] is an identical statement' (OP, 22:109; trans. A.T.). Since Kant infers God's existence from our awareness of the moral law in us in the form of the categorical imperative – or indeed from the very idea of God – Wimmer contends that in the *Opus postumum* Kant endorses a version of the ontological proof for the existence of God.[14] Relatedly, Kant expresses the idea that existence follows analytically from the concept of God, being part of its 'grammar' (mark the *avant-la-lettre* Wittgensteinian flavour to the idea): '*God* is not a thing existing outside me,' he avers, 'but my own *thought*. It is unreasonable to ask *whether* there is a *God*. A *verbum personale* belongs to the grammar' (OP, 21:153; trans. A.T.). And: 'Reason inevitably creates objects for itself. Hence everything that thinks has a God' (OP, 21:83). Yet the concern arises that if Kant endorses the ontological argument in his post-critical theology, not only does the doctrine of the postulates of pure practical reason need to be put aside, but he also turns to the kind of metaphysics that he criticized throughout his entire philosophical career. One does not have to think, however, that Kant indeed endorses the argument. Below are some reasons for this conviction.

First, even if his argument for the existence of God is based on the concept of God, it does not mean that the argument is ontological. In the critical period, Kant comes up with the 'moral concept of God' (V-Phil-Th/Pölitz, 28:1071), which includes the following determinations: 'a *holy lawgiver*, a *benevolent sustainer of the world*, and a *just judge*' (V-Phil-Th/Pölitz, 28:1073;

cf. RGV, 6:139), 'the supreme lawgiver of an ethical community, with respect to whom all *true duties*, hence also the ethical, must be represented as *at the same time* his commands' and 'one who knows the heart' (RGV, 6:99; cf. SF, 7:10). The moral concept of God represents the sovereign of an ethical state the aim of which is twofold: to reinforce individuals' struggle against radical evil and to enable the realization of the highest good – a moral world in which nature meets the ends of morality. But if the moral concept of God presupposes the idea of the highest good, then existence is not analytically contained in this concept but postulated as the condition of the real possibility of the moral ideal. Thus, the moral concept of God would be derived from the doctrine of the postulates of pure practical reason, Kant being far from replacing the doctrine with the ontological proof – *pace* Adickes and Wimmer.

Second, Kant may claim that we need to think of God as existing without thereby establishing that it indeed follows from this thought that God exists. The above-adduced textual evidence from the *Opus postumum* shows that he takes the idea of God to be an indispensable component of rational thought. As 'the idea... of a reason which constitutes itself into a thought object' (OP, 21:27), the idea of God is a necessary condition of our rationality. If the idea of God forms part of the idea of reason, it should emerge in the course of reflection on our rational activity. The claim that our reason constitutively depends on the idea of God echoes Leibniz's claim that we arrive at the idea of God in the course of self-reflective acts, which are themselves contingent on our ability to know necessary truths.[15] In this construal, our having the idea of God would be a corollary of our rationality, without this fact necessarily entailing the divine existence.

Third, assuming that the late Kant replaces the doctrine of postulates with directly inferring the existence of God from the categorical imperative in our moral-practical reason, this does not yet turn his argument into an ontological proof in the sense espoused by Wimmer, earlier to be found in Anselm, Descartes and Leibniz. There are at least two ways in which this inference could be construed. First, we could think of it in causal-explanatory terms, on analogy with Descartes's theistic argument in Meditation Three in his *Meditations on First Philosophy*.[16] On this reading, the existence of God would explain the fact of our awareness of the moral law. God would figure here as the cause of the moral law in us, one who has 'implanted' in us moral awareness. Yet this reading runs the risk of compromising the autonomy of practical reason, for the moral law might then be conceived as the divine law we are obliged to follow, rather than the law we legislate for ourselves. Thus, an alternative way of reading Kant's inference to the existence of God from our awareness of the moral law should be proposed. This alternative interpretation would be based on the idea of God as 'personification' of the moral law and would establish a conceptual relation between the idea of God and that of the moral law. Such a relation can be thought of as analytic, though, only if there is something 'divine' about the moral law itself. The 'deification' of morality would allow establishing the 'existence' of God without recourse to the Anselmian ontological argument and a relapse into dogmatic metaphysics. This is because it would allow conceiving of the divine as immanent to human reason, thus without illegitimately positing the transcendent God of the dogmatic metaphysicians. The last option seems to capture the purport of textual evidence most adequately.

7.3. An argument for the divinity of reason

Kant's argument for the 'existence' of God (as an idea of reason) based on the awareness of the moral law in us, mistakenly associated with the ontological argument, draws on what we earlier described as identification of God with practical reason. The case for the 'divinity' of reason in the *Opus postumum*, to be presented in this section, rests on two pillars: textual evidence and an argument from the autonomy of practical reason. In what follows, we shall start with some discussion of Kant's text and proceed to the autonomy argument afterwards.

There are passages dispersed through Kant's late unfinished work which corroborate the claim that he veers towards identifying God with practical reason:

(i) Categorical imperative which our reason expresses [*ausspricht*] through the divine. Freedom under laws, duties as divine commands. There is a God (OP, 22:104).

(ii) A being who has only rights and no duties (moral-practical reason according to its laws and principles), *God* (OP, 22:50).

(iii) Thus the idea of moral practical reason in the categorical imperative is the ideal of God (OP, 22:54).

(iv) The holy Ghost judges, punishes and absolves through the categorical imperative of duty, by means of moral-practical reason.

(v) There is a God in moral-practical reason, that is, in the idea of the relation of man to right and duty. But not as a being outside man (OP, 22:60).

(vi) There is a fact of moral-practical reason: the categorical imperative, which commands for nature freedom under laws and through which freedom itself demonstrates the principle of its own possibility: the commanding subject is God (OP, 21:21).

Kant attributes to practical reason and God several essential features which they apparently share. First, they both 'command' the moral law or duties to us, as can be gathered from quotes (i), (ii), (iii) and (vi). Second, as legislators, reason and God are not subject to the laws themselves (ii). Legislating the moral law, practical reason manifests divinity, because it represents the 'holy will', that is, a will that does not need imperatives because it is 'not capable of any maxim conflicting with' the law (KpV, 5:32). Furthermore, reason takes over the role of God in that it judges our actions – a function symbolized by the Third Person of the Trinity (iv), interpreted in light of the 'moral concept of God' (see 7.1). Finally, if we regard our duties as divine commands, the idea of God emerges from our attitude to the duties (cf. v). The 'divinity' of reason would thereby follow from the kind of attitude we manifest to the law it legislates.

Let us proceed to the argument from autonomy. To remind: Kant says that 'autonomy of the will is the sole principle of all moral laws and of duties in keeping with them; heteronomy of choice… not only does not ground any obligation at all but is instead opposed to the principle of obligation and to the morality of the will' (KpV, 5:33). Following a law determining an object external to the will implies the will's heteronomy and actions guided by heteronomous principles do not qualify as moral: 'Autonomy of the will is the property of the will by which it is a law to itself (independently of any property of the objects of volition).… the… principle of autonomy is the sole principle of morals' (GMS, 4:440). Thus, if the law we are supposed to follow originated in the divine as opposed to our will, our actions, motivated heteronomously, could never be moral. The idea of divine legislation for our will is thus incompatible with the autonomy of the will, as much as would be the idea of deriving the moral law from the laws of nature. Hence, Kant's reference to God as legislator of the moral law cannot imply the divine origin of the moral law but rather constitutes an attempt to 'deify' practical reason in its role of moral legislator. The idea of autonomy as the foundation of morality, which Kant promotes in the critical writings, would thus result in the identification of God and practical reason in the *Opus postumum*. Christopher Insole interprets this move as a 'shift away from… Christianised Platonism', expressed by Kant 'in highly religious terms, explaining that we are divine, insofar as we give the moral law to ourselves'. According to Insole:

> The traditional theological concept of theosis involves the human being becoming divine by virtue of divine action and participation in the Godhead. Kant's final reflections curiously parallel a sort of theosis, except with an important difference. We become divine, but by virtue of our own action, and

by virtue of our participation in the moral law. We have a sort of theosis whereby as we become divine, God is eclipsed and vanishes, or dissolves into us.[17]

There are a number of problems with the autonomy argument which can be summarized by the claim that the consequences of the argument amount to reducing religion to ethics, Kant's God being assigned the status of a mere by-product of our rational activity. In the remaining part of this section, we shall go through some possible charges against the autonomy argument as formulated above.

First, as Norbert Fischer has pointed out, the autonomy of practical reason is grounded in the 'fact of reason', which makes every rational being endowed with the status of an end in itself, and this fact is 'given', not invented by us.[18] Our awareness of the moral law is not of our own making, although it is within our power to subordinate our capacity of choice (*Willkür*) to the moral law. For one can prescribe a law to oneself or follow the law without being its author: for example, that the principle of non-contradiction is binding for us as rational thinkers does not imply that it is of our own making, even though one's resolution is required to consistently abide by it. Thus, on Fischer's account, the idea of the divine legislation of the moral law is compatible with the autonomy of practical reason without this implying the 'deification' of reason.

Second, since the moral law binds every rational being and every rational will is a legislator, God can be thought of as legislator of the moral law without this posing any threat to the autonomy of my will or of the will of any other rational being. Accordingly, being legislator of the moral law does not make human reason a divine entity, the more so that Kant associates with God properties that he would not predicate of human reason. For example, he refers to God as a 'being, which has unrestricted power over nature and freedom under laws of reason' (OP, 22:117). Surely, human reason does not exercise unrestricted power over nature, otherwise bringing about the moral world – the highest good – would not be claimed by Kant to surpass human capacities.

Third, there is a sense of the 'deification' of reason which does not necessitate identifying human reason with God or making God 'dissolve into us', to use Insole's turn of phrase. To illustrate the point: in Book X of the *Nicomachean Ethics*, Aristotle features the intellect as 'something divine' in man and equates life dedicated to truth-seeking with the divine life.[19] Early Christian authors, such as Philo of Alexandria and Justin, would find affinities between the ancient conceptions of reason as λογος and the biblical Λογος representing Christ.[20]

According to Leibniz, God has an infinite reason from which human reason differs only in its deductive capacities: whereas all truths are provable for the divine mind, though some of them require an infinite number of steps, the human mind operates in a finitistic way, hence the distinction between necessary and factual (contingent) truths obtains only from the finite perspective.[21] Also, many eighteenth-century deists considered reason divine, claiming that it originates from God as divine light (*lux divina*) implanted in every human being and enabling us to cognize God.[22]

The foregoing objections to the autonomy argument support an account of God as moral lawgiver that does not challenge Kant's doctrine of autonomy, and which therefore does not encourage identifying God with practical reason. But the problem with these objections is that they seem to build on an idea of God as either the cause of the moral law, who has, as it were, implanted the law in us, or as a rational being which differs from us only with regard to the extent of its rational powers. In the critical period, Kant was clear that establishing a causal connection between God and human rationality may undermine the autonomy of practical reason (cf. 2.4). Besides, the idea of such a connection could be legitimately endorsed only if it had practical but not theoretical purport, but it is not obvious yet what exactly this practical purport would amount to. To address this issue, we shall later turn to Kant's account of practical self-positing and the role of the idea of God in it. In the next section, we will see that even if Kant did not rule out a certain kind of divine causality in the moral world, he rejected the view on which God could affect the human will without this compromising its autonomy.

7.4. Human freedom and the divine will

According to the argument in 7.3, the autonomy of practical reason rules out the divine legislation of the moral law unless God and reason are considered one and the same thing. However, in light of some textual evidence, other than the evidence supporting the 'divinity' of reason, Kant seems to endorse both the divine legislation and the distinction between human reason and God. He says, for example: 'A being who is originally universally lawgiving for nature and freedom, is God. Not only the highest *being*, but also the highest *understanding* – *good* (with respect to holiness). *Ens summum, summa intelligentia, summum bonum*' (OP, 21:14). Kant attributes to God properties such as '*summa intelligentia*', which, considering his views on the limitedness of our cognitive capacities, he would never predicate of human reason, but he also describes God as the author of the moral law and, if one may so put it, the first cause in the moral world. Yet, given that he posits autonomy as the principle of all moral action, there must also be a way in which God and autonomy could be put together without this making his account of human action internally incoherent. As we shall see, though, while divine moral legislation can in some sense be accommodated within Kant's account of freedom, there is also a sense in which God and autonomy prove to be mutually exclusive.

Accordingly, the idea of God as the author of the moral law does not conflict with Kant's conception of transcendental freedom, which he defines as 'absolute causal spontaneity beginning from itself a series of appearances that runs according to natural laws' (KrV, A 446/B 474). This is because freedom in the transcendental sense implies independence from causal relations in the *empirical* world and conditions the possibility of the subject's initiating new causal chains in the domain of appearances without her action being determined by any occurrence in the domain of empirical causes. But, given Kant's distinction between the noumenal and the phenomenal, to be free from empirical causality does not mean to be free from all kinds of causality. Thus, the subject's ability to exercise spontaneity in the empirical world does not preclude the possibility of God's action on the subject, let alone the divine authorship of the principles of the subject's action. The point here would be quite straightforward and well known from the history of Western metaphysics: God *creates* human beings free and human beings exercise freedom in relation to other creatures.

Yet, contends Kant, even if God authored the moral law and equipped human beings with the capacities requisite to follow the law, he cannot make anyone moral: 'Animals can be *made* by God, because there is, indeed, in them a *spiritus* and even *anima* (*immateriale*), but not *mens*, as free will. *Whether God could also give [geben könne] man a good will?* No, rather, that requires freedom' (OP, 21:34). Kant rejects the idea that moral action as such invites collaboration between the human and the divine will. Thereby he stands in clear opposition not only to Nicolas Malebranche and the occasionalists who advocated the view that the human will is inefficacious when it comes to motivating morally good actions, and hence in need of permanent divine assistance.[23] He also rejects the view that moral action results from the 'concurrence' of the finite human will with the will of God. For, as the above quote suggests, divine action on the human will would restrict the latter's freedom. Thus, *pace* Augustine,[24] for Kant morally good actions can be solely of the subject's own making. As he avers, 'God cannot concur in the causality of freely acting beings towards his moral ends in this world, for he must not be regarded as *causa* of their free actions' (HN, 18:474). God cannot determine the subject's will without thereby thwarting the subject's freedom. In Pölitz lecture notes on religion, one can read:

> Now in general speculative reason cannot comprehend the freedom of creatures, nor can experience prove it; but our practical interest requires us to presuppose that we can act according to the idea of freedom. Yet even if it is true that our will can decide something independently of every natural cause, it is still not in the least conceivable how God might concur in our actions despite our freedom, or how he could concur as a cooperating cause of our will; for then *eo ipso* we would not be the author of our own actions, or at least not wholly so.... even if our reason cannot deny the possibility of this *concursus*, it still sees that such an effect would have to *be a miracle of the moral world*.
> (V-Phil-Th/Pölitz, 28:1106–7)

The above passage does not rule out the possibility of the divine legislation of the moral law in the sense of God's being the origin of the law – the first cause in the moral world. Rather, it states that we cannot comprehend how God, or the divine will, could provide a concomitant cause of our actions. Given that Kant rejected the compatibilist account of freedom, as we have seen in 2.4, what he finds inconceivable in divine 'concurrence' is the coexistence of our freedom with any kind of divine causality on our moral agency. Accordingly, Kant does not subscribe to the Augustinian view that whatever good or right thing I do, it is God who, as it were, acts through me, so that the goodness of my action is to be owed to Him. To draw on a biblical metaphor, in Kant's view, God cannot 'incline my heart' without infringing upon and actually nullifying my freedom. Were he to do so, I would not be able to act morally. Hence, Kant's rejection of divine concurrence marks, as Insole has put it,

> a far more significant rupture with the Christian tradition than any supposed crisis in belief in the existence of God. Kant believes in God. It is our freedom in relation to such a God that he cannot believe in, at least in a traditional sense. If we are to be free, the will must have no external efficient cause, and no external object.[25]

Insole notices, however, that although Kant rejects concurrence in a 'traditional' sense of the term, he is 'more open to the possibility of divine–human concurrence, particularly when talking about the divine *assistance* that is available to human beings when they struggle to be moral.'[26] In his view, Kant refers to '*concursus*' within the 'mere conservationist' rather than concurrentist framework, which means that he allows for God's cooperation with the human will to the extent that 'God can supplement the action of the creature by removing impediments to the creature's free action,'[27] rather than by providing 'an immediate cause' of the creature's actions so that an action would have two causes: the human and the divine.[28] Kant does not, therefore, deny that God might act towards safeguarding the conditions of our moral life, but rejects God's immediate involvement in our actions. God could thus perform the kind of tasks that exceed human capacities, without giving any succour to finite agents in their own specific tasks. The divine concurrence so understood is also needed if the ideal of the highest good – a world in which nature would be fit for realizing moral ends – is to be actualized:

> The *concursus* of God with freedom (insofar as freedom is morally determined), in order to make nature concordant with freedom and the moral law, can also be considered as lying in the order of nature and must be so considered.... The correspondence of divine providence with the perfection of the world in accordance with laws of nature is called a *concursus* with freedom and morality. He imparts capacity, opportunities, and incentives for the good.
>
> (HN, 18:479)

The above quote concerning divine *concursus* comes from the early 1780s, while the latest theological passages of the *Opus postumum* are dated early 1800s. The earlier texts promote the view of God that bears a resemblance to the deist God, because they suggest that he is not immediately involved with creatures, having imparted to them existence and requisite capacities. This way God would also compensate for the creatures' deficiencies and provide what is needed for the finite rational beings to exercise their freedom. Yet in his final work Kant seems to have abandoned this apparently deist outlook and conferred some of the 'divine' properties on the subject's rational capacities that motivate the subject to act and judge her actions accordingly. He says:

> There is a being in me, which is different from me and which stands in an efficient causal relation (*nexus effectivus*) toward myself (*agit, facit, operatur*); itself free (that is, not being dependent upon the laws of nature in space and time) it judges me inwardly (justifies or condemns); and I, man, am this being myself – it is not some substance outside me. What is most surprising is that this causality is a determination [of my will] to action in freedom ([that is], not as a natural necessity).
>
> (OP, 21:25)

What justifies this transition from the close-to-deist conception of God to the notion of 'God in us' (strikingly resembling Edelmann's conception of God as reason, cf. 5.3.4)? One of the reasons of the transition might be that the 'deist' view does not cohere with Kant's account of autonomy. For in the moral world in which God would act as its 'designer', the subject's freedom could only be partial, at least in the sense that the very exercise of this freedom would hinge upon God's having authored the moral law: had the moral law not been legislated by God, the finite rational beings would not be able to act in accordance with it. But autonomy is incompatible with the origin of the subject's moral motivation lying outside the subject's will. Thus, the autonomy of practical reason cannot consist in merely endorsing the moral law as the primary motive for the subject's will but must also include the very act by means of which the law is established. Autonomy does not express itself in the affirmation of a reality preordained by the divine being but in creating the reality on one's own. Also, note that Kant attributes to the 'being in me', which he equates with 'myself' – or should we rather say, with the rational part of my nature – the function of a judge. This move significantly transforms the conception of the highest good as the unity of happiness and the worthiness to be happy (i.e. morality). For now, it seems that a transcendent God is not requisite to judge my inner moral disposition. The idea of the highest good framed in terms of what Lawrence Pasternack has called the Principle of Proportionate Distribution[29] apparently falls.

Yet again the worry emerges that by replacing God with a function of human reason, Kant makes the idea of God ultimately superfluous. In what follows, we shall address this worry arguing that despite Kant's 'deification' of practical reason, the idea of God remains an irremovable component of his new version of transcendental philosophy.

7.5. The divinity of reason revisited

In its legislative function, human reason, as Kant construes it, can be said to replace God. In Yovel's words: 'Despite finitude – and also because of it – human reason takes over the role of God as legislator for both nature and morality.'[30] Thus, God could be dispensed with as the source of the natural and the moral order. Indeed, as we have seen, in their interpretations of the *Opus postumum*, Cortina and Insole suggest that for the late Kant God becomes superfluous. On this construal, without openly endorsing an atheistic position, Kant would eventually remove the concept of God from his philosophy.

This eliminativist reading faces problems when we confront it with textual evidence. Yet this evidence should be accommodated without this implying the endorsement of the metaphysical commitments incurred by such readings as those offered by Fischer and Wimmer. In what follows, we shall look at some arguments against eliminating the idea of God from Kant's late theological doctrine which do not necessitate accepting these commitments.

First, the idea of God forms part of Kant's revised conception of transcendental philosophy, understood as 'a system of ideas, which are themselves problematic (not assertoric), but which must nevertheless be thought as possible forces affecting reason: God, the world, and man in the world, subject to the law of duty' (OP, 21:83). Just like in the *Critique of Pure Reason*, Kant does not state here that we can become cognitively acquainted with the objects of the ideas of God, the world and 'I', but only that we can form problematic concepts of these objects (cf. KrV, A 339/B 397). Thus, we can think of God, even though we cannot prove God's existence (cf. KrV, B 310). In the *Opus postumum* account of transcendental philosophy, the idea of God provides one of the 'moving forces' of reason (OP, 22:118), which makes it possible for reason to acquire the idea of itself (cf. OP, 21:27), thus consider itself as its own object.

This takes us to the second point providing the reason why the idea of God does not turn out to be redundant for Kant. This is because of the place of the idea in the doctrine of practical self-positing (*Selbstsetzungslehre*). Though the name of the doctrine has been coined by scholars,[31] fascicles 7 and 1 abound in expressions such as 'the subject posits itself' (OP, 22:11, 96), 'the subject constitutes itself' (OP, 22:12), 'I posit myself as…' (OP, 22:32), 'the subject makes itself into an object' (OP, 22:79, 88) and 'the subject constitutes itself a priori into an object' (OP, 21:14). Without defining the notion of positing, Kant devotes separate considerations to theoretical and practical self-positing, which cover the accounts of the subject's constituting itself as an object of sensible intuition and as a person, respectively.

According to Giovanni Pietro Basile, God plays in practical self-positing a role analogous to the role ether plays in theoretical self-positing.[32] As a category of physics and an *a priori* concept of our mind, ether provides a transcendental *material* condition of the subject's experiencing itself in space and time ('the subject posits itself as object [*dabile*]' [OP, 22:28]). Likewise, Kant employs the idea of God when he spells out the conditions of the process whereby the subject 'makes itself into a person' (OP, 22:54). The idea provides a 'material' condition insofar as it enables the subject to represent *itself* as a person – 'a being who has rights and is conscious of them' (OP, 22:49), and so a member of an ethical state.

With the concept of ether, space can be construed as a dynamic field of 'moving forces' affecting the subject, and the subject can be thought of as an object representable in space.[33] The idea of God, in turn, would enable the subject to think of itself as an object in the 'moral space' – an analogue of the ethical state in the *Religion* (RGV, 6:94f.) and the kingdom of ends in the *Groundwork* (GMS, 4:433f.). God and ether would thus account for the objective side of self-positing: for the subject's constituting itself both as an object of empirical cognition – an embodied 'ego' – and as a member of the ethical community, subordinated to the moral law which binds all rational beings without exception. The idea of God would bring with it the 'space' of the 'moving forces' of morality, that is, such forces which 'affect' the subject's moral agency.

Third, the idea of God cannot be superfluous insofar as it originates from reason's reflection on its own legislative activity. In the act of moral lawgiving, pure practical reason gives to itself an *a priori*, necessarily binding law valid for all rational beings. Legislating for the entire community of rational agents, practical reason transcends its individual dimension, acting as a universal legislator. Accordingly, the idea of God becomes requisite for reason to authorize its self-transcending move. God in the *Opus postumum* would thus represent the universal and absolute dimension of the moral command; as Mathieu has put the point, God would provide a 'hypostasis of the absoluteness of moral duty'.[34] What Kant would 'deify' then would be practical reason in its function or aspect of a *universal* legislator. The point here is that the idea of God is 'given' together with the universal aspect of reason; thus, the very exercise of reason in its morally legislative function would relate it to the divine. As Kant says: 'There is a fact of moral-practical reason; the categorical imperative, which commands for nature freedom under laws and through which freedom itself demonstrates the principles of its own possibility; the commanding subject is God' (OP, 21:21). Yet, despite establishing human reason's constitutive dependence on God, Kant does not posit the divine existence outside the human mind, but rather only shows that it is legitimate to *think* of God as transcendent.

The corollary of placing God within the immanence of practical reason, if one may so put it, might amount to sidetracking the idea of the highest good as requisite to postulate the existence of God. Briefly: in the *Opus postumum*, Kant envisages a much shorter route from morality to religion than he did in the critical period. However, the idea of the highest good does not disappear from his philosophical vocabulary; indeed, it frequently emerges in the company of two other expressions, all of which refer to God: '*ens summum, summa intelligentia, summum bonum*'. These three predicates jointly appear in a number of places (e.g. OP, 22:116–117, 54, 58, 21:13–14, 19, 29, 33, 79, 91). In several passages Kant explains what divine properties each of the superlatives is supposed to connote, namely an 'omnipotent being (*ens summum*)... omniscient (*summa intelligentia*) and omnibenevolent (*summum bonum*)' (OP, 22:48); or, '*Ens summum, summa intelligentia, summum bonum* (understanding, judgment, reason)' (OP, 21:11); or, 'What does reason think in the *idea of God*? A being who *knows* everything, is *capable* of everything, and *wills* what is good (*ens summum, summa intelligentia, summum bonum*). The *highest wisdom*' (OP, 21:50). Kant also emphasizes that, construed in this way, God is an entity of reason: '*Ens summum, summa intelligentia, summum bonum* is an *ens rationis*' (OP, 22:123). Clearly, the '*summum bonum*' does not serve here as a basis for the postulate of the existence of God, because by establishing the constitutive dependence of practical reason on God, Kant would make the doctrine of postulates – though not the *idea of God* – superfluous.

There is an important consequence of what looks like Kant's abandonment of the critical doctrine of the postulates of pure practical reason. Namely, while in the critical period he would urge that the possibility of the realization of the highest good requires the 'presuppositions' of the existence of God and 'a future life' (KrV, A 811/B 839), in the *Opus postumum* he leaves it up to the subject to realize the moral ideal not in any future world but in *this* empirical world where we live as embodied beings. For in the draft of his unfinished work, Kant assigns to the subject the role of the junction between the domain of freedom and the domain of nature: 'God, the world, and I: the thinking being in the world who connects them' (OP, 21:36). Accordingly, to draw on Palmquist's interpretation of Kant's philosophy as a 'system of perspectives',[35] the shift between the critical writings and the *Opus postumum* would consist in a change of perspectives: from the judicial one, pertaining to religion, to a perspective that could be labelled anthropological (in the sense of transcendental – not empirical – anthropology). In Kant's new version of transcendental philosophy, the human being would provide a nexus between science and morality – the domain of theoretical and the domain of practical reason, respectively. Morality would become definitively elevated to the status of religion.

Yet the problem that this change of perspectives may generate is one of consistency. For if the new perspective involves what Wimmer refers to as the 'anthropologization of the concept of God'[36] – as it does because God becomes now a hypostasis of practical reason, representing its universal legislative dimension – how does it fit with Kant's doctrine of practical self-positing discussed earlier, in which the idea of God was taken as constitutive of moral personality itself? In this doctrine, the idea of God would condition the emergence of moral agency, thus, it would ground what the human being is as a moral being, and thereby also the possibility of bringing about the moral ideal in the empirical world. Wimmer contends that the theological fascicles of the *Opus postumum* express two opposite tendencies: one which prioritizes anthropology over theology and one which does the reverse.[37] Which of the tendencies is more basic? Opting for any of them requires adopting a foundationalist stance, but could not such a stance be overcome in favour of one which reconciles the apparent opposites? In the final section, we shall inquire into the possibility of removing what may look like a discrepancy between the theological and the anthropological perspectives, without this necessarily implying the need to embrace a foundationalist agenda. To that end, let us zoom in on some of the cryptic passages in which Kant mentions Spinoza's name.

7.6. Kant's 'moral panentheism' and Spinoza

In what seems to be the most obscure passages in the whole corpus of his works, Kant collates Spinoza, transcendental idealism, the Malebranchean doctrine of vision in God and his own moral theory. For example, he says: 'According to Spinoza, I see myself in God who is legislative within *me*' (OP, 22:54). 'The subject of the categorical imperative... is God. It cannot be denied that such a being exists; yet it cannot be asserted that it exists outside rationally thinking man. In him – the man who thinks morally according to our own commands of duty – we live (*sentimus*), move (*agimus*) and have our being (*existimus*)' (OP, 22:55; cf. OP, 22:118). A few paragraphs later one can read: 'According to Spinoza's transcendental idealism, we intuit ourselves in God. The categorical imperative does not presuppose a highest commanding substance as outside me, but lies within my own reason' (OP, 22:56). Due to the sketchy character of Kant's remarks, we shall not wage a systematic reconstruction of his argument, yet it seems that the general direction in which his thought could be seen as developing can be outlined.

Accordingly (I), featuring the relation between God and human beings, Kant uses spatial metaphors and says that God is 'in us' – '*Est deus in nobis*' (OP, 22:130)[38] – and that we are 'in God'. Whereas the first metaphor draws on the conception of God as the 'subject' that legislates the moral law for us, that is, practical reason in its function of moral legislator, the second evokes the 'space' of the 'moving forces' of morality (cf. 7.5). In one of the passages quoted above,

Kant refers to the moral space paraphrasing the Acts of the Apostles where Paul says (attributing these words to 'poets'): 'For in him we live and move and have our being' (Act 17,28). Paul's words invoke God, 'the Lord of heaven and earth' and the Creator. In his paraphrase, Kant replaces Paul's reference to God with the phrase 'the man who thinks morally' (*dem moralisch nach Pflichtgeboten unserer selbst denkenden Menschen*) (OP, 22:55). This looks like a clear indication that Kant places anthropology before theology as the foundation of the new transcendental philosophy. But does he really do so?

The morally thinking man could be construed as the 'Son of God' that figures in the *Religion* and that embodies the *ideal* human being, according to Kant: 'the prototype of a humanity well-pleasing to God' (RGV, 6:119). Kant's appeal to the passage from the Acts would then emphasize the vital role of the ideal in our moral life: residing in our reason (RGV, 6:62), the ideal is to motivate the improvement which we have a duty to undertake to overcome the evil propensity we have fallen into as a result of our choice. The ideal is both immanent, hence 'in us', given together with our practical rationality, and transcendent, determining the goal of the development of our moral agency. Therefore, Kant's late construal of the relation between 'man' and 'God' could be defined as 'moral panentheism', to use a term proposed by Stephen Palmquist.[39] On this account, the pride of place would be conferred neither on theology nor on anthropology, but both would be seen as inextricably intertwined: even as a projection of our practical rationality, the moral ideal embodied by the 'Son of God' represents a reality which transcends the merely human condition. In a slogan, neither God nor the human being can be completely understood in separation from one another.

(II) The metaphor of 'God in us' can also be read against the background of what we have featured as Kant's 'deification' of reason in the *Opus postumum*. According to Burkhard Tuschling, for example, Kant 'elevates' his transcendental idealism to 'a speculative Spinozism that not only approaches the works of the young Hegel but agrees with them as to some systematically central and foundational points'.[40] The 'deification' of reason would consist in Kant's elevating reason to the rank of the creator of nature and morality. Kant's subject would be akin in this respect to Spinoza's God and his transcendental idealism would thereby approximate 'Spinoza's transcendental idealism' (OP, 22:56). But, as Mathieu and De Flaviis have argued, there are significant differences between Kant and Spinoza. Mathieu contends that Kant eschews the kind of absolute idealism that would be espoused later by Hegel, because he emphasizes the finitude of the subject constituting the empirical and the moral realms. As finite, the subject only contributes the forms of cognition, which then become the forms of the objects of cognition, but its faculties are still dependent on objects for acquiring the 'matter' of cognition.[41] This means that the subject could not enjoy representations of *objects* in the absence of the 'input' from the objects themselves which, in a way unknown to us, affect our mind. Similarly, De Flaviis holds that the Kantian subject approximates Spinoza's God in its creative activity as the 'author of God, the world and itself',[42] yet only insofar as it generates the ideas of metaphysics without bringing about any realities corresponding to them.

However, all three authors – Tuschling, Mathieu and De Flaviis – seem to overlook Kant's distinction between practical and theoretical reason, as well as the fact that Kant tends to put Spinoza's 'transcendental idealism' together with the 'categorical imperative', thus together with his moral theory. This juxtaposition, odd as it may seem, does not make Kant into a Spinozist but might suggest a 'deification' of practical rationality. For Kant, the autonomy of practical reason cannot suffer limitations in the form of dependence on external objects. Moreover, exercising autonomy, practical reason generates the idea of God since in the act of moral legislation reason transcends both its finitude and particularity. It is thus only as legislator of the moral law that the Kantian subject can be likened to Spinoza's God. Kant 'deifies' an aspect of humanity, but not the human being as such.

Finally (III), in the passages where he mentions Spinoza's name, Kant employs the metaphor of 'seeing in God'. The metaphor derives from Malebranche's theory of cognition, and we can gather from the Inaugural Dissertation (1770) that Kant was well aware of its original *locus* (cf. MSI, 2:410), though in the *Opus postumum* he would associate it with Lichtenberg's reading of Spinoza (cf. OP, 22:55). In *The Search after Truth* (1674), Malebranche argued that we perceive, or cognize, everything – from particulars through abstract concepts and general truths to eternal laws – 'in God', that God has ideas of all things and is the 'place' of all minds, just like space is the place of all bodies.[43] Arguing for his conception of vision in God, Malebranche draws on the idea of divine '*concourse*', according to which 'our souls depend on God in all ways'[44] and which echoes the doctrine of occasionalism regarding the relation between the human and the divine will (cf. 7.4). Also, insofar as our cognition presupposes the idea of the infinite, contends Malebranche, it must be mediated by the divine mind which alone can comprehend this idea. Without going into the details of this argument – such as, for instance, the conflation of the infinite with the indefinite – Malebranche's position can be captured as the idea that God, or the divine mind, is the necessary condition of the possibility of human cognition. To 'perceive' anything, we must thus participate in the mind of God. Yet this 'participation' in the mind of God shall also guarantee that what *we* perceive is 'perceived' by the divine mind. In this way, rendering God a 'mediator' in human cognition, a necessary condition of its possibility, Malebranche attributes to finite human subjects the capacity of cognizing things from the divine point of view.

Spinoza develops a similar account of human cognition in the *Ethics*. The immediate objects of our cognition, on his account, are not private mental representations, but things that anyone can have cognitive access to and that are thus independent from particular minds, because as modes of substance considered under the attribute of thought they constitute the divine mind. It is noteworthy that neither Malebranche nor Spinoza endorses the idea, characteristic, for example, of Locke's theory of cognition, that we can cognize objects only by means of ideas in our minds.[45] The divine mind considered as the 'place' of ideas for Malebranche, or God considered under the attribute of thought for Spinoza, is supposed to guarantee direct access to truth and knowledge.

Given his critique of the dogmatic metaphysics, there is no way in which we could associate Kant's theory of cognition with the doctrine of vision in God advocated by Malebranche and, in a sense, also Spinoza. Yet, as stated before, Kant refers to 'vision in God' in the context of his doctrine of 'practical self-positing', thus remaining within the domain of practical reason, in relation to which the association can indeed be drawn between his and Malebranche and Spinoza's conceptions. Kant's equivalent of direct access to truth and knowledge, posited by these conceptions, would be provided by the 'fact of reason', that is, our awareness of the moral law in the form of the categorical imperative (cf. KpV, 5:31). Through the categorical command of the moral law direct access to God would be ensured to reason.

In the *Opus postumum*, Kant derives the 'existence' of God from the 'fact' at issue but also stipulates that God exists as an '*ens rationis*' – an idea of reason. The idea of God emerges insofar as practical reason exercises autonomy, and it warrants the move towards the universal perspective implicated in reason's legislation of the moral law for itself. As has been stated, the idea of God enables our reason to transcend itself, as it were. Thus, for Kant, God can be said to condition the possibility of our moral agency, but it is also our moral agency, or practical rationality, that makes any reference to God possible – and in the light of which such reference can be considered meaningful. This way, the unity between God and rational autonomy, as well as between theology and anthropology, becomes finally established.

Concluding remarks

The aim of this book has been to analyse Kant's views on religion against the background of debates on the relation between Enlightenment and religion. More specifically, Kant's views have been set against the radical Enlightenment inspired primarily by Spinoza's thought and construed in terms of the critique of revealed religion – as opposed to religion established on rational tenets. It has been argued that given his approach to 'historical faith' as expedient for reinforcing commitment to 'pure moral faith' and 'the religion of reason', Kant approximates the radical Enlightenment's critique of revealed religion. Though it would be too far-fetched to say that Kant himself was a Spinozist, we can contend that with his account of religion he belongs to the rationalist, heterodox current nurtured by a Spinozist impulse that also shaped many a radical religious reformer of the European and the Trans-Atlantic Enlightenment: the Koerbagh brothers and Jarig Jelles, John Toland, Carl Friedrich Bahrdt, Thomas Paine, Johann Christian Edelmann, Hermann Samuel Reimarus and Gotthold Ephraim Lessing – to mention but a few.[1]

The argument of this book has been developed in seven chapters – here is a brief overview of their conclusions:

1. Setting the stage for a debate on Kant and the radical Enlightenment, I established that Kant, as much as the radical enlighteners, was a critic of *revealed* religion. In particular, his critique would allow the recognition of a potential conflict between religion based on historical revelation and morality. 'Mercenary faith', or the 'religion of service', according to Kant, encourages the conviction that being immoral is compatible with being religious, as it places apparent duties to God, that is, such duties that are related to the cultic aspects of religiosity, above genuine – moral – duties. Kant was also sensitive to the threat of 'spiritual despotism' exerted by both political and ecclesiastical authority to curb the free use of reason by citizens and members of congregations. Yet his critique of revealed religion

is just a prelude to a positive programme of 'reforming' religion by setting up its rational foundations.

2. Kant prepares the ground for this programme by removing the residue of theistic metaphysics which he attempted to construct before the 'Copernican revolution'. To discredit this metaphysics, and distance himself from his earlier endeavours, he charges it with being conducive to Spinozist consequences. Analysing Kant's pre-critical 'possibility proof', I argued that Kant's self-attribution of Spinozism was based not so much on noticing that his account of the relation between God and possibilities, called grounding, involved the conflation of inherence with causation, but rather on his rebuttal of the compatibilist notion of freedom and the notion of grounding as double causality. Since divine creation instantiates the relation of grounding thus conceived, the critical Kant would not endorse the theistic doctrine of creation insofar as it compromises freedom understood as an indispensable prerequisite of moral agency. Kant's critical project would therefore encourage the recognition of the discrepancy between theistic metaphysics and rational autonomy.

3. Arguably, this recognition would make it possible for Kant to accommodate a variety of unbelief within his critical philosophy. Indeed, in the third *Critique*, as well as in various notes, he entertained the possibility of a 'virtuous atheist', a description he associated with Spinoza. Though in principle Kant rejected atheism as an attitude thwarting one's moral pursuits – that is, the promotion of the highest good – and internally inconsistent, he came close to admitting that 'sceptical atheism' may be compatible with the critical standpoint. Just like Kant, the virtuous unbeliever rejects theoretical arguments for the existence of God and, abiding by the moral law nevertheless, prioritizes practical over theoretical rationality. The main point of contention between Kant and the sceptic turned out thus to lie in their *conceptions* of theistic faith. Accepting a variety of unbelief would make Kant a more 'radical' enlightener than was, for instance, Locke.

4. Subsequently, I proceeded to compare the accounts of the primacy of the practical in Kant and Spinoza. Drawing on a common pattern of thought running through the writings of the two thinkers – their recognition of human finitude and the critique of a certain type of metaphysics – I reconstructed their arguments bringing out the crucial role of practical rationality. For Kant, practical reason allows establishing the reality of freedom, based on our awareness of the moral law. Practical rationality

paves thus the way for the realization of the interest of reason as such. For Spinoza, in turn, we have shown that insofar as it aims at entertaining adequate ideas, cognition cannot be separated from causal efficacy, and so action. It is when we act that we can exercise critical thinking, which protects us from the illusions of the speculative metaphysician and the ignorance of the 'common man'. The pragmatic aspects in Kant and Spinoza connect their ideas with the radical Enlightenment as a project of a thoroughgoing reform of the patterns of human thought and action.

5. Marking the radical and heterodox tendencies in Kant's thought, there is a critique of revelation, which I then investigated. I argued that even if the *Religion* is read as an attempt to 'translate' the key Christian doctrines into the language of 'pure moral faith', crucial tenets are left over which cannot be thus translated. One of such tenets would be the Incarnation: in Kant's rational religion Jesus could be construed either as a virtuous teacher of morality or as an ideal – a divine-like 'prototype' of a morally perfect humanity, accessible to us through our own reason – but not as a historical figure and an idea of reason jointly. The idea of the 'Son of God' as a rational ideal took Kant close to Johann Christian Edelmann's account of the biblical Λογος rendered as 'reason', and hence to those heterodox theologians who would conceive of Christianity as a religion that can be arrived at without the mediation of revelation – thus, as a natural or universal religion. But, whereas for Edelmann our 'participation' in the divine would be contingent upon our rationality alone, Kant would envisage the 'deification' of humanity as the end-stage and the goal of our moral development. Kant's account of secularization – *avant la lettre* – was teleological.

6. Given that Kant perceived religious institutions as a means of furthering the moral improvement of human beings mired in 'radical evil', he construed the church as itself involved in the process of attaining rational autonomy by finite agents, which he associated with enlightenment. Yet, since he also featured the church as a project of an ethical community under divine moral legislation, Kant should be considered a representative of what intellectual historians have recently called the 'religious Enlightenment', rather than its 'secular' counterpart. If creating a moral world was the end of enlightenment which would require a community governed by the divine law to be brought about, the ideal of a '(divine) ethical state on earth' (RGV, 6:122) would be anything but secular. I suggested, though, that even the 'theological' readings of the highest

good cannot wipe out the fact that Kant attributed a 'this-worldly' purpose to the ethical community in the form of a church – namely, the moral improvement of finite rational agents. Regardless of the reading of the highest good, the tension remained between human autonomy and divine sovereignty in the ethical state, which Kant would attempt to overcome in his final unfinished work published as the *Opus postumum*.

7. I proposed that overcoming the tension between human autonomy and divine sovereignty in the ethical state required a radical step that Kant eventually took in his final work and that consisted in identifying practical reason and the moral domain with God – or 'deifying' practical reason. However, this move did not result in rendering the idea of God redundant. Generated by practical reason as a projection of its legislative power, the idea of God would help reason ascertain its authority as moral lawgiver. Moreover, as part of the doctrine of practical self-positing, Kant thought that the idea is requisite for the subject to constitute herself as a person: a member of the ethical community for which she is a legislator while herself being bound by the law legislated by every other rational agent. The idea of God as sovereign of the ethical state allows such a perspective on the autonomy of the subject which warrants the universality of self-legislation. This way, autonomy becomes the foundation of an ethical community – the very same community which, in the form of a 'church', would realize the goal of enlightenment. The conflict between autonomy and God's sovereignty would thereby eventually dissolve, for the divine turns out to constitute moral autonomy and moral autonomy would constitute the divine. Thus, Kant's moral religion transforms into a religion of morality.

On a final note: given that the Enlightenment, especially its radical variety, would often be perceived as bringing along a secularizing tendency, the question may arise whether Kant's account of religion fits with this perception. As I have tried to show, valid reasons can be adduced to regard Kant as a contributor to secularization defined for instance by Ian Hunter as 'an epochal transition from a culture of religious belief to one of rational autonomy'.[2] Such a reading, though, may inspire objections. It might be incoherent, one could claim, since I have assimilated Kant with radical religious reformers, hence (at least some of them) protagonists of the so-called religious Enlightenment that did not champion unbelief together with the criticism of religious institutions. Accordingly, doubts can emerge whether the reading advanced here does not necessitate that we turn back to 'traditional' interpretations of Kant's religion which assessed it as a failed enterprise, thwarted by the cognitive strictures which the critical philosophy has brought to the fore (cf. 5.2.4). Does the reading proposed in this book eventually ignore what has been dubbed 'affirmative' or 'religious' interpretations advocated, for example, by Stephen Palmquist, Lawrence Pasternack, Nathan Jacobs and Christopher Firestone, and more recently by Allen Wood in his *Kant and Religion*?[3]

The above objections, however, overlook the possibility that radical religious reforms could go hand in hand with the secularizing trend, even if as their unintended byproduct. More to the point, there is no discrepancy between the affirmative reading of Kant's religion and my claim concerning Kant's contribution to secularization. For Kant's idea of a rational religion – a moral faith originating in and justified by reason rather than revelation and its purported manifestations in history – converges with the idea of 'rational autonomy' as the foundation of culture within which some space for religion is made. To give an example: Pasternack, himself a proponent of the affirmative reading, admits that when it comes to interpreting revelation, Kant makes reason entitled to appraise the contents and determine the soteriological value of revealed and ecclesiastical doctrines. In evaluating these doctrines, avers Pasternack, 'one should hardly expect from Kant deference to any claim of authority over reason itself.... Hence, it is not the biblical theologian but the philosopher who ultimately holds privilege over the doctrines essential to our salvation.'[4] For Kant, as much as for Spinoza's friend and medical doctor, Lodewijk Meijer (cf. 5.1), it is philosophy that assumes the role of '*S. Scripturae interpres*'. It is thus not in denying religion but in the reversal of the order of significance between reason and faith – or in reconceiving the relation of constitutive dependence between these two authorities – that the secularizing potential of Kant's thought on religion should be sought.

Notes

Introduction

1 See, e.g., Ayaan Hirsi Ali, *Nomad. From Islam to America: A Personal Journey through the Clash of Civilizations* (New York: Free Press, 2010), 206; John Paul II, 'Address of His Holiness John Paul II at the Conclusion of the International Colloquium on "Enlightenment Today"', https://www.vatican.va/content/john-paul-ii/en/speeches/1996/august/documents/hf_jp-ii_spe_19960810_illuminismo-oggi.html [Accessed 19 November 2021].
2 Margaret C. Jacob, *The Secular Enlightenment* (Princeton: Princeton University Press, 2019), 1–2.
3 David Sorkin, *The Religious Enlightenment. Protestants, Jews and Catholics from London to Vienna* (Princeton: Princeton University Press, 2008), 3.
4 Jonathan I. Israel, *Enlightenment Contested. Philosophy, Modernity and the Emancipation of Man, 1670–1752* (Oxford: Oxford University Press, 2006), 11.
5 Leo Strauss, *Spinoza's Critique of Religion* (New York: Schocken Books, 1982), 35.
6 Jonathan I. Israel, 'Leo Strauss and the Radical Enlightenment', in *Reading between the Lines – Leo Strauss and the History of Early Modern Philosophy*, ed. Winfried Schröder (Berlin: De Gruyter, 2015), 17.
7 See, e.g., Stephen R. Palmquist, 'Does Quakerism Qualify as Kantian Enlightened Religion?', in *Between Secularization and Reform: Religion in the Enlightenment*, ed. Anna Tomaszewska (manuscript).
8 Steven Lestition, 'Kant and the End of the Enlightenment in Prussia', *The Journal of Modern History* 65, no. 1 (1993): 58.
9 Ibid., 112.
10 Allen W. Wood, 'Ethical Community, Church and Scripture', in *Die Religion innerhalb der Grenzen der bloßen Vernunft*, ed. Otfried Höffe (Berlin: Akademie Verlag, 2011), 149.
11 Allen W. Wood, *Kant and Religion* (Cambridge: Cambridge University Press, 2020), 188.
12 Gordon E. Michalson, *Kant and the Problem of God* (Oxford: Blackwell, 1999), 1.

Chapter 1

1. For an account of the Enlightenment as secular, i.e., 'an eighteenth-century movement of ideas and practices that made the secular world its point of departure', see Jacob, *The Secular Enlightenment*, 1. For the idea of the religious Enlightenment, which 'made possible new iterations of faith', see Sorkin, *The Religious Enlightenment*, 3.
2. Frederik Stjernfelt, '"Radical Enlightenment": Aspects of the History of a Term', in *Reassessing the Radical Enlightenment*, ed. Steffen Ducheyne (London: Routledge, 2017), 96.
3. See Margaret Jacob, *The Radical Enlightenment: Pantheists, Freemasons and Republicans* (London: George Allen and Unwin, 1981), ch. 7; Margaret Jacob, 'How Radical Was the Enlightenment? What Do We Mean by Radical?', *Diametros* 40 (2014): 99–114.
4. Martin Mulsow, *Moderne aus dem Untergrund. Radikale Frühaufklärung in Deutschland 1680–1720* (Hamburg: Felix Meiner Verlag, 2002), 29–30.
5. Gianni Paganini, 'Enlightenment before the Enlightenment: Clandestine Philosophy', *Ethica e politica / Ethics and Politics* 20, no. 3 (2018): 183–200. See also: Gianni Paganini, Margaret C. Jacob and John Christian Laursen (eds.), *Clandestine Philosophy. New Studies on Subversive Manuscripts in Early Modern Europe, 1620–1823* (Toronto: University of Toronto Press, 2020).
6. Israel, *Enlightenment Contested*, 866.
7. Ibid., 46.
8. Jonathan I. Israel, 'Spinoza and Early Modern Theology', in *The Oxford Handbook of Early Modern Theology, 1600–1800*, ed. Ulrich L. Lehner, Richard A. Muller, and Anthony G. Roeber (New York: Oxford University Press, 2016), 579.
9. Jonathan I. Israel, '"Radical Enlightenment" – Peripheral, Substantial, or the Main Face of the Trans-Atlantic Enlightenment (1650–1850)', *Diametros* 40 (2014): 73.
10. Cf. Charles Taylor, *A Secular Age* (Cambridge MA: Harvard University Press, 2007), 25–6, 307.
11. Jonathan I. Israel, *Radical Enlightenment. Philosophy and the Making of Modernity 1650–1750* (New York: Oxford University Press, 2001), 11.
12. Israel, *Enlightenment Contested*, 808.
13. For a discussion of a position along these lines, see Gianni Paganini, 'The Way of Clandestinity. Radical Cartesianism and Deism in Robert Challe (1659–1721)', in *Between Secularization and Reform. Religion in the Enlightenment*, ed. Anna Tomaszewska (manuscript).
14. Also, on the basis of an interpretation of Kant as an anti-imperialist thinker, a case can be made for his support of racial equality. See Sankar Muthu, *Enlightenment against Empire* (Princeton: Princeton University Press, 2003).

15 Kant distinguishes, however, between freedom of thought and speech, on the one hand, and freedom of expression, on the other. For an argument for this distinction, see Geert Van Eekert, 'Freedom of Speech, Freedom of Self-Expression, and Kant's Public Use of Reason', *Diametros* 54 (2017): 118–37.
16 Jonathan I. Israel, *Democratic Enlightenment: Philosophy, Revolution, and Human Rights* (Oxford: Oxford University Press, 2011), 724.
17 Heinrich Heine, *On the History of Religion and Philosophy in Germany. And Other Writings* (Cambridge: Cambridge University Press, 2007), 78–9.
18 Ibid., 87.
19 Michalson, *Kant and the Problem of God*, 1.
20 On the ethical purport of religion in the public sphere, see Mehmet R. Demiray, 'Public Religion and Secular State: A Kantian Approach', *Diametros* 54 (2017): 30–55. See also: Katrin Flikschuh, 'Gottesdienst und Afterdienst: die Kirche als öffentliche Institution?', in *Immanuel Kant: Die Religion innerhalb der Grenzen der bloßen Vernunft*, ed. Otfried Höffe (Berlin: Akademie Verlag, 2011), 193–209, for a discussion of the 'public' form of the Kantian church.
21 For a proposal of 'political secularism' along these lines, see Jocelyn Maclure and Charles Taylor, *Secularism and Freedom of Conscience* (Cambridge, MA: Harvard University Press, 2011).
22 Strauss, *Spinoza's Critique of Religion*, 35.
23 Israel, 'Leo Strauss and the Radical Enlightenment', 14.
24 Ibid., 17.
25 Strauss, *Spinoza's Critique of Religion*, 38.
26 'The Sacred Books were not the work of a single writer, nor were they written for a people of a single age; they were written by a number of men of different characters and different generations over a period of time which, taking them all into account, will be found to extend to about two thousand years, and perhaps much longer.' Benedictus de Spinoza, 'Theological-Political Treatise', in *Complete Works* (Indianapolis: Hackett Publishing Co., 2002), 514. On the authorship of the Pentateuch specifically, see ibid., 478.
27 See Winfried Schröder, *Athen und Jerusalem. Die philosophische Kritik am Christentum in Antike und Neuzeit* (Stuttgart-Bad Cannstatt: Frommann-Holzboog, 2011), 71–84.
28 Strauss, *Spinoza's Critique of Religion*, 37–52. For the Epicurean origins of religious criticism, see also Alan Ch. Kors, *Epicureans and Atheists in France, 1650-1729* (Cambridge: Cambridge University Press, 2016).
29 Strauss, *Spinoza's Critique of Religion*, 40.
30 Attempts to 'defang [the religious impulse] of bellicosity' are described in: Jacob, 'How Radical Was the Enlightenment?'. For further developments in this area, illustrated by stories about individuals working towards secularization yet without openly advocating atheism, see Jacob, *The Secular Enlightenment*, ch. 3.

31 Charles Voysey (ed.), *Fragments from Reimarus Consisting in Brief Critical Remarks on the Object of Jesus and His Disciples as Seen in the New Testament* (London: Williams and Norgate, 1879).
32 Winfried Schröder, *Ursprünge des Atheismus: Untersuchungen zur Metaphysik- und Religionskritik des 17. und 18. Jahrhunderts*, 2nd edn (Stuttgart-Bad Cannstatt: Frommann-Holzboog, 2012), 21–44.
33 Iac. Frid. Reimmann, *Historia universalis atheismi et atheorum falso & merito suspectorum apud jvdæos, ethnicos, christianos, mvhamedanos* (Hildesiæ: Apud Lvdolphvm Schroeder, 1725).
34 See Dominic Erdozain, 'A Heavenly Poise: Radical Religion and the Making of the Enlightenment', *Intellectual History Review* 27, no. 1 (2017): 71–96.
35 Schröder, *Ursprünge des Atheismus*, 404–16.
36 See Ulrich L. Lehner, *The Catholic Enlightenment. The Forgotten History of a Global Movement* (New York: Oxford University Press, 2016). Israel vents scepticism with regard to the notion of the Catholic Enlightenment and presents its adherents as *anti-philosophes* who fought not only against the radical critics of the religious and political status quo, but also against other moderate enlighteners, especially some of the deists, e.g., Voltaire, Rousseau and Montesquieu. The Catholic authors would argue that the deistic arguments against the radicals are ineffective and their doctrines internally inconsistent. Israel, *Democratic Enlightenment*, 151–8.
37 Taylor, *A Secular Age*, 270.
38 Johann Christian Edelmann, to be discussed in Chapter 5, and in a sense also Kant represent such a position.
39 See Henri Krop, 'The Secularism of Spinoza and His Circle', in *The Sources of Secularism: Enlightenment and Beyond*, ed. Anna Tomaszewska and Hasse Hämäläinen (Cham: Palgrave Macmillan, 2017), 73–99. A similar organization and attitude to religious faith could be found among the English Quakers. See, e.g., Leslie Stevenson, 'Kant's Approach to Religion Compared with Quakerism', in *Kant and the New Philosophy of Religion*, ed. Chris L. Firestone and Stephen R. Palmquist (Bloomington: Indiana University Press, 2006), 210–29.
40 Israel, 'Leo Strauss and the Radical Enlightenment', 17.
41 James J. DiCenso, *Kant, Religion, and Politics* (Cambridge: Cambridge University Press, 2011), 269.
42 Israel, *Radical Enlightenment*, 174.
43 Israel, *Democratic Enlightenment*, 10.
44 Moses Krakauer, *Zur Geschichte des Spinozismus in Deutschland während der ersten Hälfte des achtzehnten Jahrhunderts* (Breslau: S. Schottlaender, 1881), 1 (trans. A.T.).
45 Walter Sparn, '*Formalis Atheus?* Die Krise der protestantischen Orthodoxie, gespiegelt in ihrer Auseinandersetzung mit Spinoza', in *Spinoza in der Frühzeit*

seiner religiösen Wirkung, ed. Karlfried Gründer and Wilhelm Schmidt-Biggemann (Heidelberg: L. Schneider Verlag, 1984), 29.
46 Manfred Walther, *Spinoza in Deutschland. Von G.W. Leibniz bis zu Carl Schmidt. Philosophie – Wissenschaft – Ideologie* (Heidelberg: Universitätsverlag Winter, 2018), 253.
47 Friedrich Heman, 'Kant und Spinoza', *Kant-Studien* 5, no. 1–3 (1901): 276 (trans. A.T.).
48 Omri Boehm, *Kant's Critique of Spinoza* (New York: Oxford University Press, 2014), chs. 2 and 3.
49 In view of recent research, the *Opus postumum* cannot be ignored as a worthless product of a demented mind, however cryptic some remarks contained in it might seem. The fascicles collected later by Kant scholars into one volume are but preparatory notes for a work which he would never complete, and it is likely that some apparently contradictory remarks contained in the notes figure as parts of arguments modelled as antinomies. For a detailed account of the scholarship on Kant's 'final synthesis' see Giovanni Pietro Basile, *Kants* Opus postumum *und seine Rezeption* (Berlin: De Gruyter, 2013).
50 Giuseppe De Flaviis, *Kant e Spinoza* (Firenze: Sansoni Editore, 1986), 15 (trans. A.T.).
51 Max Grunwald, *Spinoza in Deutschland. Gekrönte Preisschrift* (Berlin: Verlag von S. Calvary, 1897), 16 (trans. A.T.).
52 Spinoza, 'Theological-Political Treatise', 526.
53 Ibid., 392.
54 The idea of Spinoza's circle originates from: Koenraad O. Meinsma, *Spinoza und sein Kreis* (Berlin: Karl Schnabel Verlag, 1909).
55 The views held by these figures will be discussed in Chapter 5.
56 Yirmiyahu Yovel, *Kant and the Philosophy of History* (Princeton: Princeton University Press, 1980), 215.
57 See Winfried Schröder, '*Spinozam tota armenta in Belgio sequi ducem*: The Reception of the Early Dutch Spinozists in Germany', in *Disguised and Overt Spinozism around 1700*, ed. Wiep van Bunge and Wim Klever (Leiden: Brill, 1996), 159, 167.

Chapter 2

1 Michela Massimi, 'Kant on the Ideality of Space and the Argument from Spinozism', in *Kant's* Critique of Pure Reason, ed. James R. O'Shea (New York: Cambridge University Press, 2017), 74.

2   See Boehm, *Kant's Critique of Spinoza*; Andrew Chignell, 'Kant, Modality, and the Most Real Being', *Archiv für Geschichte der Philosophie* 91 (2009): 157–92; Andrew Chignell, 'Kant, Real Possibility and the Threat of Spinoza', *Mind* 121, no. 483 (2012): 635–75. According to Beth Lord, 'Friedrich Heinrich Jacobi was among the first to "read Kant Spinozistically"', in *Kant and Spinozism. Transcendental Idealism and Immanence from Jacobi to Deleuze* (Basingstoke: Palgrave Macmillan, 2011), 20. Lord considers Jacobi's interpretation to be a misreading.
3   Jacob Freudenthal, 'On the History of Spinozism', *The Jewish Quarterly Review* 8, no. 1 (1895): 58.
4   This term is used throughout Kant scholarship. See, e.g., Nicholas Stang, 'Kant's Possibility Proof', *History of Philosophy Quarterly* 27, no. 3 (2010): 275–99.
5   See Gottfried W. Leibniz, *Discourse on Metaphysics and the Monadology* (New York: Dover Publications, Inc., 2005), 14–15.
6   For an account of Leibniz's logic, see Benson Mates, *The Philosophy of Leibniz. Metaphysics and Language* (New York: Oxford University Press, 1986). On Kant's use of the doctrine of complete concept in the possibility argument, see Martin Schönfeld, *The Philosophy of the Young Kant* (Oxford: Oxford University Press, 2000), 197–208.
7   This leads to counterintuitive consequences: for example, when I suggest to my husband that *he* should have booked the flights earlier (meaning that the flights *could* have been booked earlier *by him*), what I say makes no sense, unless the person I refer to in the counterfactual statement is a *counterpart* of my husband.
8   Kant distinguishes between two kinds of positing (*Setzung*): absolute and relative. The distinction maps the existential ('There is an x') and the predicative ('x is F') uses of the verb 'to be'.
9   Compare Kant's critical slogan: 'Thoughts without content are empty, intuitions without concepts are blind' (KrV, A 51/B 75). Kant's real *vs.* logical possibility distinction is a likely predecessor of the dualism of intuitions and concepts on which the epistemological argument of the first *Critique* largely rests. See Paul Guyer, 'Absolute Idealism and the Rejection of Kantian Dualism', in *The Cambridge Companion to German Idealism*, ed. Karl Ameriks (New York: Cambridge University Press, 2000), 37–56.
10 See Peter Yong, 'God, Totality and Possibility in Kant's Only Possible Argument', *Kantian Review* 19, no. 1 (2014): 27–51.
11 According to this condition, 'positive predicates', i.e. those that designate real properties of objects, 'must be such that they can be co-instantiated by a really possible thing'. Chignell, 'Kant, Modality, and the Most Real Being', 174–5. Chignell's real harmony condition recalls Leibniz's notion of compossibility. Leibniz uses this notion in his doctrine of God creating the world by choosing the maximum set of internally consistent predicates that will be actualized jointly.

On compossibility as a criterion of God's choosing the best possible world, see Lloyd Strickland, *Leibniz's* Monadology. *A New Translation and Guide* (Edinburgh: Edinburgh University Press, 2014), 116.

12 Chignell, 'Kant, Modality, and the Most Real Being', 175.
13 This term derives from Boehm, *Kant's Critique of Spinoza*, 24. Chignell speaks instead of 'fundamental predicates', that is, predicates that are 'both *unanalysable* and *positive*'. 'Kant, Modality and the Most Real Being', 166.
14 Frederick C. Beiser, *The Fate of Reason. German Philosophy from Kant to Fichte* (Cambridge MA: Harvard University Press, 1987), 11–12.
15 See Allen W. Wood, *Kant's Rational Theology* (Ithaca: Cornell University Press, 1978), 70–1. See also Boehm, *Kant's Critique of Spinoza*, 27–8.
16 Michael Della Rocca, 'Razing Structures to the Ground', *Analytic Philosophy* 55, no. 3 (2014): 276-94.
17 Lord, *Transcendental Idealism and Immanence*, 5–6.
18 Yitzhak Melamed, 'Spinoza's Deification of Existence', in *Oxford Studies in Early Modern Philosophy*, Vol. 6, ed. Daniel Garber and Donald Rutherford (Oxford: Oxford University Press, 2013), 76.
19 Heman, 'Kant und Spinoza', 290 (trans. A.T.).
20 Pierre Bayle, *Historical and Critical Dictionary. Selections* (Indianapolis: The Bobbs-Merrill Company, Inc., 1965), 301 (italics A.T.). Lord argues that Bayle misread Spinoza by flouting the distinction between *natura naturans* and *natura naturata*. She emphasizes that though Spinoza's God comprises the totality of being, he cannot be understood as the sum total of things constituting the empirical world. *Kant and Spinozism*, 13.
21 Boehm, *Kant's Critique of Spinoza*, 37 (italics A.T.).
22 See Beiser, *The Fate of Reason*, 11. Frederick E. England, *Kant's Conception of God. A Critical Exposition of Its Metaphysical Development together with a Translation of the* Nova Dilucidatio (New York: Humanities Press, 1968), 57–61.
23 Cf. Martin Moors, 'Die Bestimmungsgestalt von Kants Gottesidee und Gemeinschaftsprinzip', in *Proceedings of the Sixth International Kant Congress*, ed. Gerhard Funke and Thomas Seebohm (Lanham: Center for Advanced Research in Phenomenology and University Press of America, 1989), 49–66.
24 Kant rejects *causa sui* because he denies that a thing which exists absolutely necessarily can have its ground of existence ('To say that something has the ground of its existence within itself is absurd' [PND, 1:394]). This rules out the application of the principle of sufficient reason to the necessary being: God does not have a *ratio essendi*, an antecedently determining reason, since the very possibility of the existence of God implies the he exists.
25 Compare Spinoza's definitions of substance and mode in Part One of the *Ethics*. Benedictus de Spinoza, 'Ethics', in *Complete Works* (Indianapolis: Hackett Publishing Co., 2002), 217.

26 Boehm, *Kant's Critique of Spinoza*, 31.
27 Yong, 'God, Totality and Possibility', 43.
28 Noam Hoffer, 'The Relation between God and the World in the Pre-Critical Kant: Was Kant a Spinozist?', *Kantian Review* 21, no. 2 (2016): 185–210.
29 Christopher Insole, 'Intellectualism, Relational Properties and the Divine Mind in Kant's Pre-Critical Philosophy', *Kantian Review* 16, no. 3 (2011): 400.
30 Kant's polemic with Leibniz is masked as an attack on Spinoza's conflation of inherence with causal dependence e.g. in *On a Discovery whereby Any New Critique of Pure Reason Is to Be Made Superfluous by an Older One*. See Heman, 'Kant und Spinoza', 297–302.
31 Spinoza, 'Ethics', 217.
32 On Kant's pre-critical compatibilism, see Christopher Insole, *Kant and the Creation of Freedom. A Theological Problem* (Oxford: Oxford University Press, 2013), 61–7.
33 See Nicholas Rescher, 'Noumenal Causality', in *Proceedings of the Third International Kant Congress*, ed. Lewis White Beck (Dordrecht: D. Reidel Publishing Co., 1972), 462–70. See also Insole, *Kant and the Creation of Freedom*, 94–112.
34 For a discussion of Kant on theological determinism, see Kimberly Brewer, Eric Watkins, 'A Difficulty Still Awaits: Kant, Spinoza, and the Threat of Theological Determinism', *Kant-Studien* 103, no. 2 (2012): 163–87.
35 Insole, *Kant and the Creation of Freedom*, 88–9.
36 On the relation between Newton's metaphysical conception of space and the Christian dogma, see Christopher Insole, 'Kant's Transcendental Idealism and Newton's Divine Sensorium', *Journal of the History of Ideas* 72, no. 3 (2011): 413–36.

Chapter 3

1 See Andree Hahmann, 'Pflichtgemäß, aber töricht! Kant über Spinozas Leugnung der Vorsehung', in *Das Leben der Vernunft. Beiträge zur Philosophie Kants*, ed. Dieter Hüning, Stefan Klingner, and Carsten Ork (Berlin: De Gruyter, 2013), 477.
2 Jonathan I. Israel, *Locke, Spinoza and the Philosophical Debate Concerning Toleration in the Early Enlightenment (c. 1670–c. 1750)* (Amsterdam: Koninklijke Nederlandse Akademie van Wetenschappen, 1999), 11. For an exposition of Locke's arguments against 'atheism', see Diego Lucci, *John Locke's Christianity* (Cambridge: Cambridge University Press, 2021), 192–5.
3 Michael Czelinski-Uesbeck, *Der tugendhafte Atheist. Studien zur Vorgeschichte der Spinoza-Renaissance in Deutschland* (Würzburg: Königshausen und Neumann, 2007), 101.
4 Bayle, *Historical and Critical Dictionary*, 288.

5 Ibid., 300.
6 Ibid., 308.
7 Ibid., 295.
8 Czelinski-Uesbeck, *Der tugendhafte Atheist*, 101.
9 Ibid., 109–11.
10 Bayle, *Historical and Critical Dictionary*, 405. See also Czelinski-Uesbeck, *Der tugendhafte Atheist*, 106–7.
11 See also Leslie Stevenson, 'Opinion, Belief or Faith, and Knowledge', in *Inspirations from Kant: Essays* (Oxford: Oxford University Press, 2011), 80.
12 For an excellent discussion of Kant's moral argument, see Courtney Fugate, 'The Highest Good and Kant's Proof(s) of God's Existence', *History of Philosophy Quarterly* 31, no. 2 (2014): 137–58.
13 Hahmann, 'Pflichtgemäß, aber töricht', 493–4.
14 Bernd Dörflinger, 'Führt Moral unausbleiblich zur Religion? Überlegungen zu einer these Kants', in *Kants Metaphysik und Religionsphilosophie*, ed. Norbert Fischer (Hamburg: Felix Meiner Verlag, 2004), 221 (trans. A.T.).
15 Gabriele Tomasi, 'God, the Highest Good, and the Rationality of Faith: Reflections on Kant's Moral Proof of the Existence of God', in *The Highest Good in Kant's Philosophy*, ed. Thomas Höwing (Berlin: De Gruyter, 2016), 125.
16 Lara Denis, 'Kant's Criticism of Atheism', *Kant-Studien* 94 (2003): 212.
17 Ibid., 210.
18 Lawrence Pasternack, 'Restoring Kant's Conception of the Highest Good', *Journal of the History of Philosophy* 55, no. 3 (2017): 435–68.
19 Ibid., 439, 449, 455–6.
20 Ibid., 445.
21 Secular conceptions of the highest good can be traced back to: Andrews Reath, 'Two Conceptions of the Highest Good', *Journal of the History of Philosophy* 26, no. 4 (1988): 593–619.
22 John Hare, 'Kant on the Rational Instability of Atheism', in *Kant and the New Philosophy of Religion*, ed. Chris L. Firestone and Stephen R. Palmquist (Bloomington: Indiana University Press, 2006), 71.
23 For more objections against Kant's ethicotheology, see Eddis N. Miller, *Kant's Religion within the Boundaries of Mere Reason* (London: Bloomsbury, 2015), 135–7.
24 Johann Heinrich Schulz (1739–1823), nicknamed 'Ponytail' for wearing a 'pigtail' instead of a wig during his sermons, was a Prussian cleric who fell victim of the edict on religion issued by Johann Christoph von Wöllner, a minister of the conservative king Frederick William II, and 'was dismissed for preaching an unorthodox form of religious rationalism to ordinary people'. Michael J. Sauter, *Visions of the Enlightenment. The Edict on Religion of 1788 and the Politics of the Public Sphere in Eighteenth-Century Prussia* (Leiden: Brill, 2009), 50. Sauter discusses Schulz's views in chapter 2 of his book.

25 Lord, *Kant and Spinozism*, ch. 1.
26 See Hermann Timm, *Gott und die Freiheit. Studien zur Religionsphilosophie der Goethezeit*, Vol. 1: *Die Spinozarenaissance* (Frankfurt am Main: Vittorio Klostermann, 1974), 421–39.
27 Andrew Chignell, 'Belief in Kant', *Philosophical Review* 116, no. 3 (2007): 336.
28 On Chignell's definition, 'theoretical belief involves freely holding an assent on account of its non-epistemic but still in some important sense *theoretical* merits'. Ibid., 349. Those theoretical merits might be related, for example, to the coherence and unity of the whole system of knowledge.
29 Ibid., 334.
30 Both kinds of theology constitute modes of the rational cognition of God, but whereas transcendental theology develops its concepts of the divine from 'pure understanding and reason' (V-Phil-Th/Pölitz, 28:999), natural theology describes God in anthropocentric terms. Hence, 'in transcendental theology we represent God as *cause of the world*; in natural theology as *author of the world*, i.e., as a living God, as a free being' (V-Phil-Th/Pölitz, 28:1001).
31 Chignell, 'Belief in Kant', 349.
32 For the distinction between cognition and knowledge in Kant, see Chris L. Firestone and Nathan Jacobs, *In Defense of Kant's* Religion (Bloomington: Indiana University Press, 2008), 110–12, and Chris L. Firestone, *Kant and Theology at the Boundaries of Reason* (Farnham: Ashgate, 2009), 35–9. According to Firestone and Jacobs, Kant does not rule out the possibility of cognizing (*erkennen*) supersensible objects, but only dismisses the idea that we could know (*wissen*) such objects. For cognition, it suffices that one be 'able to get something in mind', i.e. to acquire a representation with determinate content, whereas knowledge requires that a representation be accompanied by a corresponding intuition of an object. On this account, cognition of the existence of God, without yielding knowledge, constitutes a variety of 'pure cognition (or "the cognition of reason")' which 'refer[s] to the proper objects of rational faith'.
33 Antony Flew, 'The Presumption of Atheism', *Canadian Journal of Philosophy* 2, no. 1 (1972): 30. According to Palmquist, 'Flew is a good example of the approach to philosophy that Kant regards as harmful to the best interests of humanity: an uncritical trust in the all-sufficiency of logic plus empirical evidence to prove or disprove any and every point at issue... and a neglect of the perspectival difference between human beings... and God.' Palmquist observes that Flew targets his argument mostly at Catholic theologians, such as Aquinas, 'who share his own bias for the power of theoretical reason.' Stephen R. Palmquist, *Kant's Critical Religion. Volume Two of Kant's System of Perspectives* (Aldershot: Ashgate, 2000), 439. I concur with Palmquist's assessment of Flew's approach to theistic belief: the demands that Flew imposes upon the believer are too stringent to be met

because meeting them would require demonstrating theistic claims with the accuracy comparable to that of mathematical proofs, which might be unattainable because of the differences between the respective subject matters.

34 I am grateful to Hasse Hämäläinen for suggesting that the sceptical atheist might be interpreted in this way.

35 Palmquist suggests that 'enthusiasm' should be replaced by 'delirium' as the translation of '*Schwärmerei*' and defines delirium as 'a trance-like state (similar to reverie, but more negative), manifesting itself in extreme forms as mania'. Palmquist goes on to add that 'Kantian *Schwärmerei* refers not (necessarily) to excessive emotion, but to any form of (e.g., romantic) delirium that usurps the place that belongs to *rigorous argument*'. Stephen R. Palmquist, *Comprehensive Commentary on Kant's* Religion within the Bounds of Bare Reason (Chichester: John Wiley & Sons, 2016), 520–1. Yet one may wonder whether 'delirium' is an adequate word for what Kant labels as '*philosophische Schwärmerei*'. Anyway, also the word 'enthusiasm' does not convey an important sense of *Schwärmerei*, a noun which derives from '*schwärmen*' meaning 'to swarm' (usually of bees in a hive), which aptly describes an incited crowd participating in a demonstration or a religious ceremony.

36 Gregory R. Johnson, 'The Tree of Melancholy. Kant on Philosophy and Enthusiasm', in *Kant and the New Philosophy of Religion*, ed. Chris L. Firestone and Stephen R. Palmquist (Bloomington: Indiana University Press, 2006), 54.

37 Anthony J. La Vopa, 'The Philosopher and the *Schwärmer*: On the Career of a German Epithet from Luther to Kant', in *Enthusiasm and Enlightenment in Europe, 1650–1850*, ed. Lawrence E. Klein and Anthony J. La Vopa (San Marino, CA: Huntington Library, 1998), 105.

38 Ibid., 95. See also Johnson, 'The Tree of Melancholy', 45.

39 John Zammito argues that in the *Pantheismusstreit* Kant defends enlightenment against *Sturm und Drang* and attempts to take over the role of the key figure in the German Enlightenment after the deaths of Lessing and Mendelssohn. He would thus write the essay with a view to advertising his critical philosophy among the intellectual elites of Berlin. See 'Herder, Kant, Spinoza und die Ursprünge des deutschen Idealismus', in *Herder und die Philosophie des deutschen Idealismus*, ed. Marion Heinz (Amsterdam: Rodopi, 1997), 117.

40 For a reading of Kant's critique of dogmatic metaphysics as not only an epistemological, but also a political enterprise, see DiCenso, *Kant, Religion, and Politics*, 32–9.

41 See Beiser, *The Fate of Reason*, 44–5, 60–1; Jacob, *The Secular Enlightenment*, 197–8.

42 Stephen R. Palmquist, *Kant and Mysticism. Critique as the Experience of Baring All in Reason's Light* (Lanham: Lexington Books, 2019), 49.

43 Ibid., 51.
44 Jacob, *The Radical Enlightenment*, 223.
45 For biographical details illustrating this claim, see Palmquist, *Kant and Mysticism*, 69–70.
46 Cf. ibid., 73–4.
47 Palmquist dedicates the third part of *Kant and Mysticism*, titled 'The *Opus postumum* as an Experiment in Critical Mysticism', to this late unfinished project of Kant.
48 Palmquist, *Kant and Mysticism*, 51.
49 Ibid., 57. In part one of his book Palmquist argues that Swedenborg's mysticism played the formative role in Kant's turn to critical philosophy.

Chapter 4

1 See Walter Eckstein, 'The Religious Element in Spinoza's Philosophy', *The Journal of Religion* 23, no. 3 (1943): 153–63.
2 Jonathan I. Israel, *A Revolution of the Mind. Radical Enlightenment and the Intellectual Origins of Modern Democracy* (Princeton: Princeton University Press, 2010), 21.
3 Ibid., 36.
4 Ibid., 33.
5 Eckart Förster, *The Twenty-Five Years of Philosophy. A Systematic Reconstruction*, trans. Brady Bowman (Cambridge, MA: Harvard University Press, 2012), 75.
6 Ibid., 78.
7 Ibid., 83.
8 Spinoza, 'Ethics', 278.
9 Edwin Curley, *Behind the Geometrical Method. A Reading of Spinoza's Ethics* (Princeton: Princeton University Press, 1988), 5–6.
10 René Descartes, *Principles of Philosophy*, trans. Valentine R. Miller, Reese P. Miller (Dordrecht: Kluwer Academic Publishers, 1982), xxiv.
11 Ibid., xvii.
12 See ibid., xxv.
13 Ibid., xxiv.
14 See Spinoza, 'Ethics', 245.
15 Ibid., 217.
16 Ibid., 250–2.
17 See, e.g., the following definition: 'by attribute I mean every thing that is conceived in itself and through itself, so that its conception does not involve the conception of any other thing.' Benedictus de Spinoza, 'The Letters', in *Complete Works* (Indianapolis: Hackett Publishing Co., 2002), 762 (Letter 3).

18 Spinoza, 'Ethics', 320.
19 See ibid., 372–3.
20 Palmquist, *Kant's Critical Religion*, 12.
21 Spinoza, 'Treatise on the Emendation of the Intellect', in *Complete Works* (Indianapolis: Hackett Publishing Co., 2002), 11.
22 Spinoza, 'Ethics', 279. Also: Spinoza, 'Treatise on the Emendation', 18.
23 Ibid., 20.
24 See Spinoza, 'Ethics', 255.
25 Gilles Deleuze, *Spinoza: Practical Philosophy* (San Francisco: City Lights Books, 1988), 18–19.
26 Ibid., 19.
27 Spinoza, 'Treatise on the Emendation', 23.
28 Spinoza, 'Ethics', 226.
29 Ibid., 240.
30 Ibid., 242.
31 Ibid., 269–70.
32 Spinoza, 'Theological-Political Treatise', 388.
33 Ibid., 404–5.
34 See, e.g., Wayne Waxman, *Kant's Model of the Mind. A New Interpretation of Transcendental Idealism* (Oxford: Oxford University Press, 1991).
35 Spinoza, 'Ethics', 376–8.
36 Ibid., 267.
37 Firestone and Jacobs, *In Defense of Kant's* Religion, 112.
38 Ibid., 110.
39 Spinoza, 'Ethics', 247.
40 Michael Della Rocca, *Spinoza* (New York: Routledge, 2008), 110.
41 René Descartes, *Meditations on First Philosophy. With Selections from the Objections and Replies*, trans. and ed. John Cottingham (Cambridge: Cambridge University Press, 1996), 40 (italics A.T.).
42 Spinoza, 'Ethics', 217.
43 Cf. ibid., 233.
44 Benedictus de Spinoza, 'Short Treatise on God, Man and His Well-Being', in *Complete Works* (Indianapolis: Hackett Publishing Co., 2002), 101.
45 Spinoza, 'Theological-Political Treatise', 567.
46 Stuart Hampshire, 'Spinoza's Theory of Human Freedom', *The Monist* 55, no. 4 (1971): 566.
47 Spinoza, 'Ethics', 221.
48 Ibid., 264.
49 Ibid., 218.
50 Spinoza, 'Theological-Political Treatise', 444.

51 Ibid., 446.
52 Yirmiyahu Yovel, *Spinoza and Other Heretics. The Adventures of Immanence* (Princeton: Princeton University Press, 1989), 12.
53 Leszek Kołakowski, 'The Two Eyes of Spinoza', in *The Two Eyes of Spinoza and Other Essays on Philosophers*, ed. Zbigniew Janowski (South Bend: St. Augustine's Press, 2004), 6.
54 Spinoza, 'Ethics', 259.
55 Yirmiyahu Yovel, *Kant's Philosophical Revolution. A Short Guide to the* Critique of Pure Reason (Princeton: Princeton University Press, 2018), 7.
56 Nancy Levene, 'Spinoza the Radical', in *Reassessing the Radical Enlightenment*, ed. Steffen Ducheyne (London: Routledge, 2017), 114.
57 Spinoza, 'Ethics', 230.
58 Ibid., 283.
59 Cf. ibid., 283–4.
60 As argued, for example, in Della Rocca, *Spinoza*.
61 Spinoza, 'Ethics', 333.
62 Etienne Balibar, *Spinoza and Politics*, trans. Peter Snowdon (London: Verso, 2008), 102.
63 Spinoza, 'Theological-Political Treatise', 518.
64 Ibid.
65 For a thorough treatment of Spinoza's life and views in the context of religious strife – the Thirty Years War, the conflict between the Remonstrants and the Anti-Remonstrants, the Cocceians and the Voetians – see Steven Nadler, *Spinoza. A Life* (New York: Cambridge University Press, 1999), esp. ch. 11.
66 Colin McLear, 'On the Transcendental Freedom of the Intellect', *Ergo: An Open Access Journal of Philosophy* 7, no. 2 (2020): 35–104.
67 On freedom as the condition of the imputability of actions to the subject, see Henry E. Allison, 'We Can Act Only under the Idea of Freedom', *Proceedings and Addresses of the American Philosophical Association* 71, no. 2 (1997): 39–50.
68 Ralph C.S. Walker, 'The Primacy of Practical Reason', in *The Palgrave Kant Handbook*, ed. Matthew C. Altman (London: Palgrave Macmillan, 2017), 194.
69 Israel, *A Revolution of the Mind*, 178.
70 Ibid., 157.

Chapter 5

1 According to Wilhelm Dilthey, by the time Kant received the royal rescript, 'no one in Germany would have done so much as he did for the cultivation of a serious religiosity (*einer ernsten Religiosität*).' 'Der Streit Kants mit der Zensur über

das Recht freier Religionsforschung', in *Die Jugendgeschichte Hegels und andere Abhandlungen zur Geschichte des deutschen Idealismus* (Göttingen: Vandenhoeck und Ruprecht, 1990), 307 (trans. A.T.). See also Allen W. Wood, 'General Introduction', in Immanuel Kant, *Religion and Rational Theology*, ed. Allen. W. Wood and George Di Giovanni (New York: Cambridge University Press, 1996), xvii–xix.

2   Ian Hunter defends Wöllner's edict as 'a typical instrument of the Prussian state's long-standing policy of supervising the religious peace while remaining neutral between the rival confessions'. *Rival Enlightenments. Civil and Metaphysical Philosophy in Early Modern Germany* (Cambridge: Cambridge University Press, 2003), 342. See also Ian Hunter, 'Kant's *Religion* and Prussian Religious Policy', *Modern Intellectual History* 2, no. 1 (2005): 1–27. According to Sauter, although 'there is no doubt that Woellner spoke very critically of the Enlightenment… if judged by contemporary standards, the edict itself was politically moderate, as it only prescribed what preachers could say before their congregations and did not interfere in academic debate'. Besides, 'like his anti-edict opponents Woellner was a product of Prussia's most important enlightened institutions – both state and public.' *Visions of the Enlightenment*, 24. James Schmidt notices in turn that 'the controversy that greeted the edicts might better be seen as a consequence of differing interpretations of one of the most central concepts in the European Enlightenment: religious toleration'. 'German Enlightenment', https://open.bu.edu/ds2/stream/?#/documents/28872/page/1 [Accessed 15 October 2020].

3   Hunter, 'Kant's *Religion*', 14.

4   Ibid., 11.

5   Ibid., 9.

6   Here are some examples: Andreas Wissowatius, *Religio rationalis seu de rationis judicio, in controversiis etiam theologicis, ac religiosis, adhibendo, tractatus* (1685), Hermann Alexander Röell, *Oratio inauguralis de religione rationali. Dicta, quoque per tempus licuit, solenniter Franekerae Frisiorum in templo academico* (1686), John Locke, *The Reasonableness of Christianity, as Delivered in the Scriptures* (1695), Matthew Tindal, *Christianity as Old as the Creation: Or, the Gospel, a Republication of the Religion of Nature* (1730), Johann Christian Edelmann, *Die Göttlichkeit der Vernunft, in einer kurtzen Anweisung zu weiterer Untersuchung der ältesten und vornehmsten Bedeutung des Wortes ΛΟΓΟΣ* (1742), Hermann Samuel Reimarus, *Die vornehmsten Wahrheiten der natürlichen Religion in zehn Abhandlungen auf eine begreifliche art erkläret und gerettet* (1754), Johann Salomo Semler, *Theologische Briefe. Dritte Sammlung. Nebst einem Versuch über den freien Ursprung der christlichen Religion* (1782), Carl Friedrich Bahrdt, *Catechismus der natürlichen Religion, als Grundlage eines jeden Unterrichts in der Moral und Religion* (1795).

7   See, e.g., Henri Krop, 'The *Philosophia S. Scripturae Interpres* between Humanist Scholarship and Cartesian Science: Lodewijk Meijer and the Emancipatory Power of Philology', in *The Dutch Legacy: Radical Thinkers of the 17th Century and the Enlightenment*, ed. Sonja Lavaert and Winfried Schröder (Leiden: Brill, 2017), 90–120.
8   Leszek Kołakowski, *Świadomość religijna i więź kościelna: studia nad chrześcijaństwem bezwyznaniowym XVII wieku* (Warszawa: Wydawnictwo Naukowe PWN, 2009), 150 (trans. A.T.).
9   Hunter, 'Kant's *Religion*', 6.
10 See Ian Hunter, 'Secularization: The Birth of a Modern Combat Concept', *Modern Intellectual History* 12, no. 1 (2014): 1–32.
11 See, e.g., Sparn, '*Formalis Atheus?*'.
12 Beiser, *The Fate of Reason*, 50–1.
13 Other members of the 'circle' include Jarig Jelles, who authored the preface to Spinoza's *Opera posthuma*, where he argued that Spinoza's philosophical views concord with Christianity, and Adriaan Koerbagh, the author of *Een Bloemhof van allerley lieflijkheyd*, who urged that only those contents should be preserved from Scripture that 'agree with reason', since all else 'is for us useless and void, and can therefore be rejected without scruples'. Meinsma, *Spinoza und sein Kreis*, 359 (trans. A.T.).
14 See Schröder, *Ursprünge des Atheismus*, 21–44; see also Winfried Schröder, 'The Charge of Religious Imposture in Late Anti-Christian Authors and their Early Modern Readers', *Intellectual History Review* 28, no. 1 (2018): 23–34; Kors, *Epicureans and Atheists*.
15 Cf. Heine, *On the History of Religion*, 78–9.
16 See Allen W. Wood, 'Kant's Deism', in *Kant's Philosophy of Religion Reconsidered*, ed. Philip J. Rossi and Michael J. Wreen (Bloomington: Indiana University Press, 1991), 2.
17 For the metaphor of core (*Kern*) and husk (*Hülse*), see Dilthey, 'Der Streit Kants mit der Zensur', 295–7.
18 Palmquist, *Kant's Critical Religion*, 122.
19 Firestone and Jacobs, *In Defense of Kant's* Religion, 66 and 24. See also Firestone, *Kant and Theology*, 58–9.
20 An analogous formulation can be found in RGV, 6:84, where Kant stipulates that 'a moral religion' should be 'cast not in dogmas and observances but in the heart's disposition to observe all human duties as divine commands'.
21 For the discussion of Kant's 'definition' in light of the distinction between religion defined as a bond between creatures and the Creator (Lactantius) and religion defined as conscientious observance (Cicero), see Gabriele Tomasi, *La voce e lo sguardo: metafore e funzioni della coscienza nella dottrina Kantiana della virtù* (Pisa: Edizioni ETS, 1999), 158–70.

22 Reza Mosayebi has called this feature 'ethical motivation agnosia' (*ethische Motivagnosie*). 'Die "Definition" der Vernunftreligion', in *Immanuel Kant: Die Religion innerhalb der Grenzen der bloßen Vernunft*, ed. Otfried Höffe (Berlin: Akademie Verlag, 2011), 257–9.
23 Israel, *Democratic Enlightenment*, 310. Bahrdt also served time in prison for 'having published a scandalous play against the Prussian prime minister'. Jacob, *The Secular Enlightenment*, 203.
24 Carl Friedrich Bahrdt, *Catechismus der natürlichen Religion als Grundlage eines jeden Unterricht in der Moral und Religion*, Zweite Auflage (Görlitz: Hermsdorf und Anton, 1795), 4 (here and in the remaining passages of this work – trans. A.T.).
25 Ibid., 5.
26 *Bahrdts neues Christenthum, oder letztes Vermächtniß an Freund und Feinde* (Frankfurt, 1790), 27 (here and in the remaining passages – trans. A.T.).
27 Bahrdt, *Catechismus*, 40.
28 Ibid., 10.
29 Ibid., 12.
30 Ibid., 63–4.
31 *Neues Christenthum*, 31.
32 Bahrdt, *Catechismus*, 2–5.
33 *Neues Christenthum*, 24.
34 Carl Friedrich Bahrdt, *Würdigung der natürlichen Religion* (Halle, 1791), 9 (italics. A.T.; trans. A.T.).
35 *Neues Christenthum*, 25.
36 Ibid., 26–7.
37 Ibid., 27.
38 See the fifth out of seven tenets of the universal faith formulated by Spinoza in chapter 14 of *Theological-Political Treatise*: 'Worship of God and obedience to him consists solely in justice and charity, or love towards one's neighbours.' Spinoza, 'Theological-Political Treatise', 518.
39 Bahrdt, *Catechismus*, 59–63.
40 Firestone, *Kant and Theology*, 1.
41 See Stephen R. Palmquist, 'Does Kant Reduce Religion to Morality?', *Kant-Studien* 83, no. 2 (1992): 132–3; Palmquist, *Kant's Critical Religion*, 118–19.
42 Ibid., 122–3.
43 Ibid., 120.
44 Ibid., 137.
45 Ibid., 136n.
46 Ibid., 137.
47 Yovel, *Kant and the Philosophy of History*, 210.

48 Otfried Höffe, 'Philosophische Grundsätze der Schriftauslegung: Ein Blick in den *Streit der Fakultäten*', in *Immanuel Kant. Die Religion innerhalb der Grenzen der bloßen Vernunft* (Berlin: Akademie Verlag, 2011), 238 (trans. A.T.).
49 For Kant's references to Reimarus's 'book on natural religion' see BDG, 2:161. According to Israel, Kant held Reimarus's *Die vornehmsten Wahrheiten der natürlichen Religion* (1754) in high esteem at least for a decade after its publication. See Jonathan I. Israel, 'The Philosophical Context of Hermann Samuel Reimarus' Radical Bible Criticism', in *Between Philology and Radical Enlightenment: Hermann Samuel Reimarus (1694–1768)*, ed. Martin Mulsow (Leiden: Brill, 2011), 189. For a useful comparison of Kant's and Reimarus's ideas on religion, see Manfred Kuehn, 'Kant's Jesus', in *Kant's* Religion within the Boundaries of Mere Reason. *A Critical Guide*, ed. Gordon E. Michalson (Cambridge: Cambridge University Press, 2014), 156–74. According to Kuehn, Kant approximates the 'Neologists' (or neologians), a group of theologians who attempted to 'empty' revealed religion 'of all historical content and to fill it with purely rational content instead'. Ibid., 157.
50 Spinoza, 'Theological-Political Treatise', 478.
51 For an account of Spinoza's argument challenging the authenticity of the Gospels, see Edwin Curley, 'Resurrecting Leo Strauss', in *Reading between the Lines – Leo Strauss and the History of Early Modern Philosophy*, ed. Winfried Schröder (Berlin: De Gruyter, 2015), 129–70.
52 Otfried Höffe, 'Holy Scriptures within the Boundaries of Mere Reason: Kant's Reflections', in *Kant's* Religion within the Boundaries of Mere Reason. *A Critical Guide*, ed. Gordon E. Michalson (Cambridge: Cambridge University Press, 2014), 15.
53 Firestone and Jacobs, *In Defense of Kant's* Religion, 48. The authors mention Bernard Reardon and John Hare as working under the assumption of this thesis.
54 Lawrence R. Pasternack, *Kant on* Religion within the Boundaries of Mere Reason (London: Routledge, 2014), 6–8.
55 Höffe, 'Holy Scriptures within the Boundaries', 20.
56 Allen W. Wood, 'The Evil in Human Nature', in *Kant's* Religion within the Boundaries of Mere Reason. *A Critical Guide*, ed. Gordon E. Michalson (Cambridge: Cambridge University Press, 2014), 32.
57 Leslie Stevenson, 'Kant on Grace', in *Kant's* Religion within the Boundaries of Mere Reason. *A Critical Guide*, ed. Gordon E. Michalson (Cambridge: Cambridge University Press, 2014), 129–30.
58 See Wood, 'The Evil in Human Nature', 32n.
59 For a detailed account of the connection between evil and human nature in Kant, see Firestone and Jacobs, *In Defense of Kant's* Religion, 134–41.

60 Kant calls a will that does not succumb to non-moral incentives and 'is of itself necessarily in accord with the [moral] law' a divine and a holy will (GMS, 4:414). See also KpV, 5:32.
61 Kuehn, 'Kant's Jesus', 171.
62 Zbigniew Janowski, *Cartesian Theodicy. Descartes' Quest for Certitude* (Dordrecht: Kluwer, 2000), 140.
63 See, e.g., Pasternack, *Kant on* Religion, 133–7.
64 Palmquist, *Comprehensive Commentary*, 153.
65 Given this ambiguity in Kant's notion of Jesus, it does not seem accurate enough to claim, as Kuehn does, that 'Jesus is for Kant both a philosophical teacher who taught by example and doctrine, and a "model" or "symbol of humanity": an idea'. Kuehn, 'Kant's Jesus', 172. It would be more accurate to say that for Kant Jesus is *either* the teacher of morality *or* the idea of moral perfection, but not both at once.
66 Wood, *Kant and Religion*, 151.
67 See Curley, 'Resurrecting Leo Strauss', 163–4.
68 Firestone and Jacobs, *In Defense of Kant's* Religion, 163.
69 Ibid., 165.
70 Ibid., 163.
71 See ibid., 164–5.
72 Christopher Insole, *The Intolerable God: Kant's Theological Journey* (Grand Rapids: Eerdmans, 2016), 114.
73 Christopher Insole, *Kant and the Divine. From Contemplation to the Moral Law* (New York: Oxford University Press, 2020), 203.
74 Ibid., 204.
75 Leo Bäck, *Spinozas erste Einwirkungen auf Deutschland* (Berlin: Mayer & Müller, 1895), 35.
76 The frontispiece of *Die Göttlichkeit der Vernunft* features the opening line of John's Gospel in translation revamped thus: 'In the beginning there was reason (*Vernunft*) / and reason was with God / and God was the reason' (all passages from Edelmann's book are in my translation – A.T.).
77 Johann Christian Edelmann, *Die Göttlichkeit der Vernunft* (Berleburg, 1742), 28–38.
78 Ibid., 16–17.
79 Ibid., 56.
80 Ibid., 170.
81 Ibid., 103.
82 Ibid., 6.
83 Ibid., 172.
84 Ibid., 184.
85 Ibid., 147–8.
86 Ibid., 26.

87   Ibid., 96.
88   Ibid., 77. Edelmann defines sin as everything that is against reason.
89   Ibid., 6.
90   Ibid., 21.
91   Ibid., 14.
92   Ibid., 12.
93   Ibid., 29.
94   Spinoza, 'Ethics', 219, 238.
95   Edelmann, *Die Göttlichkeit der Vernunft*, 111.
96   Edelmann (ibid., 34.) reasons thus: if one has the concept (*Begriff*) of a thing, one conceives of the thing, so it is not inconceivable. We have the concept of God, therefore God is not inconceivable, although his invisible essence can be 'unclear (*confus*)' to us. Note that Edelmann does not say that we have *knowledge* of God. Of course, the idea that we can cognize God on the basis of his concept or idea in our mind is not exclusively Spinoza's: it can be found, in particular, in Descartes, Malebranche and Leibniz.
97   Ibid., 108–9.
98   Johann Christian Edelmann, *Abgenöthigtes jedoch Andern nicht wieder aufgenöthigtes Glaubens-Bekentniß* (s.l., 1746), 101, 122–3.
99   Steven Nadler, *A Book Forged in Hell: Spinoza's Scandalous Treatise and the Birth of the Secular Age* (Princeton: Princeton University Press, 2011).
100 Freudenthal, 'On the History of Spinozism', 17.
101 Bäck, *Spinozas erste Einwirkungen*, 7f.
102 Freudenthal, 'On the History of Spinozism', 43; Lord, *Kant and Spinozism*, 5–6, 11–16.
103 Schröder, '*Spinozam tota armenta*'; Grunwald, *Spinoza in Deutschland*, 19; Michael J. Sauter, 'Preaching, a Ponytail, and an Enthusiast: Rethinking the Public Sphere's Subversiveness in Eighteenth-Century Prussia', *Central European History* 37, no. 4 (2004): 550–60.
104 Freudenthal, 'On the History of Spinozism', 46.
105 Bäck, *Spinozas erste Einwirkungen*, 38 (all passages from this work are in my translation – A.T.).
106 Ibid., 56.
107 Ibid., 67.
108 Ibid., 85.
109 Freudenthal, 'On the History of Spinozism', 55.
110 For an account of Spinoza's interpretation of revealed religions as various forms of 'a philosophical religion', see Carlos Fraenkel, *Philosophical Religions from Plato to Spinoza. Reason, Religion, and Autonomy* (Cambridge: Cambridge University Press, 2012).

111 Spinoza, 'Theological-Political Treatise', 391.
112 Ibid., 470.
113 Ibid., 392.
114 See ibid., 403, 457.
115 Yovel, *Spinoza and Other Heretics*, 12. For Spinoza's definition of the 'intellectual love of God', see 'Ethics', 377–8. By making use of Yovel's distinction, we do not subscribe to his portraying Spinoza as a secular philosopher inimical to Christianity. An opposed view would be that of Graeme Hunter who contends that 'Spinoza's radicalism is still internal to Protestant Christianity'. In this section, stress is put, however, on Spinoza's rationalization of Christianity, rather than his abiding by the tenets of Protestantism, and secularization might be a side-effect of this rationalization. See Graeme Hunter, *Radical Protestantism in Spinoza's Thought* (London: Routledge, 2017), 182.
116 Spinoza, 'Theological-Political Treatise', 388.
117 See ibid., 404.
118 Ibid., 392.
119 Ibid., 506.
120 Ibid., 427–8.
121 Ibid., 398–9.
122 Ibid., 398.
123 Ibid., 404.
124 Ibid., 398.
125 Ibid., 399.
126 Ibid., 431.
127 Spinoza, 'The Letters', 875 (Letter 42: from Jacob Ostens to Lambert de Velthuysen).
128 Nadler, *A Book Forged in Hell*, 172.
129 Spinoza, 'Ethics', 377–9.
130 A similar suggestion can be found in: Wiep van Bunge, *Spinoza Past and Present. Essays on Spinoza, Spinozism, and Spinoza Scholarship* (Leiden: Brill, 2012), 78–9, 114–17.
131 Hunter, *Radical Protestantism in Spinoza's Thought*.
132 Pasternack, *Kant on* Religion, 3–4.
133 Firestone and Jacobs, *In Defense of Kant's* Religion, 219.
134 Palmquist, *Comprehensive Commentary*, 38. For a discussion of pure rationalism see ibid., 388–94; for arguments that Kant inclines towards this stance, see ibid., 409.
135 Wood, 'Kant's Deism', 11. Wood, *Kant and Religion*, 18–19, esp. 18 n. 17.
136 Peter Byrne, *Kant on God* (Aldershot: Ashgate, 2007), 154, 159–62, 169.
137 Yovel, *Kant and the Philosophy of History*, 216.

Chapter 6

1. Israel, *Enlightenment Contested*, 669.
2. Ibid., 663.
3. John Toland, *Christianity Not Mysterious: Or, a Treatise Shewing, That There Is Nothing in the Gospel Contrary to Reason, Nor above It: And That No Christian Doctrine Can Be Properly Call'd a Mystery* (London: S. Buckley, 1696), 166.
4. Paul-Henry Thiry, Baron d'Holbach, *The System of Nature* (Kitchener: Batoche Books, 2001), 142.
5. For an illuminating explanation of Kant's views on afterlife, see Aaron Bunch, 'The Resurrection of the Body as a "Practical Postulate". Why Kant Is Committed to Belief in an Embodied Afterlife', *Philosophia Christi* 12, no. 1 (2010): 46–60.
6. Kant's idea that the church infuses the public life with moral values figures as a premise in the argument for the public presence of religion in a state otherwise respecting the principles of political secularism, proposed by Demiray in 'Public Religion and Secular State'. Demiray draws on some insights on the moral relevance of religious institutions formulated in Onora O'Neill, 'Kant on Reason and Religion', in *Tanner Lectures on Human Values* 18, ed. Grethe B. Peterson (Utah: Utah University Press, 1997), 267–308.
7. To describe moral conversion, Kant also uses other phrases such as 'the putting on of the new man' (RGV, 6:197n.) and 'rebirth' (RGV, 6:47, 197n.).
8. By the end of his essay, Fugate makes a brief remark on the ethical community, but does not develop it. See Fugate, 'The Highest Good and Kant's Proof(s)', 152–3.
9. Pasternack, *Kant on Religion*, 7.
10. Ibid., 8.
11. See Lawrence Pasternack, 'The Ethical Community in Kant's Pure Rational System of Religion: Comments on Rossi's *The Ethical Commonwealth in History*', *Philosophia* 49, no. 5 (2021): 1–16. For the source text, see Philip J. Rossi, *The Ethical Commonwealth in History. Peace-Making as the Moral Vocation of Humanity* (Cambridge: Cambridge University Press, 2019).
12. Gordon E. Michalson, 'The Ambiguity of Kant's Concept of the Visible Church', *Diametros* 17, no. 65 (2020): 85.
13. For an explanation of Kant's conception of the highest good, see 3.3.
14. Moses Mendelssohn, 'Über die Frage: Was heißt aufklären?', in *Was ist Aufklärung? Thesen und Definitionen*, ed. Erhard Bahr (Stuttgart: Philipp Reclam), 3–8.
15. Andreas Riem, *Ueber Aufklärung. Ob sie dem Staate – der Religion – oder überhaupt gefährlich sey, und seyn könne? Erstes Fragment* (Berlin, 1788), 4 (trans. A.T.).
16. Reath, 'Two Conceptions', 601.
17. Ibid., 619.
18. Yovel, *Kant and the Philosophy of History*, 30.

19 Ibid., 72–3.
20 O'Neill, 'Kant on Reason and Religion', 306.
21 Taylor, *A Secular Age*, 539f.
22 See, e.g., Jeffrey D. Burson, *The Culture of Enlightening: Abbé Claude Yvon and the Entangled Emergence of the Enlightenment* (Notre Dame: University of Notre Dame Press, 2019); Jeffrey D. Burson, 'The Interlacing of Secular Implications and Sacred Discourse in the French Enlightenment: Toleration and Freedom of Expression in the Works of Abbé Claude Yvon', in *The Sources of Secularism: Enlightenment and Beyond*, ed. Anna Tomaszewska and Hasse Hämäläinen (Cham: Palgrave Macmillan, 2017), 169–87; Harm Klueting, 'The Catholic Enlightenment in Austria or the Habsburg Lands', in *A Companion to the Catholic Enlightenment in Europe*, ed. Ulrich Lehner and Michael Printy (Leiden: Brill, 2010), 127–64.
23 The name of the kind of the category is provided in square brackets.
24 Palmquist thinks that the term *Lauterkeit* in the German original of Kant's text should be rendered as 'integrity', not 'purity', because the latter refers to the lack of sensible content which does not have to be foreign to religion. See Stephen R. Palmquist, 'How Political Is the Kantian Church?', *Diametros* 17, no. 65 (2020): 100. It seems that whereas 'purity' captures the nature of motivation behind joining an ethical community by a rational agent, 'integrity' designates a feature of the character of an individual which the ethical community is to reinforce.
25 Wojciech Kozyra, 'The Gospel of the New Principle: The Marcionian Leitmotif in Kant's Religious Thought in the Context of Thomas Morgan and the German Enlightenment', in *Between Secularization and Reform: Religion in the Enlightenment*, ed. Anna Tomaszewska (manuscript).
26 Nicholas Tampio, 'Pluralism in the Ethical Community', in *Kant's* Religion within the Boundaries of Mere Reason. A Critical Guide, ed. Gordon E. Michalson (Cambridge: Cambridge University Press, 2014), 175–92, see esp. 188–91.
27 This point has also been argued from a sociological point of view. See Graeme Smith, 'Talking to Ourselves: An Investigation into the Christian Ethics Inherent in Secularism', in *The Sources of Secularism. Enlightenment and Beyond*, ed. Anna Tomaszewska and Hasse Hämäläinen (Cham: Palgrave Macmillan, 2017), 229–44.
28 DiCenso, *Kant, Religion, and Politics*, 249.
29 Ibid., 259.
30 See Stephen R. Palmquist, 'Kant's Prudential Theory of Religion: The Necessity of Historical Faith for Moral Empowerment', *Con-Textos Kantianos* 1 (2015): 57–76.
31 John E. Hare, *The Moral Gap. Kantian Ethics, Human Limits, and God's Assistance* (Oxford: Clarendon Press, 1996), 34.
32 Ibid., 7.
33 Cf. ibid., 35.
34 Pasternack, *Kant on* Religion, 31f.

Chapter 7

1. See Bryan W. Hall, *The Post-Critical Kant. Understanding the Critical Philosophy through the Opus postumum* (New York: Routledge, 2015), 12.
2. See Vittorio Mathieu, *L'Opus postumum di Kant* (Napoli: Bibliopolis, 1991), 258; also De Flaviis emphasizes that scholars no longer share this hypothesis of Karl Krause and Hans Vaihinger. *Kant e Spinoza*, 246.
3. See Lord, *Kant and Spinozism*, 156f.
4. Reiner Wimmer, *Kants kritische Religionsphilosophie* (Berlin: De Gruyter, 1990), 258–9.
5. Mathieu, *L' Opus postumum*, 268.
6. '[I]t was Thee I sought, not according to the understanding of the mind, by which Thou didst will us to stand above brutes, but according to fleshly sensation. But, *Thou wert deeper within me* than my innermost depths and higher than my highest parts.' Saint Augustine, *Confessions* (Washington, DC: The Catholic University of America Press, 1966), 60.
7. See Insole, *The Intolerable God*, 130–2. Insole envisages the late developments as following from Kant's earlier ideas. The significant change that would come about is that Kant, overcome by mental infirmity, would now cease to restrain his thoughts, so that his mind would be 'flooded' by their consequences. Cf. ibid., 136.
8. Cf. Eckart Förster, *Kant's Final Synthesis. An Essay on the Opus postumum* (Cambridge MA: Harvard University Press, 2000), 147.
9. Adela Cortina, 'Die Auflösung des religiösen Gottesbegriffs im *Opus postumum* Kants', *Kant-Studien* 75, no. 3 (1984): 280–93.
10. '[I]t is illegitimate, from the point of view of scholarship, to extract separate passages and consider them in isolation; rather, one should interpret one passage on the basis of the other and of the whole background of thought… In the case of a number of reflections, Kant leaves out the most essential, which he states in other places, but which remains the background of his thought, although he does not attend to it, it is not readily available in his memory, or at least he does not expressly assert it.' Erich Adickes, *Kants* Opus postumum (Vaduz: Topos Verlag, 1978), 772 (trans. A.T.).
11. On God as identical with the moral domain, or the 'field' of relations between rational moral agents, see Tomasz Kupś, *Opus postumum Immanuela Kanta* (Toruń: Wydawnictwo Naukowe Uniwersytetu Mikołaja Kopernika, 2016), ch. 5.
12. Hans Vaihinger, *The Philosophy of As If: A System of the Theoretical, Practical and Religious Fictions of Mankind* (London: Routledge, 1965), 318.
13. Adickes, *Kants* Opus postumum, 776.
14. For an argument supporting this interpretation, see Wimmer, *Kants kritische Religionsphilosophie*, 259–70. By contrast, according to Vittorio Mathieu, Kant

departs from the Anselmian tradition despite proposing an argument that the existence of God should directly follow from the 'fact of reason': 'God exists certainly and necessarily as a principle in accordance with which I should behave, *as my thought or idea*.' *La filosofia trascendentale e l'*Opus postumum *di Kant* (Torino: Edizioni di 'Filosofia', 1958), 419 (trans. and italics A.T.).

15 In § 30 of the *Monadology* Leibniz says: 'It is... through the knowledge of necessary truths and their abstractions that we are raised to *reflexive acts*, which make us think of what is called the *self*, and consider that this or that is within us.... in thinking of ourselves, we think of being, of substance, of the simple and the compound, of the immaterial and of God himself, by conceiving that what is limited in us is boundless in him. And these reflexive acts provide the main objects of our reasoning.' Strickland, *Leibniz's* Monadology, 19–20.

16 'And indeed it is no surprise that God, in creating me, should have placed this idea [of God – A.T.] in me to be, as it were, the mark of the craftsman stamped on his work.' Descartes, *Meditations on First Philosophy*, 35.

17 Insole, *The Intolerable God*, 133. See also Insole, *Kant and the Creation of Freedom*, 169–70.

18 Norbert Fischer, 'Kants Idee *est Deus in nobis* und ihr Verhältnis zu Meister Eckhart. Zur Beziehung von Gott und Mensch in Kants kritischer Philosophie und bei Eckhart', in *Meister Eckhart als Denker*, ed. Wolfgang Erb and Norbert Fischer (Stuttgart: Kohlhammer, 2017), 373.

19 *The Complete Works of Aristotle*, ed. Jonathan Barnes, Vol. 2 (Princeton: Princeton University Press, 1995), 1861 (EN, 1177b).

20 See Damian Mrugalski, *Logos. Filozoficzne i teologiczne źródła idei wczesnochrześcijańskiej* (Kraków: Wydawnictwo WAM, 2006).

21 See Strickland, *Leibniz's* Monadology, §§ 31–3.

22 Schröder, *Ursprünge des Atheismus*, 308–9.

23 According to Malebranche, the human will, like any finite thing, cannot be causally efficacious without divine concurrence: 'If men held, of themselves, the power to love the good, we could say they had some power, but men can only love because God wills them to and because His will is efficacious. Men can only love because God incessantly pushes them toward the good in general... It is not they who move themselves toward the good in general, it is God who moves them.... Now it appears to me quite certain that the will of minds is incapable of moving the smallest body in the world; for it is clear that there is no necessary connection between our will to move our arms, for example, and the movement of our arms. It is true that they are moved when we will it, and that thus we are the natural cause of the movement of our arms. But *natural* causes are not true causes; they are only *occasional* causes that act only through the force and efficacy of the will of God.' Nicolas Malebranche, *The Search after Truth* (Cambridge: Cambridge University Press, 1997), 449.

24 Augustine denies the Pelagian claim that 'God's grace is given in accordance with our deserts' and contends that 'we see that it is given, and given daily, not only where there are no previous good deserts but even where there are many previous evil deserts. Yet clearly, once grace has been given, our deserts begin to be good, though only by means of it. For if grace were to withdraw itself, human beings would fall, no longer raised up but cast down by free choice. Accordingly, even when someone begins to have good deserts, he ought not attribute them to himself, but rather to God.' Augustine, *On the Free Choice of the Will, On Grace and Free Choice, and Other Writings* (New York: Cambridge University Press, 2010), 150–2.
25 Insole, *The Intolerable God*, 151.
26 Insole, *Kant and the Creation of Freedom*, 194 (italics A.T.).
27 Ibid., 215.
28 Ibid., 200.
29 See Pasternack, 'Restoring Kant's Conception of the Highest Good'.
30 Yovel, *Spinoza and Other Heretics*, 7. Yovel's observation that Kant replaces God with human reason as legislator for nature and freedom is important especially in the context of the early modern philosophy in which the description of God as the author of the laws of nature is crucial for thinkers such as Descartes, Newton, Locke, Leibniz and Berkeley.
31 For more on the history of the term, see Stephen Howard, 'The Transition within the Transition: The *Übergang* from the *Selbstsetzungslehre* to the Ether Proofs in Kant's *Opus postumum*', *Kant-Studien* 110, no. 4 (2019): 595–617.
32 Basile, *Kants* Opus postumum *und seine Rezeption*, 171–2.
33 See Förster, *Kant's Final Synthesis*, 102–13.
34 Mathieu, *La filosofia trascendentale*, 418.
35 Palmquist, *Kant's Critical Religion*, 45–6.
36 Wimmer, *Kants kritische Religionsphilosophie*, 228–9 (trans. A.T.).
37 Ibid., 224. While the first tendency would be pursued by Hegel, the second one would be developed by nineteenth-century thinkers such as Ludwig Feuerbach, Karl Marx and Friedrich Nietzsche.
38 Kant's late idea of 'God in us' has inspired some scholars to attribute mysticism to him, even if in a 'critical' guise. See Fischer, 'Kants Idee *est Deus in nobis*'; Palmquist, *Comprehensive Commentary*, e.g. 145, 149.
39 See Stephen R. Palmquist, 'Kant's Moral Panentheism', *Philosophia* 36 (2008): 17–28.
40 Burkhard Tuschling, 'Transzendentaler Idealismus ist Spinozismus – Reflexionen von und über Kant und Spinoza', in *Spinoza im Deutschland des achtzehnten Jahrhunderts*, ed. Eva Schürman, Norbert Waszek, and Frank Weinreich (Stuttgart-Bad Cannstatt: Frommann-Holzboog, 2002), 140–1 (trans. A.T.).
41 Mathieu, *La filosofia trascendentale*, 400–1.

42 De Flaviis, *Kant e Spinoza*, 261 (trans. A.T.).
43 Malebranche, *The Search after Truth*, 230 (cf. ibid., 235).
44 Ibid., 235.
45 Ibid., 230.

Conclusion

1 For a discussion of the influence of Spinozist ideas on the thinkers listed, see in particular: Krop, 'The Secularism of Spinoza and His Circle'; Ian Leask, 'Toland, Spinoza, and the Naturalisation of Scripture', in *Ireland and the Reception of the Bible: Social and Cultural Studies*, ed. Brad Anderson and Jonathan Kearney (London: Bloomsbury, 2018), 227–42; Israel, *Democratic Enlightenment*; Rüdiger Otto, 'Johann Christian Edelmann's Criticism of the Bible and its Relation to Spinoza', in *Disguised and Overt Spinozism around 1700*, ed. Wiep van Bunge and Wim Klever (Leiden: Brill, 1996), 171–88; Jonathan I. Israel, 'Spinoza and the Religious Radical Enlightenment', in *The Intellectual Consequences of Religious Heterodoxy, 1600–1750*, ed. Sarah Mortimer and John Robertson (Leiden: Brill, 2012), 181–203; Jacob, *The Secular Enlightenment*, esp. 178–203.
2 Hunter, 'Secularization', 2.
3 According to Firestone and Palmquist, 'theologically affirmative interpretations of Kant, contrary to their negative counterparts, typically hold that Kant's philosophy provides a rationale for God-talk, God-thought, and even God-experience.' Chris L. Firestone, Stephen R. Palmquist, 'Editors' Introduction', in *Kant and the New Philosophy of Religion*, ed. Chris L. Firestone and Stephen R. Palmquist (Bloomington: Indiana University Press, 2006), 3. Thus, 'any scholar who interprets Kant as *affirming* theology and/or religion *and* interprets that affirmation as a position *worthy of being affirmed* by theologians and/or religious believers belongs to the group or *trend*' that endorses the affirmative interpretation. Ibid., 28. See also Palmquist, *Comprehensive Commentary*, 38n. Firestone has termed Palmquist's a 'religious interpretation' in Firestone, *Kant and Theology*, 59.
4 Lawrence Pasternack, 'Kant's "Appraisal" of Christianity: Biblical Interpretation and the Pure Rational System of Religion', *Journal of the History of Philosophy* 53, no. 3 (2015): 505.

Bibliography

1. The works of Immanuel Kant

Kants gesammelte Schriften. Edited by Royal Prussian Academy of Sciences. Berlin: De Gruyter, 1900–. https://korpora.zim.uni-duisburg-essen.de/kant/verzeichnisse-gesamt.html [Accessed 22 March 2022].

'A New Elucidation of the First Principles of Metaphysical Cognition'. 1755. In *Theoretical Philosophy, 1755–1770*, translated and edited by David Walford in collaboration with Ralf Meerbote, 1–45. New York: Cambridge University Press, 1992 (PND, 1).

'Universal Natural History and Theory of the Heavens, or Essay on the Constitution and the Mechanical Origin of the Whole Universe according to Newtonian Principles'. 1755. In *Natural Science*, edited by Eric Watkins, translated by Lewis White Beck, Jeffrey B. Edwards, Olaf Reinhardt, Martin Schönfeld, and Eric Watkins, 182–308. Cambridge: Cambridge University Press, 2012 (NTH, 1).

'Metaphysik Herder'. 1762-4. In *Lectures on Metaphysics*, translated and edited by Karl Ameriks and Steve Naragon, 3–16. New York: Cambridge University Press, 1997 (V-Met/Herder, 28).

'Attempt to Introduce the Concept of Negative Magnitudes into Philosophy'. 1763. In *Theoretical Philosophy, 1755–1770*, translated and edited by David Walford in collaboration with Ralf Meerbote, 203–41. New York: Cambridge University Press, 1992 (NG, 2).

'The Only Possible Argument in Support of a Demonstration of the Existence of God'. 1763. In *Theoretical Philosophy, 1755–1770*, translated and edited by David Walford in collaboration with Ralf Meerbote, 107–201. New York: Cambridge University Press, 1992 (BDG, 2).

'Observations on the Feeling of the Beautiful and Sublime'. 1764. In *Observations on the Feeling of the Beautiful and Sublime and Other Writings*, edited by Patrick Frierson and Paul Guyer, with an introduction by Patrick Frierson, 11–62. New York: Cambridge University Press, 2011 (GSE, 2).

'On the Form and Principles of the Sensible and the Intelligible World'. 1770. In *Theoretical Philosophy, 1755–1770*, translated and edited by David Walford in collaboration with Ralf Meerbote, 373–416. New York: Cambridge University Press, 1992 (MSI, 2).

'Metaphysik L_1'. Mid-1770s. In *Lectures on Metaphysics*, translated and edited by Karl Ameriks and Steve Naragon, 19–106. New York: Cambridge University Press, 1997 (V-Met-L1/Pölitz, 28).

Critique of Pure Reason. 1781/7. Translated and edited by Paul Guyer and Allen W. Wood. New York: Cambridge University Press, 1998 (KrV, A/B).

'Review of Schulz's Attempt at an Introduction to a Doctrine of Morals for All Human Beings Regardless of Different Religions'. 1783. In *Practical Philosophy*, translated and edited by Mary J. Gregor, 1–10. New York: Cambridge University Press, 1996 (RezSchulz, 8).

Eberhard, Johann August, and Immanuel Kant, *Preparation for Natural Theology. With Kant's Notes and the Danzig Rational Theology Transcript*. 1783/4. Edited by Courtney D. Fugate and John Hymers. London: Bloomsbury, 2016 (V-Th/Baumbach, 28).

'An Answer to the Question: What Is Enlightenment?'. 1784. In *Practical Philosophy*, translated and edited by Mary J. Gregor, 11–22. New York: Cambridge University Press, 1996 (WA, 8).

'Moral Philosophy: Collins's Lecture Notes'. 1784–5. In *Lectures on Ethics*, edited by Peter Heath and Jerome B. Schneewind, translated by Peter Heath, 37–222. New York: Cambridge University Press, 1997 (V-Mo/Collins, 27).

'Groundwork of the Metaphysics of Morals'. 1785. In *Practical Philosophy*, translated and edited by Mary J. Gregor, 37–108. New York: Cambridge University Press, 1996 (GMS, 4).

'What Does It Mean to Orient Oneself in Thinking?'. 1786. In *Religion and Rational Theology*, translated and edited by Allen W. Wood and George Di Giovanni, 1–18. New York: Cambridge University Press, 1996 (WDO, 8).

'Critique of Practical Reason'. 1788. In *Practical Philosophy*, translated and edited by Mary J. Gregor, 133–271. New York: Cambridge University Press, 1996 (KpV, 5).

'On a Discovery whereby Any New Critique of Pure Reason Is to Be Made Superfluous by an Older One'. 1790. In *Theoretical Philosophy after 1781*, edited by Henry Allison and Peter Heath, translated by Gary Hatfield, Michael Friedman, Henry Allison, and Peter Heath, 271–336. New York: Cambridge University Press, 2002 (ÜE, 8).

Critique of the Power of Judgment. 1790. Edited by Paul Guyer, translated by Paul Guyer and Eric Matthews. New York: Cambridge University Press, 2002 (KU, 5).

Critique of Judgement. 1790. Translated by James C. Meredith, revised, edited and introduced by Nicholas Walker. New York: Oxford University Press, 2007 (KU, 5).

'Metaphysik L_2'. 1790–1 (?). In *Lectures on Metaphysics*, translated and edited by Karl Ameriks and Steve Naragon, 299–354. New York: Cambridge University Press, 1997 (V-Met-L2/Pölitz, 28).

'On the Miscarriage of All Philosophical Trials in Theodicy'. 1791. In *Religion and Rational Theology*, translated and edited by Allen W. Wood and George Di Giovanni, 19–37. New York: Cambridge University Press, 1996 (MpVT, 8).

'On the Common Saying: That May Be Correct in Theory, but It Is of No Use in Practice'. 1793. In *Practical Philosophy*, translated and edited by Mary J. Gregor, 273–309. New York: Cambridge University Press, 1996 (TP, 8).

'Religion within the Boundaries of Mere Reason'. 1793/4. In *Religion and Rational Theology*, translated and edited by Allen W. Wood and George Di Giovanni, 39–215. New York: Cambridge University Press, 1996 (RGV, 6).

'Kant on the Metaphysics of Morals: Vigilantius's Lecture Notes'. 1793–4. In *Lectures on Ethics*, edited by Peter Heath and Jerome B. Schneewind, translated by Peter Heath, 249–452. New York: Cambridge University Press, 1997 (V-Ms/Vigil, 27).

'What Real Progress Has Metaphysics Made in Germany since the Time of Leibniz and Wolff?'. 1793/1804. In *Theoretical Philosophy after 1781*, edited by Henry Allison, Peter Heath, translated by Gary Hatfield, Michael Friedman, Henry Allison, and Peter Heath, 337–424. New York: Cambridge University Press, 2002 (FM, 20).

'The End of All Things'. 1794. In *Religion and Rational Theology*, translated and edited by Allen W. Wood and George Di Giovanni, 217–31. New York: Cambridge University Press, 1996 (EAD, 8).

'Toward Perpetual Peace'. 1795. In *Practical Philosophy*, translated and edited by Mary J. Gregor, 311–51. New York: Cambridge University Press, 1996 (ZeF, 8).

'The Metaphysics of Morals'. 1797. In *Practical Philosophy*, translated and edited by Mary J. Gregor, 353–603. New York: Cambridge University Press, 1996 (MS, 6).

'The Conflict of the Faculties'. 1798. In *Religion and Rational Theology*, translated and edited by Allen W. Wood and George Di Giovanni, 233–327. New York: Cambridge University Press, 1996 (SF, 7).

'Preface to Reinhold Bernhard Jachmann's *Examination of the Kantian Philosophy of Religion*'. 1800. In *Religion and Rational Theology*, translated and edited by Allen W. Wood and George Di Giovanni, 329–34. New York: Cambridge University Press, 1996 (PKR, 8).

'Lectures on the Philosophical Doctrine of Religion'. 1817. In *Religion and Rational Theology*, translated and edited by Allen W. Wood and George Di Giovanni, 335–451. New York: Cambridge University Press, 1996 (V-Phil-Th/Pölitz, 28).

Opus postumum. 1938. Edited, with an introduction and notes, by Eckart Förster, translated by Eckart Förster and Michael Rosen. New York: Cambridge University Press, 1993 (OP, 21–22).

Lectures on Logic, translated and edited by J. Michael Young. New York: Cambridge University Press, 1992 (Log, 9).

Correspondence, translated and edited by Arnulf Zweig. New York: Cambridge University Press, 1999 (Br, 10–13).

Notes and Fragments. Edited by Paul Guyer, translated by Curtis Bowman, Paul Guyer, Frederick Rauscher. New York: Cambridge University Press, 2005 (HN, 14–23; Refl, 14–19).

2. Secondary literature

Adickes, Erich. *Kants Opus postumum*. 1920. Reprinted. Vaduz: Topos Verlag, 1978.
Allison, Henry E. 'We Can Act Only under the Idea of Freedom'. *Proceedings and Addresses of the American Philosophical Association* 71, no. 2 (1997): 39–50.
Aristotle. *The Complete Works of Aristotle*. Vol. 2. The revised Oxford translation. Edited by Jonathan Barnes. Princeton: Princeton University Press, 1995.

Augustine, Saint. *Confessions*. Translated by Vernon J. Bourke. Washington, DC: The Catholic University of America Press, 1966.

Augustine, Saint. *On the Free Choice of the Will, On Grace and Free Choice, and Other Writings*. Edited and translated by Peter King. New York: Cambridge University Press, 2010.

Bahrdt, Carl Friedrich. *Bahrdts neues Christenthum, oder letztes Vermächtniß an Freund und Feinde*. Frankfurt, 1790.

Bahrdt, Carl Friedrich. *Würdigung der natürlichen Religion*. Halle: Francke und Bispink, 1791.

Bahrdt, Carl Friedrich. *Catechismus der natürlichen Religion als Grundlage eines jeden Unterricht in der Moral und Religion*. Zweite Auflage. Görlitz: Hermsdorf und Anton, 1795.

Balibar, Etienne. *Spinoza and Politics*. Translated by Peter Snowdon. London: Verso, 2008.

Basile, Giovanni Pietro. *Kants Opus postumum und seine Rezeption*. Berlin: De Gruyter, 2013.

Bayle, Pierre. *Historical and Critical Dictionary. Selections*. Translated, with an introduction and notes, by Richard H. Popkin. Indianapolis: The Bobbs-Merrill Company, Inc., 1965.

Bäck, Leo. *Spinozas erste Einwirkungen auf Deutschland*. Berlin: Mayer & Müller, 1895.

Beiser, Frederick C. *The Fate of Reason. German Philosophy from Kant to Fichte*. Cambridge MA: Harvard University Press, 1987.

Biblia Sacra. Iuxta Vulgatam Versionem. 1969. Edited by Robert Weber and Roger Gryson. Stuttgart: Deutsche Bibelgesellschaft, 2007.

Boehm, Omri. *Kant's Critique of Spinoza*. New York: Oxford University Press, 2014.

Brewer, Kimberly, and Eric Watkins. 'A Difficulty Still Awaits: Kant, Spinoza, and the Threat of Theological Determinism'. *Kant-Studien* 103, no. 2 (2012): 163–87.

Bunch, Aaron. 'The Resurrection of the Body as a "Practical Postulate". Why Kant Is Committed to Belief in an Embodied Afterlife'. *Philosophia Christi* 12, no. 1 (2010): 46–60.

Burson, Jeffrey D. *The Culture of Enlightening: Abbé Claude Yvon and the Entangled Emergence of the Enlightenment*. Notre Dame: University of Notre Dame Press, 2019.

Burson, Jeffrey D. 'The Interlacing of Secular Implications and Sacred Discourse in the French Enlightenment: Toleration and Freedom of Expression in the Works of Abbé Claude Yvon'. In *The Sources of Secularism: Enlightenment and Beyond*, edited by Anna Tomaszewska and Hasse Hämäläinen, 169–87. Cham: Palgrave Macmillan, 2017.

Byrne, Peter. *Kant on God*. Aldershot: Ashgate, 2007.

Chignell, Andrew. 'Belief in Kant'. *Philosophical Review* 116, no. 3 (2007): 323–60.

Chignell, Andrew. 'Kant, Modality, and the Most Real Being'. *Archiv für Geschichte der Philosophie* 91 (2009): 157–92.

Chignell, Andrew. 'Kant, Real Possibility and the Threat of Spinoza'. *Mind* 121, no. 483 (2012): 635–75.

Cortina, Adela. 'Die Auflösung des religiösen Gottesbegriffs im *Opus postumum* Kants'. *Kant-Studien* 75, no. 3 (1984): 280–93.

Curley, Edwin. *Behind the Geometrical Method. A Reading of Spinoza's Ethics*. Princeton: Princeton University Press, 1988.

Curley, Edwin. 'Resurrecting Leo Strauss'. In *Reading between the Lines: Leo Strauss and the History of Early Modern Philosophy*, edited by Winfried Schröder, 129–70. Berlin: De Gruyter, 2015.

Czelinski-Uesbeck, Michael. *Der tugendhafte Atheist. Studien zur Vorgeschichte der Spinoza-Renaissance in Deutschland*. Würzburg: Königshausen und Neumann, 2007.

De Flaviis, Giuseppe. *Kant e Spinoza*. Firenze: Sansoni Editore, 1986.

Deleuze, Gilles. *Spinoza: Practical Philosophy*. San Francisco: City Lights Books, 1988.

Della Rocca, Michael. *Spinoza*. New York: Routledge, 2008.

Della Rocca, Michael. 'Razing Structures to the Ground'. *Analytic Philosophy* 55, no. 3 (2014): 276–94.

Demiray, Mehmet R. 'Public Religion and Secular State: A Kantian Approach'. *Diametros* 54 (2017): 30–55.

Denis, Lara. 'Kant's Criticism of Atheism'. *Kant-Studien* 94, no. 2 (2006): 198–219.

Descartes, René. *Principles of Philosophy*. 1644. Translated, with explanatory notes, by Valentine Rodger Miller and Reese P. Miller. Dordrecht: Kluwer Academic Publishers, 1982.

Descartes, René. *Meditations on First Philosophy. With Selections from the Objections and Replies*. 1641. Translated and edited by John Cottingham. Cambridge: Cambridge University Press, 1996.

DiCenso, James J. *Kant, Religion, and Politics*. Cambridge: Cambridge University Press, 2011.

Dilthey, Wilhelm. 'Der Streit Kants mit der Zensur über das Recht freier Religionsforschung'. In *Die Jugendgeschichte Hegels und andere Abhandlungen zur Geschichte des deutschen Idealismus*, edited by Herman Nohl, 285–309. Göttingen: Vandenhoeck und Ruprecht, 1990.

Dörflinger, Bernd. 'Führt Moral unausbleiblich zur Religion? Überlegungen zu einer These Kants'. In *Kants Metaphysik und Religionsphilosophie*, edited by Norbert Fischer, 207–23. Hamburg: Felix Meiner Verlag, 2004.

Eckstein, Walter. 'The Religious Element in Spinoza's Philosophy'. *The Journal of Religion* 23, no. 3 (1943): 153–63.

Edelmann, Johann Christian. *Die Göttlichkeit der Vernunft, in einer kurtzen Anweisung zu weiterer Untersuchung der ältesten und vornehmsten Bedeutung des Wortes ΛΟΓΟΣ*. Berleburg, 1742.

Edelmann, Johann Christian. *Abgenöthigtes jedoch Andern nicht wieder aufgenöthigtes Glaubens-Bekentniß*. S.l., 1746.

England, Frederick E. *Kant's Conception of God. A Critical Exposition of Its Metaphysical Development Together with a Translation of the* Nova Dilucidatio. New York: Humanities Press, 1968.
Erdozain, Dominic. 'A Heavenly Poise: Radical Religion and the Making of the Enlightenment'. *Intellectual History Review* 27, no. 1 (2017): 71–96.
Firestone, Chris L. *Kant and Theology at the Boundaries of Reason*. Farnham: Ashgate, 2009.
Firestone, Chris L., and Nathan Jacobs. *In Defense of Kant's Religion*. Bloomington: Indiana University Press, 2008.
Firestone, Chris L., and Stephen R. Palmquist. 'Editors' Introduction'. In *Kant and the New Philosophy of Religion*, edited by Chris L. Firestone and Stephen R. Palmquist, 1–39. Bloomington: Indiana University Press, 2006.
Fischer, Norbert. 'Kants Idee *est Deus in nobis* und ihr Verhältnis zu Meister Eckhart. Zur Beziehung von Gott und Mensch in Kants kritischer Philosophie und bei Eckhart'. In *Meister Eckhart als Denker*, edited by Wolfgang Erb and Norbert Fischer, 367–406. Stuttgart: Kohlhammer, 2017.
Flew, Antony. 'The Presumption of Atheism'. *Canadian Journal of Philosophy* 2, no. 1 (1972): 29–46.
Flikschuh, Katrin. 'Gottesdienst und Afterdienst: die Kirche als öffentliche Institution?'. In *Immanuel Kant: Die Religion innerhalb der Grenzen der bloßen Vernunft*, edited by Otfried Höffe, 193–209. Berlin: Akademie Verlag, 2011.
Förster, Eckart. *Kant's Final Synthesis. An Essay on the* Opus postumum. Cambridge MA: Harvard University Press, 2000.
Förster, Eckart. *The Twenty-Five Years of Philosophy. A Systematic Reconstruction*. Translated by Brady Bowman. Cambridge MA: Harvard University Press, 2012.
Fraenkel, Carlos. *Philosophical Religions from Plato to Spinoza. Reason, Religion, and Autonomy*. Cambridge: Cambridge University Press, 2012.
Freudenthal, Jacob. 'On the History of Spinozism'. *The Jewish Quarterly Review* 8, no. 1 (1895): 17–70.
Fugate, Courtney. 'The Highest Good and Kant's Proof(s) of God's Existence'. *History of Philosophy Quarterly* 31, no. 2 (2014): 137–58.
Grunwald, Max. *Spinoza in Deutschland. Gekrönte Preisschrift*. Berlin: Verlag von S. Calvary, 1897.
Guyer, Paul. 'Absolute Idealism and the Rejection of Kantian Dualism'. In *The Cambridge Companion to German Idealism*, edited by Karl Ameriks, 37–56. New York: Cambridge University Press, 2000.
Hahmann, Andree. 'Pflichtgemäß, aber töricht! Kant über Spinozas Leugnung der Vorsehung'. In *Das Leben der Vernunft. Beiträge zur Philosophie Kants*, edited by Dieter Hüning, Stefan Klingner, and Carsten Ork, 477–505. Berlin: De Gruyter, 2013.
Hall, Bryan W. *The Post-Critical Kant. Understanding the Critical Philosophy through the* Opus postumum. New York: Routledge, 2015.

Hampshire, Stuart. 'Spinoza's Theory of Human Freedom'. *The Monist* 55, no. 4 (1971): 554–66.

Hare, John E. *The Moral Gap. Kantian Ethics, Human Limits, and God's Assistance.* Oxford: Clarendon Press, 1996.

Hare, John E. 'Kant on the Rational Instability of Atheism'. In *Kant and the New Philosophy of Religion*, edited by Chris L. Firestone and Stephen R. Palmquist, 62–78. Bloomington: Indiana University Press, 2006.

Heine, Heinrich. *On the History of Religion and Philosophy in Germany. And Other Writings.* Edited by Terry Pinkard, translated by Howard Pollack-Milgate. Cambridge: Cambridge University Press, 2007.

Heman, Friedrich. 'Kant und Spinoza'. *Kant-Studien* 5, no. 1–3 (1901): 273–339.

Hirsi Ali, Ayaan. *Nomad. From Islam to America: A Personal Journey through the Clash of Civilizations.* New York: Free Press, 2010.

Hoffer, Noam. 'The Relation between God and the World in the Pre-Critical Kant: Was Kant a Spinozist?'. *Kantian Review* 21, no. 2 (2016): 185–210.

Howard, Stephen. 'The Transition within the Transition: The *Übergang* from the *Selbstsetzungslehre* to the Ether Proofs in Kant's *Opus postumum*'. *Kant-Studien* 110, no. 4 (2019): 595–617.

Höffe, Otfried. 'Holy Scriptures within the Boundaries of Mere Reason: Kant's Reflections'. In *Kant's* Religion within the Boundaries of Mere Reason. *A Critical Guide*, edited by Gordon E. Michalson, 10–30. Cambridge: Cambridge University Press, 2014.

Höffe, Otfried. 'Philosophische Grundsätze der Schriftauslegung: Ein Blick in den *Streit der Fakultäten*'. In *Immanuel Kant. Die Religion innerhalb der Grenzen der bloßen Vernunft*, edited by Otfried Höffe, 231–48. Berlin: Akademie Verlag, 2011.

Hunter, Graeme. *Radical Protestantism in Spinoza's Thought.* London: Routledge, 2017.

Hunter, Ian. *Rival Enlightenments. Civil and Metaphysical Philosophy in Early Modern Germany.* Cambridge: Cambridge University Press, 2003.

Hunter, Ian. 'Kant's *Religion* and Prussian Religious Policy'. *Modern Intellectual History* 2, no. 1 (2005): 1–27.

Hunter, Ian. 'Secularization: The Birth of a Modern Combat Concept'. *Modern Intellectual History* 12, no. 1 (2014): 1–32.

Insole, Christopher. 'Intellectualism, Relational Properties and the Divine Mind in Kant's Pre-Critical Philosophy'. *Kantian Review* 16, no. 3 (2011): 399–427.

Insole, Christopher. 'Kant's Transcendental Idealism and Newton's Divine Sensorium'. *Journal of the History of Ideas* 72, no. 3 (2011): 413–36.

Insole, Christopher. *Kant and the Creation of Freedom.* Oxford: Oxford University Press, 2013.

Insole, Christopher. *The Intolerable God: Kant's Theological Journey.* Grand Rapids: Eerdmans, 2016.

Insole, Christopher. *Kant and the Divine. From Contemplation to the Moral Law.* New York: Oxford University Press, 2020.

Israel, Jonathan I. *Locke, Spinoza and the Philosophical Debate Concerning Toleration in the Early Enlightenment (c. 1670–c. 1750)*. Amsterdam: Koninklijke Nederlandse Akademie van Wetenschappen, 1999.

Israel, Jonathan I. *Radical Enlightenment. Philosophy and the Making of Modernity 1650–1750*. New York: Oxford University Press, 2001.

Israel, Jonathan I. *Enlightenment Contested. Philosophy, Modernity, and the Emancipation of Man 1670–1752*. New York: Oxford University Press, 2006.

Israel, Jonathan I. *A Revolution of the Mind. Radical Enlightenment and the Intellectual Origins of Modern Democracy*. Princeton: Princeton University Press, 2010.

Israel, Jonathan I. *Democratic Enlightenment: Philosophy, Revolution, and Human Rights*. Oxford: Oxford University Press, 2011.

Israel, Jonathan I. 'The Philosophical Context of Hermann Samuel Reimarus' Radical Bible Criticism'. In *Between Philology and Radical Enlightenment: Hermann Samuel Reimarus (1694–1768)*, edited by Martin Mulsow, 183–200. Leiden: Brill, 2011.

Israel, Jonathan I. 'Spinoza and the Religious Radical Enlightenment'. In *The Intellectual Consequences of Religious Heterodoxy, 1600–1750*, edited by Sarah Mortimer and John Robertson, 181–203. Leiden: Brill, 2012.

Israel, Jonathan I. '"Radical Enlightenment" – Peripheral, Substantial, or the Main Face of the Trans-Atlantic Enlightenment (1650–1850)'. *Diametros* 40 (2014): 73–98.

Israel, Jonathan I. 'Leo Strauss and the Radical Enlightenment'. In *Reading between the Lines – Leo Strauss and the History of Early Modern Philosophy*, edited by Winfried Schröder, 9–28. Berlin: De Gruyter, 2015.

Israel, Jonathan I. 'Spinoza and Early Modern Theology'. In *The Oxford Handbook of Early Modern Theology, 1600–1800*, edited by Ulrich L. Lehner, Richard A. Muller, Anthony G. Roeber, 577–93. New York: Oxford University Press, 2016.

Jacob, Margaret C. *The Radical Enlightenment: Pantheists, Freemasons and Republicans*. London: George Allen and Unwin, 1981.

Jacob, Margaret C. 'How Radical Was the Enlightenment? What Do We Mean by Radical?'. *Diametros* 40 (2014): 99–114.

Jacob, Margaret C. *The Secular Enlightenment*. Princeton: Princeton University Press, 2019.

Janowski, Zbigniew. *Cartesian Theodicy. Descartes' Quest for Certitude*. Dordrecht: Kluwer, 2000.

John Paul II, 'Address of His Holiness John Paul II at the Conclusion of the International Colloquium on "Enlightenment Today"', https://www.vatican.va/content/john-paul-ii/en/speeches/1996/august/documents/hf_jp-ii_spe_19960810_illuminismo-oggi.html [Accessed 19 November 2021].

Johnson, Gregory R. 'The Tree of Melancholy. Kant on Philosophy and Enthusiasm'. In *Kant and the New Philosophy of Religion*, edited by Chris L. Firestone and Stephen R. Palmquist, 43–61. Bloomington: Indiana University Press, 2006.

Klueting, Harm. 'The Catholic Enlightenment in Austria or the Habsburg Lands'. In *A Companion to the Catholic Enlightenment in Europe*, edited by Ulrich Lehner and Michael Printy, 127–64. Leiden: Brill, 2010.

Kołakowski, Leszek. 'The Two Eyes of Spinoza'. In *The Two Eyes of Spinoza and Other Essays on Philosophers*, edited by Zbigniew Janowski, translated by Agnieszka Kołakowska et al., 1–15. South Bend: St. Augustine's Press, 2004.

Kołakowski, Leszek. *Świadomość religijna i więź kościelna: studia nad chrześcijaństwem bezwyznaniowym XVII wieku*. Warszawa: Wydawnictwo Naukowe PWN, 2009.

Kors, Alan Charles. *Epicureans and Atheists in France, 1650–1729*. Cambridge: Cambridge University Press, 2016.

Kozyra, Wojciech. 'The Gospel of the New Principle: The Marcionian Leitmotif in Kant's Religious Thought in the Context of Thomas Morgan and the German Enlightenment'. In *Between Secularization and Reform: Religion in the Enlightenment*, edited by Anna Tomaszewska (manuscript).

Krakauer, Moses. *Zur Geschichte des Spinozismus in Deutschland während der ersten Hälfte des achtzehnten Jahrhunderts*. Breslau: S. Schottlaender, 1881.

Krop, Henri. 'The Secularism of Spinoza and His Circle'. In *The Sources of Secularism: Enlightenment and Beyond*, edited by Anna Tomaszewska and Hasse Hämäläinen, 73–99. Cham: Palgrave Macmillan, 2017.

Krop, Henri, 'The *Philosophia S. Scripturae Interpres* between Humanist Scholarship and Cartesian Science: Lodewijk Meijer and the Emancipatory Power of Philology'. In *The Dutch Legacy: Radical Thinkers of the 17th Century and the Enlightenment*, edited by Sonja Lavaert and Winfried Schröder, 90–120. Leiden: Brill, 2017.

Kuehn, Manfred. 'Kant's Jesus'. In *Kant's Religion within the Boundaries of Mere Reason. A Critical Guide*, edited by Gordon E. Michalson, 156–74. Cambridge: Cambridge University Press, 2014.

Kupś, Tomasz. *Opus postumum Immanuela Kanta*. Toruń: Wydawnictwo Naukowe Uniwersytetu Mikołaja Kopernika, 2016.

La Vopa, Anthony J. 'The Philosopher and the *Schwärmer*: On the Career of a German Epithet from Luther to Kant'. In *Enthusiasm and Enlightenment in Europe, 1650–1850*, edited by Lawrence E. Klein and Anthony J. La Vopa, 5–116. San Marino, CA: Huntington Library, 1998.

Leask, Ian. 'Toland, Spinoza, and the Naturalisation of Scripture'. In *Ireland and the Reception of the Bible: Social and Cultural Studies*, edited by Brad Anderson and Jonathan Kearney, 227–42. London: Bloomsbury, 2018.

Lehner, Ulrich L. *The Catholic Enlightenment. The Forgotten History of a Global Movement*. New York: Oxford University Press, 2016.

Leibniz, Gottfried W. *Discourse on Metaphysics and* The Monadology. 1686, 1714. Translated by George R. Montgomery. New York: Dover Publications, Inc., 2005.

Lestition, Steven. 'Kant and the End of the Enlightenment in Prussia'. *Journal of Modern History* 65 (1993): 57–112.

Levene, Nancy. 'Spinoza the Radical'. In *Reassessing the Radical Enlightenment*, edited by Steffen Ducheyne, 107–26. London: Routledge, 2017.

Lord, Beth. *Kant and Spinozism. Transcendental Idealism and Immanence from Jacobi to Deleuze*. Basingstoke: Palgrave Macmillan, 2011.

Lucci, Diego. *John Locke's Christianity*. Cambridge: Cambridge University Press, 2021.

Maclure, Jocelyn, Charles Taylor. *Secularism and Freedom of Conscience*. Cambridge, MA: Harvard University Press, 2011.

Malebranche, Nicolas. 'The Search after Truth'. 1674. Translated and edited by Thomas M. Lennon and Paul J. Olscamp. In *The Search after Truth with Elucidations of the Search after Truth*, xxxi–529. Cambridge: Cambridge University Press, 1997.

Massimi, Michela. 'Kant on the Ideality of Space and the Argument from Spinozism'. In *Kant's Critique of Pure Reason*, edited by James R. O'Shea, 64–82. New York: Cambridge University Press, 2017.

Mates, Benson. *The Philosophy of Leibniz. Metaphysics and Language*. New York: Oxford University Press, 1986.

Mathieu, Vittorio. *La filosofia trascendentale e l'Opus postumum di Kant*. Torino: Edizioni di 'Filosofia', 1958.

Mathieu, Vittorio. *L'Opus postumum di Kant*. Napoli: Bibliopolis, 1991.

McLear, Colin. 'On the Transcendental Freedom of the Intellect'. *Ergo: An Open Access Journal of Philosophy* 7, no. 2 (2020): 35–104.

Meinsma, Koenraad O. *Spinoza und sein Kreis: historisch-kritische Studien über holländische Freigeister*. Translated by Lisa Schneider. (The edition includes: Constantin Brunner, *Spinoza gegen Kant und die Sache der geistigen Wahrheit*.) Berlin: Karl Schnabel Verlag, 1909.

Melamed, Yitzhak. 'Spinoza's Deification of Existence'. In *Oxford Studies in Early Modern Philosophy*, edited by Daniel Garber and Donald Rutherford, 75–104. Oxford: Oxford University Press, 2013.

Mendelssohn, Moses. 'Über die Frage: was heißt aufklären?'. In *Was ist Aufklärung? Thesen und Definitionen*, edited by Erhard Bahr, 3–8. Stuttgart: Philipp Reclam, 1996.

Michalson, Gordon E. *Kant and the Problem of God*. Oxford: Blackwell, 1999.

Michalson, Gordon E. 'The Ambiguity of Kant's Concept of the Visible Church'. *Diametros* 17, no. 65 (2020): 77–94.

Miller, Eddis N. *Kant's Religion within the Boundaries of Mere Reason*. London: Bloomsbury, 2015.

Moors, Martin. 'Die Bestimmungsgestalt von Kants Gottesidee und Gemeinschaftsprinzip'. In *Proceedings of the Sixth International Kant Congress*, edited by Gerhard Funke and Thomas Seebohm, 49–66. Lanham: Center for Advanced Research in Phenomenology and University Press of America, 1989.

Mosayebi, Reza. 'Die "Definition" der Vernunftreligion'. In *Immanuel Kant: Die Religion innerhalb der Grenzen der bloßen Vernunft*, edited by Otfried Höffe, 249–70. Berlin: Akademie Verlag, 2011.

Mrugalski, Damian. *Logos. Filozoficzne i teologiczne źródła idei wczesnochrześcijańskiej*. Kraków: Wydawnictwo WAM, 2006.

Mulsow, Martin. *Moderne aus dem Untergrund. Radikale Frühaufklärung in Deutschland 1680–1720*. Hamburg: Felix Meiner Verlag, 2002.

Muthu, Sankar. *Enlightenment against Empire*. Princeton: Princeton University Press, 2003.

Nadler, Steven. *Spinoza. A Life*. New York: Cambridge University Press, 1999.

Nadler, Steven. *A Book Forged in Hell: Spinoza's Scandalous Treatise and the Birth of the Secular Age*. Princeton: Princeton University Press, 2011.

O'Neill, Onora. 'Kant on Reason and Religion'. In *Tanner Lectures on Human Values* 18, edited by Grethe B. Peterson, 267–308. Utah: Utah University Press, 1997.

Otto, Rüdiger. 'Johann Christian Edelmann's Criticism of the Bible and Its Relation to Spinoza'. In *Disguised and Overt Spinozism around 1700*, edited by Wiep van Bunge and Wim Klever, 171–88. Leiden: Brill, 1996.

Paganini, Gianni. 'The Way of Clandestinity. Radical Cartesianism and Deism in Robert Challe (1659–1721)'. In *Between Secularization and Reform. Religion in the Enlightenment*, edited by Anna Tomaszewska (manuscript).

Paganini, Gianni. 'Enlightenment before the Enlightenment: Clandestine Philosophy'. *Ethica e politica / Ethics and Politics* 20, no. 3 (2018): 183–200.

Paganini, Gianni, Margaret C. Jacob, and John Christian Laursen (eds.). *Clandestine Philosophy. New Studies on Subversive Manuscripts in Early Modern Europe, 1620–1823*. Toronto, Los Angeles: University of Toronto Press, 2020.

Palmquist, Stephen R. 'Does Kant Reduce Religion to Morality?'. *Kant-Studien* 83, no. 2 (1992): 129–48.

Palmquist, Stephen R. *Kant's Critical Religion. Volume Two of Kant's System of Perspectives*. Aldershot: Ashgate, 2000.

Palmquist, Stephen R. 'Kant's Moral Panentheism'. *Philosophia* 36 (2008): 17–28.

Palmquist, Stephen R. 'Kant's Prudential Theory of Religion: The Necessity of Historical Faith for Moral Empowerment', *Con-Textos Kantianos* 1 (2015): 57–76.

Palmquist, Stephen R. *Comprehensive Commentary on Kant's* Religion within the Bounds of Bare Reason. Chichester: John Wiley & Sons, 2016.

Palmquist, Stephen R. *Kant and Mysticism. Critique as the Experience of Baring All in Reason's Light*. Lanham: Lexington Books, 2019.

Palmquist, Stephen R. 'How Political Is the Kantian Church?'. *Diametros* 17, no. 65 (2020): 95–113.

Palmquist, Stephen R. 'Does Quakerism Qualify as Kantian Enlightened Religion?'. In *Between Secularization and Reform: Religion in the Enlightenment*, edited by Anna Tomaszewska (manuscript).

Pasternack, Lawrence R. *Kant on* Religion within the Boundaries of Mere Reason. London: Routledge, 2014.

Pasternack, Lawrence R. 'Kant's "Appraisal" of Christianity: Biblical Interpretation and the Pure Rational System of Religion'. *Journal of the History of Philosophy* 53, no. 3 (2015): 485–506.

Pasternack, Lawrence R. 'Restoring Kant's Conception of the Highest Good'. *Journal of the History of Philosophy* 55, no. 3 (2017): 435–68.

Pasternack, Lawrence. 'The Ethical Community in Kant's Pure Rational System of Religion: Comments on Rossi's *The Ethical Commonwealth in History*'. *Philosophia* 49, no. 5 (2021): 1–16.

Reath, Andrews. 'Two Conceptions of the Highest Good'. *Journal of the History of Philosophy* 26, no. 4 (1988): 593–619.

Reimmann, Iac. Frid. *Historia universalis atheismi et atheorum falso & merito suspectorum apud jvdæos, ethnicos, christianos, mvhamedanos*. Hildesiæ: Apud Lvdolphvm Schroeder, 1725.

Rescher, Nicholas. 'Noumenal Causality'. In *Proceedings of the Third International Kant Congress*, edited by Lewis White Beck, 462–70. Dordrecht: D. Reidel Publishing Co., 1972.

Riem, Andreas. *Ueber Aufklärung. Ob sie dem Staate – der Religion – oder überhaupt gefährlich sey, und seyn könne? Erstes Fragment*. Berlin: Königliche Preußische Akademische Kunst- und Buchhandlung, 1788.

Rossi, Philip J. *The Ethical Commonwealth in History. Peace-Making as the Moral Vocation of Humanity*. Cambridge: Cambridge University Press, 2019.

Sauter, Michael J. 'Preaching, a Ponytail, and an Enthusiast: Rethinking the Public Sphere's Subversiveness in Eighteenth-Century Prussia'. *Central European History* 37, no. 4 (2004): 544–67.

Sauter, Michael J. *Visions of the Enlightenment. The Edict on Religion of 1788 and the Politics of the Public Sphere in Eighteenth-Century Prussia*. Leiden: Brill, 2009.

Schmidt, James 'German Enlightenment', https://open.bu.edu/ds2/stream/?#/documents/28872/page/1 [Accessed 15 October 2020].

Schönfeld, Martin. *The Philosophy of the Young Kant*. Oxford: Oxford University Press, 2000.

Schröder, Winfried. '*Spinozam tota armenta in Belgio sequi ducem*: The Reception of the Early Dutch Spinozists in Germany'. In *Disguised and Overt Spinozism around 1700*, edited by Wiep van Bunge and Wim Klever, 157–69. Leiden: Brill, 1996.

Schröder, Winfried. *Athen und Jerusalem. Die philosophische Kritik am Christentum in Antike und Neuzeit*. Stuttgart-Bad Cannstatt: Frommann-Holzboog, 2011.

Schröder, Winfried. *Ursprünge des Atheismus: Untersuchungen zur Metaphysik- und Religionskritik des 17. und 18. Jahrhunderts*. Zweite Auflage. Stuttgart-Bad Cannstatt: Frommann-Holzboog, 2012.

Schröder, Winfried. 'The Charge of Religious Imposture in Late Anti-Christian Authors and Their Early Modern Readers'. *Intellectual History Review* 28, no. 1 (2018): 23–34.

Smith, Graeme. 'Talking to Ourselves: An Investigation into the Christian Ethics Inherent in Secularism'. In *The Sources of Secularism. Enlightenment and Beyond*, edited by Anna Tomaszewska and Hasse Hämäläinen, 229–44. Cham: Palgrave Macmillan, 2017.

Sorkin, David. *The Religious Enlightenment: Protestants, Jews, and Catholics from London to Vienna*. Princeton: Princeton University Press, 2008.

Sparn, Walter. '*Formalis Atheus?* Die Krise der protestantischen Orthodoxie, gespiegelt in ihrer Auseinandersetzung mit Spinoza'. In *Spinoza in der Frühzeit seiner Religiösen Wirkung*, edited by Karlfried Gründer and Wilhelm Schmidt-Biggemann, 27–63. Heidelberg: L. Schneider Verlag, 1984.

Spinoza, Benedictus de. 'Theological-Political Treatise'. 1670. In *Complete Works*, with translations by Samuel Shirley, edited, with introduction and notes, by Michael L. Morgan, 383–583. Indianapolis: Hackett Publishing Co., 2002.

Spinoza, Benedictus de. 'Treatise on the Emendation of the Intellect'. 1677. In *Complete Works*, with translations by Samuel Shirley, edited, with introduction and notes, by Michael L. Morgan, 1–30. Indianapolis: Hackett Publishing Co., 2002.

Spinoza, Benedictus de. 'Ethics'. 1677. In *Complete Works*, with translations by Samuel Shirley, edited, with introduction and notes, by Michael L. Morgan, 213–382. Indianapolis: Hackett Publishing Co., 2002.

Spinoza, Benedictus de. 'Short Treatise on God, Man and His Well-Being'. 1780s. In *Complete Works*, with translations by Samuel Shirley, edited, with introduction and notes, by Michael L. Morgan, 31–107. Indianapolis: Hackett Publishing Co., 2002.

Spinoza, Benedictus de. 'The Letters'. In *Complete Works*, with translations by Samuel Shirley, edited, with introduction and notes, by Michael L. Morgan, 755–959. Indianapolis: Hackett Publishing Co., 2002.

Stang, Nicholas. 'Kant's Possibility Proof'. *History of Philosophy Quarterly* 27, no. 3 (2010): 275–99.

Stevenson, Leslie. 'Kant on Grace'. In *Kant's* Religion within the Boundaries of Mere Reason. *A Critical Guide*, edited by Gordon E. Michalson, 118–36. Cambridge: Cambridge University Press, 2014.

Stevenson, Leslie. 'Opinion, Belief or Faith, and Knowledge'. In *Inspirations from Kant: Essays*, 77–94. Oxford: Oxford University Press, 2011.

Stevenson, Leslie. 'Kant's Approach to Religion Compared with Quakerism'. In *Kant and the New Philosophy of Religion*, edited by Chris L. Firestone and Stephen R. Palmquist, 210–29. Bloomington: Indiana University Press, 2006.

Stjernfelt, Frederik. '"Radical Enlightenment": Aspects of the History of a Term'. In *Reassessing the Radical Enlightenment*, edited by Steffen Ducheyne, 80–103. London: Routledge, 2017.

Strauss, Leo. *Spinoza's Critique of Religion*. 1930. Translated by Elsa M. Sinclair. New York: Schocken Books, 1982.

Strickland, Lloyd. *Leibniz's Monadology. A New Translation and Guide*. Edinburgh: Edinburgh University Press, 2014.

Tampio, Nicholas. 'Pluralism in the Ethical Community'. In *Kant's* Religion within the Boundaries of Mere Reason. *A Critical Guide*, edited by Gordon E. Michalson, 175–92. Cambridge: Cambridge University Press, 2014.

Taylor, Charles. *A Secular Age*. Cambridge MA: The Belknap Press of Harvard University Press, 2007.

Thiry, Paul-Henry, Baron d'Holbach. *The System of Nature.* 1770. Translated by H.D. Robinson. Vols. 1–2. Kitchener: Batoche Books, 2001.

Timm, Hermann. *Gott und die Freiheit. Studien zur Religionsphilosophie der Goethezeit.* Vol. 1: *Die Spinozarenaissance.* Frankfurt am Main: Vittorio Klostermann, 1974.

Toland, John. *Christianity Not Mysterious: Or, a Treatise Shewing, That There Is Nothing in the Gospel Contrary to Reason, Nor above It: and That No Christian Doctrine Can Be Properly Call'd a Mystery.* London: S. Buckley, 1696.

Tomasi, Gabriele. *La voce e lo sguardo: metafore e funzioni della coscienza nella dottrina Kantiana della virtù.* Pisa: Edizioni ETS, 1999.

Tomasi, Gabriele. 'God, the Highest Good, and the Rationality of Faith: Reflections on Kant's Moral Proof of the Existence of God'. In *The Highest Good in Kant's Philosophy*, edited by Thomas Höwing, 111–30. Berlin: De Gruyter, 2016.

Tomaszewska, Anna. 'Spinoza's God in Kant's Pre-Critical Writings: An Attempt at Localizing the "Threat"'. *Kant Studies Online* (2015): 65–102. Posted 1 September 2015. www.kantstudiesonline.net.

Tomaszewska, Anna. 'Bóg Spinozy w pismach przedkrytycznych Kanta'. In *Filozofia Oświecenia. Radykalizm – religia – kosmopolityzm*, edited by Justyna Miklaszewska and Anna Tomaszewska, 305–29. Kraków: Wydawnictwo Uniwersytetu Jagiellońskiego, 2015.

Tuschling, Burkhard. 'Transzendentaler Idealismus ist Spinozismus – Reflexionen von und über Kant und Spinoza'. In *Spinoza im Deutschland des achtzehnten Jahrhunderts*, edited by Eva Schürman, Norbert Waszek, and Frank Weinreich, 139–67. Stuttgart-Bad Cannstatt: Frommann-Holzboog, 2002.

Vaihinger, Hans. *The Philosophy of As If: A System of the Theoretical, Practical and Religious Fictions of Mankind.* 1911. Translated by Charles Kay Ogden. London: Routledge, 1965.

Van Bunge, Wiep. *Spinoza Past and Present. Essays on Spinoza, Spinozism, and Spinoza Scholarship.* Leiden: Brill, 2012.

Van Eekert, Geert. 'Freedom of Speech, Freedom of Self-Expression, and Kant's Public Use of Reason'. *Diametros* 54 (2017): 118–37.

Voysey, Charles (ed.). *Fragments from Reimarus Consisting in Brief Critical Remarks on the Object of Jesus and His Disciples as Seen in the New Testament.* London: Williams and Norgate, 1879.

Walker, Ralph C.S. 'The Primacy of Practical Reason'. In *The Palgrave Kant Handbook*, edited by Matthew C. Altman, 191–209. London: Palgrave Macmillan, 2017.

Walther, Manfred. *Spinoza in Deutschland. Von G.W. Leibniz bis zu Carl Schmidt. Philosophie – Wissenschaft – Ideologie.* Heidelberg: Universitätsverlag Winter, 2018.

Waxman, Wayne. *Kant's Model of the Mind. A New Interpretation of Transcendental Idealism.* Oxford: Oxford University Press, 1991.

Wimmer, Reiner. *Kants kritische Religionsphilosophie.* Berlin: De Gruyter, 1990.

Wood, Allen W. *Kant's Rational Theology.* Ithaca: Cornell University Press, 1978.

Wood, Allen W. 'Kant's Deism'. In *Kant's Philosophy of Religion Reconsidered*, edited by Philip J. Rossi and Michael J. Wreen, 1–21. Bloomington: Indiana University Press, 1991.

Wood, Allen W. 'General Introduction'. In Immanuel Kant, *Religion and Rational Theology*, translated and edited by Allen W. Wood and George Di Giovanni, xi–xxiv. New York: Cambridge University Press, 1996.

Wood, Allen W. 'Ethical Community, Church and Scripture'. In *Die Religion innerhalb der Grenzen der bloßen Vernunft*, edited by Otfried Höffe, 131–50. Berlin: Akademie Verlag, 2011.

Wood, Allen W. 'The Evil in Human Nature'. In *Kant's* Religion within the Boundaries of Mere Reason. A Critical Guide, edited by Gordon E. Michalson, 31–57. Cambridge: Cambridge University Press, 2014.

Wood, Allen W. *Kant and Religion*. New York: Cambridge University Press, 2020.

Yong, Peter. 'God, Totality and Possibility in Kant's Only Possible Argument'. *Kantian Review* 19, no. 1 (2014): 27–51.

Yovel, Yirmiyahu. *Kant and the Philosophy of History*. Princeton: Princeton University Press, 1980.

Yovel, Yirmiyahu. *Spinoza and Other Heretics. The Adventures of Immanence*. Princeton: Princeton University Press, 1989.

Yovel, Yirmiyahu. *Kant's Philosophical Revolution. A Short Guide to the* Critique of Pure Reason. Princeton: Princeton University Press, 2018.

Zammito, John. 'Herder, Kant, Spinoza und die Ursprünge des deutschen Idealismus'. In *Herder und die Philosophie des deutschen Idealismus*, edited by Marion Heinz, 107–44. Amsterdam: Rodopi, 1997.

Index

A
Abegg, Friedrich 146
acratic 85
action and cognition 4, 69, 83, 87
Adickes, Erich 146-9, 193 n. 10, 193 n. 13, 199
affects 70, 116-17
affirmative interpretation (reading) 169, 196
afterlife 124, 191 n. 5
Age of Lights 7, 10. *See also* Enlightenment
Age of Reason 12. *See also* Enlightenment
Allison, Henry E. 183 n. 67, 198-9
Ambrose 100
Amelius 111
Anselm 149
Anselmian 194 n. 14
  ontological argument 150
anthropocentric 73, 179 n. 30
anthropology 89, 160-2, 164
anti-Christian 90
antinomy 145
  of Pure Reason 20, 64
antiquity 8, 13
anti-Trinitarian 112
apostles 14, 103, 118
  Acts of 162
appearances 16, 42, 64, 73, 75, 84, 154
Aristotelian 61
Aristotle 15, 85, 152, 199
assent 48, 55-7, 76, 87, 98, 179 n. 28. *See also* taking something to be true
atheism 3, 11, 15-16, 21, 25, 45-8, 54-5, 60, 63-4, 68, 114, 147, 166, 172 n. 30, 177 n. 2
  presumption of 59
  sceptical 3, 60
atheist 15, 48, 50-1, 53-4, 57, 59, 63, 114
  dogmatic 49
  moral 45-7, 49-53, 57, 60, 67-8
  practical 47, 54
  righteous 20, 53, 123
  sceptical 57-9, 95, 180 n. 34
  systematic 46
  theoretical 47, 67
  virtuous 3, 166
Athenagoras 111
attribute (Spinoza's ontology) 70-1, 75, 77, 79, 181 n. 17
  of extension 35, 70, 79
  of thought 70, 79, 164
Augustine, St. 100, 144, 154, 193 n. 6, 193 n. 6, 195 n. 24, 200
Augustinian 106, 155
authoritarian 3, 18, 137
autonomy 5, 42, 96, 125-6, 128, 139-41, 153-4, 157, 163-4, 168. *See also* self-legislation
  argument from 150-3
  concept of (*also* idea of) 84, 151
  human 4, 43, 137, 139, 141, 168
  individual 138
  moral 42, 87, 126, 130, 137-8, 140, 168
  of practical reason 47, 49, 96, 125, 149-50, 152, 157, 163
  principle of 151
  of public sphere 137
  rational 4, 11, 126, 130, 164, 166-7, 169
  reason's 3, 96
  of the will 151-2

B
Bacon, Francis 19, 116
Bahrdt, Carl Friedrich 4, 10, 22, 89, 91-2, 97-8, 100, 114, 119, 165, 184 n. 6, 186 n. 24, 186 n. 27, 186 n. 32, 186 n. 34, 186 n. 39, 200
Balibar, Etienne 83, 183 n. 62, 200
Basile, Giovanni Pietro 158, 174 n. 49, 195 n. 32, 200
Bayle, Pierre 9-10, 19, 21, 34, 45-7, 54, 114, 123, 176 n. 20, 177 n. 4, 178 n. 10, 200

Bäck, Leo 110, 114, 188 n. 75, 189 n. 101,
    189 n. 105, 200
Beiser, Frederick C. 90, 176 n. 14,
    176 n. 22, 180 n. 41, 185 n. 12, 200
belief 56, 73
    and action 47
    or faith 55–6, 58, 67
    freedom of 86
    in God 20, 49, 51, 53, 55, 57–8, 95–6,
        132, 140, 147–8, 155
    in miracles 80, 120, 124
    religious 1–5, 80, 116–17, 121, 168
    in revelation 19
    theistic 58, 148, 179 n. 33
    theoretical 47, 56, 179 n. 28
Berkeley, George 25, 195 n. 30
Bible 103, 106–7, 109, 114, 117
    interpretation of 91
Bildung 130
Boehm, Omri 3, 20, 26, 35–6, 38–9,
    174 n. 48, 175 n. 2, 176 n. 13,
    176 n. 15, 176 n. 21, 177 n. 26, 200
bondage 71
Brewer, Kimberly 43, 177 n. 34, 200
Bril, Jacob 114
Bunch, Aaron 191 n. 5, 200
Burson, Jeffrey D. 192 n. 22, 200
Byrne, Peter 119, 190 n. 36, 200

C
Casaubon, Isaac 111
categorical imperative 65, 148–51, 159,
    161, 163–4
Catholic 89, 90, 107
    enlighteners 15
    Enlightenment 173 n. 36
    religion 117 (*see also religio catholica*)
    theologians 179 n. 33
causa sui 38, 78, 112, 176 n. 24
causality 37, 42, 84, 154–6
    divine 153, 155
    double 37, 40, 42–3, 166
    empirical 154
    noumenal 42
    principle of 38, 43, 82
change of heart 106–7, 126–7
charity 8, 22, 83, 98, 117, 186 n. 38
Chignell, Andrew 26, 29, 35, 55–6, 58,
    175 n. 2, 175 n. 11, 176 n. 12,
    176 n. 13, 179 n. 27, 179 n. 28,
    179 n. 31, 200–1
choice 106
    capacity of 152
    foundational 106
    free 195 n. 24
    freedom of 77
    heteronomy of 151
    power of 105
Christ 101–2, 104, 107, 109, 111, 113,
    117–18, 152
Christian 2, 44, 89, 90, 101, 105–6, 114,
    118, 167
    authors 111, 152
    church 124
    dissenters 16
    dogma 22, 101, 104, 109, 177 n. 36
    faith 104, 123–4
    heterodoxy 63
    metaphysics 8
    Platonism 110
    revelation 22, 109
    Scriptures 83
    theology 97, 100
    tradition 110, 155
    true 97–8, 111
Christianity 1, 11–13, 18, 89, 92, 101, 104,
    107–8, 118–19, 124–5, 135–6, 167,
    185 n. 13, 190 n. 115
    critique of 118
    history of 124
    institutional 91, 124
    rationalization of 190 n. 115
    Western 124
church 4, 17, 98, 104, 114, 123–39, 167–8,
    172 n. 20, 191 n. 6
    Christian 124
    critique of 123
    enlightened 4, 123, 125
    invisible 129
    officials 19, 112
    reformed 114
    and state 12, 46, 90, 128, 136–7
    true 133–5
    visible 12, 120, 125, 128, 134–5
Church Fathers 100, 111
Cicero 94, 185 n. 21
civil society 87
clandestine 8, 15, 19, 91

Clement of Alexandria 111
Collegians 22
commercium 38, 40
community 46, 126, 128–30, 134–5, 137, 159, 167
    ethical 4, 5, 12, 21, 43–4, 98, 120, 125–33, 136–40, 149, 159, 167–8, 191 n. 8, 192 n. 24
    in the form of a church 127–8
    political 86, 125, 137
compatibilist (account of freedom) 41, 79, 155, 166
complete concept 28, 175 n. 6
conatus 82
concentric circles (metaphor) 4, 91–2, 94, 100
concurrence 154–6, 194 n. 23
concurrentist 156
concursus 155–6
conservationist 156
conviction (*Überzeugung*) 47–8, 55, 57
    inner 103
Cortina, Adela 146, 157, 193 n. 9, 201
counterfeit service 124, 134
Counter-Reformation (Protestant) 90
creation (doctrine) 3, 34, 37, 40, 42–4, 166
critical thinking 2, 8, 68, 167
criticism 14, 15, 25, 48
    biblical 113
    political 8, 14
    religious 7, 13–15, 172 n. 28
    of religious institutions 168
critique 25, 81, 165–6
    of Christianity 118
    of church 123
    of dogmatic metaphysics 16, 164, 180 n. 40
    of Enlightenment 2
    of enthusiasm 62–3
    of reason 2, 21, 62, 80, 93
    of religion 8, 13, 14
    of revealed religion 1, 14–16, 90–1, 118–19, 124, 165
    of revelation 4, 13, 16, 101–2, 115, 167
    of Spinoza 45, 63
Curbachius, Adrianus (Adriaan Koerbagh) 15. *See also* Koerbagh brothers
Curley, Edwin 69, 181 n. 9, 187 n. 51, 188 n. 67, 201
Czelinski-Uesbeck, Michael 46, 177 n. 3, 178 n. 8, 178 n. 10, 201

D
Davidovich, Adina 93
De Flaviis, Giuseppe 162–3, 174 n. 50, 193 n. 2, 196 n. 42, 201
deism 15, 16, 91–2, 95
deist(s) 91–2, 114, 153, 173 n. 36
    God 11, 156–7
Deleuze, Gilles 24, 182 n. 25, 201
Della Rocca, Michael 33, 77, 176 n. 16, 182 n. 40, 183 n. 60, 201
Demiray, Mehmet R. 172 n. 20, 191 n. 6, 201
democracy 1, 67
Denis, Lara 51–2, 178 n. 16, 201
Descartes, René 19, 25, 69, 70, 72, 77–8, 149, 181 n. 10, 182 n. 41, 189 n. 96, 194 n. 16, 195 n. 30, 201
design (argument) 34
despotism 18
    spiritual 18, 165
determinism 21, 35, 40
    theological 43, 177 n. 34
Deus sive Natura. See God or Nature
Diagoras 47
DiCenso, James J. 18, 137–8, 173 n. 41, 180 n. 40, 192 n. 28, 201
Diderot, Denis 9, 87
Dilthey, Wilhelm 183 n. 1, 185 n. 17, 201
disenchantment 9
Divine Law 117, 149, 167
divine 37, 39, 65, 82, 96
    assistance 154–5
    becoming 151–2. *See also theosis*
    causality. *See* causality
    commands 94, 119, 137, 145, 150–1, 185 n. 20
    concurrence (*also concursus, concourse*) 155–6, 163, 194 n. 23
    creation 40, 42, 166
    determinations (*also* properties) 38, 156, 160
    essence 82
    existence (*also* being) 20, 33, 38, 58–9, 64, 67, 72, 79, 82, 95, 97, 108, 145, 148–9, 157, 159

freedom. *See* freedom
grace (*also* succour). *See* grace
grounding 3, 43
ideas 39
justice. *See* justice
knowledge (*also* cognition) 73–4
legislation 43–4, 96, 129, 135, 137–41, 149, 151–5, 167
light 153
mind 39–41, 65, 71, 73, 110, 118, 153, 163–4
nature 66, 108
origin of Scripture(s) 102–3, 116
person(s) 112
perspective (*also* point of view) 75, 164
presence 65
providence 8, 19, 156
reason 111, 113
revelation. *See* revelation
self-conception 110
sensorium 43
sovereign 130, 138
state 140, 167
supplement 139
thought 110
transcendence 145
understanding (*also* intellect) 40–2
will 17, 41–2, 84, 105–6, 153–5, 163, 188 n. 60
wisdom. *See* wisdom
divine, the 4, 16, 17, 65–6, 83, 103, 110, 112–13, 138, 144, 150–1, 156, 159, 167–8, 179 n. 30. *See also* God
in our reason 66
rationalization of 146
Dörflinger, Bernd 50, 178 n. 14, 201
Dryden, John 92
duty 49, 50, 53, 104, 136, 144, 146, 150, 159, 161
to abandon ethical state of nature 129
law of 158
to overcome propensity to evil 162
to perfect ourselves morally 108
to promote the highest good 131, 138
universal human 113

E
Eckstein, Walter 181 n. 1, 201
Edelmann, Johann Christian 4, 22, 91, 102, 109–14, 119, 135, 157, 165, 167, 173 n. 38, 184 n. 6, 188 n. 76, 188 n. 77, 189 n. 88, 189 n. 95, 189 n. 96, 189 n. 98, 196 n. 1, 201
Egyptians 112
Eliade, Mircea 147
embryo metaphor 135
empiricism 8
England, Frederick E. 176 n. 22, 202
enlightened values 7, 10, 15, 133, 138
enlightenment (process) 4, 55, 63, 121, 126, 130–2, 135, 137, 167–8, 180 n. 39
Enlightenment 1, 2, 4, 7, 9–13, 63, 90, 133, 165, 168, 184 n. 2
Catholic. *See* Catholic
German 19, 180 n. 39
moderate 1–3, 7, 9–13, 16
radical 1, 3, 7–10, 13, 15, 16, 18, 19, 46, 51, 64–4, 67, 87–8, 123, 165, 167
religious 1, 2, 7, 132–3, 167–8, 171 n. 1
secular 1, 7, 171 n. 1
ens
  rationis 144, 160, 164
  realissimum 109
  summum 153, 159–60. *See also* God
enthusiasm 3, 25, 46, 60–6, 66, 76, 80, 134, 180 n. 35. *See also* Schwärmerei
mystical 124
philosophical 61
Epicurus 13, 14, 47
equality 8, 9, 67, 135
racial 1, 8, 171 n. 14
Erdozain, Dominic 173 n. 34, 202
essences (possibilities) 3, 37, 39, 40
ether 143, 158–9
Ezra 14

F
fact of reason 85, 152, 164, 194 n. 14
faith 1, 10, 12, 16, 17, 22, 25, 45, 47–50, 53–6, 58–60, 67–8, 73, 83, 94–5, 97–8, 100–3, 115, 123, 135, 140, 166, 171 n. 1. *See also* belief
assertoric 95
Christian 104, 123–4

ecclesiastical 18, 94, 120, 124–5, 133, 135, 139
historical 18, 92–3, 99, 103, 124, 134, 165
and knowledge 17, 55, 71–2
mercenary 17, 165
in miracles 120
moral 3, 17, 18, 45, 56, 59, 98, 101, 104, 108, 112, 120–1, 124, 135, 139–40, 165, 167, 169
mysteries of 124
rational 17, 22, 44, 76, 101, 115, 120–1, 179 n. 32
rationalization of 90
and reason 1, 2, 9, 10, 55, 94, 111, 118, 169
religious 2, 9, 10, 12, 13, 17, 18, 22, 47, 49, 55, 93–4, 96, 119, 125, 173 n. 39
superstitious 72, 98
universal 83, 135, 186 n. 38
fanaticism 61, 63–4, 76
fatalism 25, 54, 68
feeling
  moral (towards the moral law) 64–5, 105
  of the sublime 64–5
Ficino, Marsilio 111
fideism 55, 68
fiery body 30–1
final causes 74
finitude 68, 73, 81, 157, 162–3, 166
Firestone, Christopher L. 76, 93, 99, 104, 110, 119, 169, 173 n. 39, 178 n. 22, 179 n. 32, 180 n. 36, 182 n. 37, 185 n. 19, 186 n. 40, 187 n. 53, 187 n. 59, 188 n. 68, 190 n. 133, 196 n. 3, 202–4, 209
Fischer, Norbert 152, 158, 178 n. 14, 194 n. 18, 195 n. 38, 201–2
Flew, Antony 59, 179 n. 33, 202
Flikschuh, Katrin 172 n. 20, 202
Förster, Eckart 181 n. 5, 193 n. 8, 195 n. 33, 199, 202
Fraenkel, Carlos 189 n. 110, 202
Frederick the Great 89
Fredrick William II 89, 136, 178 n. 24
free will 78, 92, 154
freedom 1–3, 20, 35–6, 40–3, 49, 50, 54, 69, 76, 78–9, 82, 84–6, 105–6, 134–7, 144, 150–1, 153–7, 159, 166, 183 n. 67
civil 86
of conscience 1, 15, 19, 90
as criterion of true church 133
divine 2
of expression 8, 126, 172 n. 15
ground of 65
idea of 54, 84, 155
as ignorance of causes 79, 80
innate 11
moral 137
and nature 68, 152–3, 156, 160, 195 n. 30
political 86, 137
reality of 85–6, 166
of the press 97
as spontaneity 42, 84, 154
of thought 8, 11, 19, 78, 130, 172 n. 15
transcendental 84, 154
of the will 73, 77, 155
freethinking 8. *See also* unbelief
Freudenthal, Jacob 26, 113–15, 175 n. 3, 189 n. 100, 189 n. 102, 189 n. 104, 189 n. 109, 202
Fugate, Courtney 127, 132, 140, 178 n. 12, 191 n. 8, 198, 202
future life 45, 47–8, 76, 124, 138, 160

G
Germany 19, 90, 110, 114, 183 n. 1
God 11, 14, 17, 20, 31, 33–6, 38–41, 44–5, 47–55, 57–8, 60, 63–5, 70, 72, 75–6, 78, 80–4, 86, 90, 92, 94–8, 102–3, 105, 107–8, 110, 112–14, 116–19, 125–6, 131–2, 135, 137, 140–1, 144–50, 152–4, 156, 158–9, 161–4, 166, 179 n. 30, 179 n. 33, 193 n. 11, 194 n. 15, 194 n. 23, 195 n. 24. *See also* the divine
as *causa sui* 78, 112, 176 n. 24
cognition of 83, 97–8, 118
concept of 62, 66, 112, 144–6, 148, 157, 160, 189 n. 96
as creator 28, 42–4, 154, 175–6 n. 11, 194 n. 16
duties to 94–5, 165
existence (being) of 2, 3, 11, 20, 26–7, 33, 39, 47, 49, 50, 52, 54, 57–60, 62–3, 65, 67, 71–2, 82, 95, 97,

131, 144–50, 158, 160, 164, 166, 176 n. 24, 179 n. 32, 194 n. 14
as ground of possibilities 36–7, 39, 40
his idea of himself 110
holiness of 97
and human freedom 43, 154–6
a hypostasis of practical reason 160
idea of 5, 21, 52, 59, 66, 95–6, 98, 112, 139, 146–51, 153, 157–61, 163, 168
 as an idea of reason 144–5, 160, 164
the ideal of the highest good 131
impossibility of 57
intuiting in (*also* seeing in, vision in) 21, 61, 65–6, 161, 163–4
as judge 144
knowledge of 22, 59, 70, 72–3, 91, 99, 100, 102, 117
as legislator (*also* lawgiver) 5, 140, 144, 151–5, 157
living 91, 95, 179 n. 30
love of 115–16, 118, 190 n. 115
mind of 61, 163
moral concept of 11, 112, 148–9, 151
the mouthpiece of 118
as a necessary substance 37
as an object of rational faith 76
as one who knows our hearts (*Herzenskündiger*) 52
a people of 129
personal 64
as personified moral law 147
as a postulate of practical reason 144, 159
as practical reason 4, 145–6, 150–1, 153, 168
presence of 61, 65–6
as reason 111–12, 157, 188 n. 76, 195 n. 30
as sovereign of the ethical community 44, 138, 168
of Spinoza 25, 33–4, 38, 163–4, 176 n. 20
as a transcendent being (*also* ens extramundanum) 38, 41, 150, 157, 159
transcendent and immanent 144
triune 112
in us 145, 157, 162, 195 n. 38
wisdom of 110, 117, 131
and the world 35, 144, 158, 160
worship of 83, 186 n. 38

God or Nature (*Deus sive Natura*) 39, 71, 73, 81, 116–18
Gospel
 of John 107, 109–11
 of Matthew 22
Gospels, the 17, 102–3, 109, 187 n. 51
Goths 112
grace 65, 106–7, 195 n. 24
 God's (*also* divine) 106, 110
Gregory of Nyssa 111
ground of possibility (*also* of possibilities) 20, 27, 40
grounds
 of beliefs 48
 epistemic 58, 87
 logical *vs.* real 38
 moral 45, 54, 58, 60
 non-epistemic 55–6, 70, 73
 objectively sufficient (objective) 12, 48, 55–6, 62
 practical 58
 subjectively sufficient (subjective) 12, 48, 55–6
Grunwald, Max 21, 174 n. 51, 189 n. 103, 202
Guyer, Paul 47, 175 n. 9, 197–9, 202

H
Hahmann, Andree 177 n. 1, 178 n. 13, 202
Hall, Bryan W. 193 n. 1, 202
Hämäläinen, Hasse 173 n. 39, 180 n. 34, 192 n. 22, 192 n. 27, 200, 205, 208
Hamann, Johann Georg 20, 62
Hampshire, Stuart 79, 182 n. 46, 203
happiness 13, 14, 50, 54, 97, 117
 as a ground of motivation 53, 127
 as an object of desire 52–3, 72, 138
 as part of the highest good 49, 51, 157
 as proportionate to morality in the highest good 50, 52, 100, 138–9
 as reward for virtue 51–2, 101, 140
Hare, John E. 53–4, 139, 178 n. 22, 187 n. 53, 192 n. 31, 203
harmony 29, 34
 real 29, 30, 175 n. 11
 of reason and nature 32
Hegel, Georg Wilhelm Friedrich 162, 195 n. 37
Heine, Heinrich 11, 13, 91, 172 n. 17, 185 n. 15, 203

Heman, Friedrich 19, 34, 174 n. 47,
    176 n. 19, 177 n. 30, 203
Herbert, Maria von 62
Herbert of Cherbury 114
Herder, Johann Gottfried 36, 62–3
heterodox 2, 10, 15, 16, 22, 91, 118, 165, 167
heterodoxy 3, 8, 15, 16, 22, 63
heteronomous 3, 17, 127, 137, 139–40, 151
heteronomy 18, 151. *See also* choice
Heydenreich, Karl Heinrich 11
highest good 49–53, 76, 93, 95, 107, 127,
    129–32, 138–40, 149, 152, 156–7,
    159–60, 166, 168
  as a duty and as an ideal 140
  religious (conceptions of) 132–3, 138
  secular (conceptions of) 52–3, 132,
    138–9, 141, 178 n. 21, 191 n. 13
Hinduism 112
Hirsi Ali, Ayaan 170 n. 1, 203
Hobbes, Thomas 19, 114
Höffe, Otfried 100, 104, 170 n. 10,
    172 n. 20, 186 n. 22, 187 n. 48, 187 n.
    52, 187 n. 55, 202–3, 206, 211
Hoffer, Noam 39, 177 n. 28, 203
d'Holbach, Paul-Henri Thiry, the baron 9,
    67, 87, 123–4, 191 n. 4, 210
holy will 146, 151, 188 n. 60
Horace (Quintus Horatius Flaccus) 131
Howard, Stephen 195 n. 31, 203
Hume, David 9, 11, 13, 25
Hunter, Graeme 119, 190 n. 115,
    190 n. 131, 203
Hunter, Ian 89, 90, 168, 184 n. 2, 184 n. 3,
    185 n. 9, 185 n. 10, 196 n. 2, 203
hypothesis (problematic assumption) 59
  theistic 57–8

I
idealism 25
  absolute 162
  transcendental 20–1, 35–6, 40, 42–3,
    73, 161–3
ideas
  adequate 4, 75, 82–3, 87, 167
  in divine mind 39, 61, 163–4
  inadequate 4, 68, 71, 73–4, 78, 80, 82
  of metaphysics 145, 163
  of reason 65
  a system of 143, 158
  theory of (Plato) 20
  transcendental 64

Ignatius of Antioch 111
illuminati 89
illusion
  of conviction 48
  metaphysical 4, 68, 76, 78–80, 83, 167
  transcendental 62
imagination 74–5, 116
  as the origin of superstitious religion
    14, 116–17
immanent frame 133
immortality 73, 86
  postulate of 11, 47, 124
Incarnation 101, 108–10, 167
Insole, Christopher 40, 43, 110, 151–2,
    155, 157, 177 n. 29, 177 n. 32,
    177 n. 33, 177 n. 35, 177 n. 36,
    188 n. 72, 188 n. 73, 193 n. 7,
    194 n. 17, 195 n. 25, 195 n. 26, 203
intellectual love of God 116, 118,
    190 n. 115
intellectualist (interpretation, reading)
    39, 40
interest of reason 85, 87, 167. *See also*
    reason
Islam 135
Israel, Jonathan I. 1, 7–11, 13, 16, 18,
    19, 51, 67, 87, 97, 123, 170 n. 4,
    170 n. 6, 171 n. 6, 171 n. 8,
    171 n. 9, 171 n. 11, 171 n. 12,
    172 n. 16, 172 n. 23, 173 n. 36,
    173 n. 40, 173 n. 42, 173 n. 43,
    177 n. 2, 181 n. 2, 183 n. 69, 186 n. 23,
    187 n. 49, 191 n. 1, 196 n. 1, 204

J
Jacob, Margaret C. 1, 7, 8, 64, 170 n. 2,
    171 n. 1, 171 n. 3, 171 n. 5,
    172 n. 30, 180 n. 41, 181 n. 44,
    186 n. 23, 196 n. 1, 204, 207
Jacobi, Friedrich Heinrich 20, 55–6, 62,
    68, 115, 175 n. 2
Jacobs, Nathan 76, 93, 104, 110, 119, 169,
    179 n. 32, 182 n. 37, 185 n. 19,
    187 n. 53, 187 n. 59, 188 n. 68,
    190 n. 133, 202
Janowski, Zbigniew 183 n. 53, 188 n. 62,
    204–5
Jelles, Jarig 16, 165, 185 n. 13
Jesus (founder of Christianity) 14, 101,
    103, 107–11, 113, 117–18, 167,
    188 n. 65

Jews 90, 112
John Damascene 111
John Paul II 170 n. 1, 204
Johnson, Gregory R. 60, 180 n. 36,
    180 n. 38, 204
judgment 48, 160
    day 104
    problematic 58
judicial (standpoint, *also* perspective) 93,
    99, 160
Julius Caesar 27
Jung-Stilling, Heinrich 62
justice 52, 139
    and charity 8, 22, 83, 98, 117,
        186 n. 38
    divine 52, 59, 140
Justin Martyr 111, 152

K
kingdom
    of ends 21, 128–9, 139, 159
    of God 4, 133–4, 140
Klueting, Harm 192 n. 22, 204
Knutzen, Matthias 15, 114
knowledge 1, 4, 25, 64, 67–74, 76, 80–3,
        87, 91, 94, 118, 130, 164
    assertoric 22, 95, 145
    vs. cognition 179 n. 32
    esoteric 89
    and faith 17, 55, 71
    of God (of the divine) 16, 22, 59, 60,
        67, 70–3, 91, 99, 100, 102, 117,
        189 n. 96
    kinds of (in Spinoza) 75–6
    of necessary truths 194 n. 15
    and religion 10
    system of 63, 68–70, 72, 179 n. 28
    theological 83
    of things in themselves (philosophy) 61
        (*Wissen*) 55–7, 59, 76, 98
Koerbagh brothers 165
Kołakowski, Leszek 80, 90, 183 n. 53,
    185 n. 8, 205
Kołłątaj, Hugo 15
Korholt, Christian 114
Kors, Alan Charles 172 n. 28, 185 n. 14,
    205
Kozyra, Wojciech 135, 192 n. 25, 205
Krakauer, Moses 19, 173 n. 44, 205
Krop, Henri 173 n. 39, 185 n. 7, 196 n. 1,
    205

Kuehn, Manfred 106, 187 n. 49, 188 n. 61,
    188 n. 65, 205
Kupś, Tomasz 193 n. 11, 205

L
La Vopa, Anthony J. 60, 180 n. 37, 205
Lactantius 94, 185 n. 21
Lau, Theodor Ludwig 115
Lavater, Johann Caspar 62, 102, 104
law of contradiction (*also* principle of
    non-contradiction) 28, 152
laws 17, 29, 30, 87, 96, 101, 120, 130,
        136–7, 146, 150–2, 156, 159, 163
    of determining ground 41
    as divine commands 145, 151
    of geometry 40
    in the kingdom of ends 128
    of morality (moral) 12, 49, 51, 57, 95,
        97, 100, 129, 137, 151
    of nature (natural) 14, 42, 69, 81, 84,
        120, 151, 154, 195 n. 30
    political 12
    public juridical 134
    of virtue. *See* virtue
Leask, Ian 196 n. 1, 205
Lehner, Ulrich L. 171 n. 8, 173 n. 36,
    192 n. 22, 204–5
Leibniz, Gottfried Wilhelm 19, 20, 27–8,
    34, 40, 114, 138, 149, 153, 175 n. 5,
    175 n. 6, 175 n. 11, 177 n. 30,
    189 n. 96, 194 n. 15, 195 n. 30, 205
Lessing, Gotthold Ephraim 20, 55, 110,
    165, 180 n. 39
Lestition, Steven 2, 170 n. 8, 205
Levene, Nancy 81, 183 n. 56, 205
Lichtenberg, Georg 115, 163
liberal way of thinking 83
libertinage érudit 91
liberty of expression 19
Locke, John 9, 19, 46, 164, 166, 177 n. 2,
    184 n. 6, 195 n. 30
Λόγος (*logos*) 102, 110–13, 152, 167
Lord, Beth 114, 175 n. 2, 176 n. 17,
    176 n. 20, 179 n. 25, 189 n. 102,
    193 n. 3, 205
love 97, 115, 134
    intellectual 116, 118, 190 n. 115
    for moral law 136
    towards one's neighbour 83, 98,
        186 n. 38
Low Countries 114

Lucci, Diego 177 n. 2, 206
Luther, Martin 15
Lutheran 89, 90, 107
Lyszincki, Casimir (Kazimierz Łyszczyński) 15

M
Maclure, Jocelyn 172 n. 21, 206
Maimonides 116, 121
Malebranche, Nicolas 15, 154, 163–4, 189 n. 96, 194 n. 23, 196 n. 43, 206
Marcionian 135
Massimi, Michela 25, 174 n. 1, 206
materialism 8, 11, 21, 25, 54
Mates, Benson 175 n. 6, 206
Mathieu, Vittorio 144, 159, 162–3, 193 n. 2, 193 n. 5, 193 n. 14, 195 n. 34, 195 n. 41, 206
Matthews, Eric 47, 198
McLear, Colin 84, 183 n. 66, 206
Meijer, Lodewijk 16, 91, 169
Meinsma, Koenraad O. 174 n. 54, 185 n. 13, 206
Melamed, Yitzhak 33, 176 n. 18, 206
Mendelssohn, Moses 20, 55, 115, 130, 180 n. 39, 191 n. 14, 206
Meredith, James 47, 198
metaphysics 21, 23, 34, 43, 69, 70, 81, 148, 154
    Baumgarten's 36
    Cartesian 78, 80
    Christian 8
    critique of. *See* critique
    dogmatic 16, 20, 25–6, 64, 73, 76, 150, 164, 180 n. 40
    ideas of 145, 163
    Kant's pre-critical 39
    Leibnizian-Wolffian 89
    rationalist 43
    Spinoza's 77, 83
    theistic 3, 11, 25, 145, 166
Michalson, Gordon E. 2, 12, 128, 139, 170 n. 12, 172 n. 19, 187 n. 49, 187 n. 52, 187 n. 56, 187 n. 57, 191 n. 12, 192 n. 26, 203, 205–6, 209, 211
micro-history 8
middle ages 8
Miller, Eddis N. 178 n. 23, 206

minority (*Unmündigkeit*) 11, 130
miracle(s) 8, 19, 120, 155. *See also* belief
modes (Spinoza's ontology) 38–9, 78, 81, 164
monism (ontology) 34, 67
Montesquieu 9, 173 n. 36
moral gap 139–40
moral law 47, 49, 50, 53, 57, 59, 64–5, 72, 84–5, 96, 100, 105, 107–8, 110, 113, 120, 128–9, 131–3, 136–7, 140, 147–57, 159, 161, 163–4, 166, 188 n. 60
morality 2, 3, 11, 12, 17, 18, 20–2, 41, 45–7, 49–55, 57, 61, 63, 71–2, 84, 87, 93, 95–6, 98–100, 104–5, 118, 125, 127–8, 131, 139–41, 146, 148–9, 151, 156, 159–61, 165, 168
    deification of 98, 147, 150
    and nature 157, 162
    and politics 7, 21, 123, 125, 137
    provisional 70
    and religion 3, 4, 45–7, 49, 96, 99–101
    teacher of 14, 108–9, 167, 188 n. 65
    and theology 3, 60, 88, 123
    universal 118, 120–1
Morgan, Thomas 135
Moses (founder of Judaism) 14
motive (*also* moving) forces 29, 30, 159, 161
    reason's (of reason) 145, 158
Mrugalski, Damian 194 n. 20, 206
Mulsow, Martin 8, 171 n. 4, 187 n. 49, 204, 206
mundus intelligibilis 52, 128
Muthu, Sankar 171 n. 14, 207
mystical 63–4, 100–1
    enthusiasm 124
    experience 63, 65–6
    solution 65
mysticism 60, 63–5, 181 n. 49, 195 n. 38
    critical 63–4

N
Nadler, Steven 118, 183 n. 65, 189 n. 99, 190 n. 128, 207
natural
    cause(s) 13, 155, 194 n. 23
    laws 42, 84, 154
    light of reason 117, 121
    necessity 156

reason 90–1
religion 97, 118–19, 121, 167, 187 n. 49
science 143
theology 57, 179 n. 30
naturalism 8, 9, 19, 119–20
nature 39, 50–3, 57, 64–9, 74, 78–9, 81,
  97–100, 114, 118, 120, 127, 131–2,
  149, 151–2, 156–7, 160. *See also*
  God or Nature
 and freedom 68, 152–3, 195 n. 30
 human 53–4, 56, 68, 81, 83, 98, 104–5,
  108–9, 111, 113, 117, 129, 132,
  187 n. 59
 law(s) of 69, 84, 151, 156, 195 n. 30
 and morality 157, 162
 realm of 50
 and reason 32
 state of 129
necessary being 27, 31–4, 36, 38–9,
  176 n. 24
need of reason 12, 58
neologians (*also* Neologists) 89, 187 n. 49
Neoplatonic(s) 14, 61, 111
New Testament 102. *See also* Gospels
Newton, Isaac 30, 43, 177 n. 36, 195 n. 30
Nicanor 47
Nicene Creed 107
nonepistemic merits 55–6

O
obedience 17, 50, 94, 116–17, 136, 145
 to God 83, 186 n. 38
 to moral law 72, 96
 to reason 111
 a way to salvation 22
occasionalism 163
occasionalists 154
O'Neill, Onora 132, 191 n. 6, 192 n. 20,
  207
ontological argument (proof) 27, 148–50
opinion (*Meinen*) 56
Origen 100, 111
original sin 22, 101, 104–5, 107
Otto, Rüdiger 196 n. 1, 207
ought-implies-can 49, 139

P
Paganini, Gianni 8, 171 n. 5, 171 n. 13, 207
Paine, Thomas 165

Palmquist, Stephen 63–5, 73, 93, 99,
  100, 107, 119, 139, 160, 162, 169,
  170 n. 7, 173 n. 39, 178 n. 22,
  179 n. 33, 180 n. 35, 180 n. 36,
  180 n. 42, 181 n. 45, 181 n. 47,
  181 n. 48, 181 n. 49, 182 n. 20,
  185 n. 18, 186 n. 41, 188 n. 64,
  190 n. 134, 192 n. 24, 192 n. 30,
  195 n. 35, 195 n. 38, 195 n. 39,
  196 n. 3, 202–4, 207, 209
panentheism 161–2
panpsychism 77, 79
pantheism 20, 64, 114
 controversy (*Pantheismusstreit*) 55,
  115, 180 n. 39
Pascal's wager 59
Pasternack, Lawrence 52, 104, 119, 128,
  132, 140, 157, 169, 178 n. 18,
  187 n. 54, 188 n. 63, 190 n. 132,
  191 n. 9, 191 n. 11, 192 n. 34,
  195 n. 29, 196 n. 4, 207–8
peace
 global 11, 18
 religious 184 n. 2
Pentateuch (Five Books) 14, 172 n. 26
persuasion (*Überredung*) 47–8, 55, 62,
  76
Philo of Alexandria 152
pietists 22, 90
Plato 20, 33, 61, 111
Platonism 110
 Christian. *See* Christian
 Christianised 151
 transcendental 110
polytheism 49
Porphyry 14
positing (*Setzung*) 27–8, 158, 175 n. 8
possible world(s) 28, 176 n. 11
possibility
 of cognition 21, 94, 163–4, 179 n. 32
 data of 38
 domain of 39
 vs. existence (*also* actuality) 27–8
 of the existence of God 57–9, 95,
  176 n. 24
 of freedom 36, 40, 84, 86, 151, 159
 internal 32, 38, 41
 logical (*also* formal) 27–9, 31, 84,
  175 n. 9

real (*also* material) 27–31, 33, 39, 84, 149, 175 n. 9
   of revelation 11, 119
postulates (of practical reason) 5, 11, 12, 47, 59, 93, 95–6, 144, 146, 148–9, 160
practical inconsistency (*absurdum practicum*) 20, 50–1
predisposition(s) (to the good) 105–6, 127
priests 14, 97, 112, 124
primacy of the practical (*also* of practical reason) 3, 12, 67–8, 73, 81, 83, 85, 87, 166
principle
   of causality 38, 43, 82
   of identity 38
   of sufficient reason 32–3, 82, 176 n. 24
Principle of Proportionate Distribution (*also* PPD) 52, 157
proof (*also* argument)
   cosmological 26, 38
   moral 49, 52–5, 95, 178 n. 12
   ontological 27, 148–50
   physico-theological 26
   possibility 3, 26–7, 33, 38, 102, 166, 175 n. 6
propensity to evil 53, 72, 96, 98, 104–7, 110, 113, 126–7, 162
prophecies 75, 117
prophets (Old Testament) 75, 107
Protestant 19, 116, 190 n. 115
   theology 2, 89
Protestantism 190 n. 115
   radical 119
prototype
   of humanity well-pleasing to God 107, 109, 113, 127, 162
   as an idea in reason 108
   as an ideal human 110
   vs. Jesus 107, 109
   of moral disposition 108, 113
   of morally perfect humanity 4, 91, 101–2, 108, 110, 112, 167
provisional moral code 70
Pseudo-Dionysius the Areopagite 52
public 137, 172 n. 20, 184 n. 2, 191 n. 6
   general 21, 25
   laws 134
   learned 124
   opinion 8
   sphere 4, 7–9, 12, 123, 125, 137, 172 n. 20
   use of reason 11, 130
Pythagoras 111

R
radical evil 53, 72, 96, 101, 104–7, 110, 113, 125, 130, 139, 149, 167
radix malorum 105
Rappolt, Friedrich 114
rationalism 55, 72, 119
   pure 119, 121, 190 n. 134
   religious 4, 89–92, 110, 115, 178 n. 24
reason 2, 4, 10, 12, 13, 16, 20, 26–7 43–4, 48, 53, 55, 57–8, 61–2, 65–6, 75, 81, 84–7, 90–5, 98–9, 101–3, 108–9, 111–16, 119–21, 127, 130–1, 135, 138, 144–6, 148–50, 153–5, 157–62, 164, 167, 169, 179 n. 30, 185 n. 13, 188 n. 76, 195 n. 30
   assertions of 58
   autonomy of 3, 96, 150, 157
   boundaries of 63, 107
   cognition of 76, 179 n. 32
   deification of 4, 96, 152, 157, 162
   divine. *See* divine
   divinity of 143, 150–1, 153, 157
   fact of 85, 152, 164, 194 n. 14
   as a faculty that legislates 68–9, 96
   and faith 1, 2, 9, 10, 55–6, 94, 111, 118
   final end of 131
   free use of 18, 97, 165
   guidance of 63, 111
   idea of. *See* God
   ideas of 65
   infinite 153
   interest of 87, 93, 167
   laws of 152
   as manifestation of divine Λόγος 111–13
   misuse of 63
   morally legislative 42, 97, 108, 137, 163, 168
   mystery of 44
   natural 90–1
   natural light of 117, 121
   and nature 9, 32
   need of 12, 58
   philosophical 4, 8, 9
   practical (use of) 4, 5, 11, 12, 21, 45, 47, 49, 50, 68–9, 71, 73, 84–5, 87–8,

93, 96, 109, 125–6, 129, 144–53,
  157, 159–61, 163–4, 166, 168
 public use of 11, 130
 pure 58, 86, 99, 143
 regulative use of 57
 and religion 7, 9, 91
 religion of 18, 22, 42, 92, 104, 109–10,
  120, 134, 165
 and revelation 13, 59, 92–3
 speculative (use of) 57, 62, 155
 theoretical 11, 12, 21, 68–9, 71, 73,
  85–6, 93, 126, 163, 179 n. 33
 unbelief of 63
Reath, Andrews 132, 138, 178 n. 21,
  191 n. 16, 208
reductionism 99, 100
reform
 Enlightenment as a project of 9, 15,
  167
 religious (*also* of religion, religious
  institutions) 2, 15, 125, 134–5, 169
 social (*also* political) 51, 133
reformation 90
Reformed (church) 89, 107
regnum gratiae 138
Reimann, Iacob Friedrich 15
Reimarus, Hermann Samuel 14, 15, 103,
  165, 184 n. 6, 187 n. 49
Reinhold, Karl Leonhard 11
religio
 catholica 83, 116–17. *See also* religion,
  universal
 vana 80, 116
 vera 116. *See also* intellectual love of
  God
religion 1–3, 7, 9, 10, 12, 14, 17–19, 21–2,
  54, 57, 59, 60, 67, 89, 91–3, 95–100,
  114–20, 124, 132–3, 136–7,
  145–8, 168–9, 172 n. 20, 192 n. 24,
  196 n. 3
 catholic 117. *See also* religion, universal
 of conscience 103
 critique of. *See* critique
 definition of 4, 91–2, 94–5, 97–8, 119,
  185 n. 21
 different kinds of 112
 edict on 90, 178 n. 24
 and Enlightenment 1, 7, 10, 165
 Enlightenment reformers of 97
 institutional 125

 Kant's philosophy of 4, 91, 110, 145
 moral 18, 101, 124, 133, 185 n. 20
 and morality 4, 45–6, 49, 95–6, 100–1,
  123, 159–60, 165
 of morality 168
 natural 97, 118–19, 121, 167, 187 n. 49
 one and only 108
 philosophical 189 n. 110
 political 115
 and politics 4, 12, 115, 123, 125, 136,
  191 n. 6
 pure faith of 12, 100, 135
 of the radical Enlightenment 64
 rational 2, 18, 23, 89, 91–2, 97, 99–101,
  103–4, 108–9, 113, 119–21, 136,
  167, 169
 and reason 7, 9, 91
 of reason 18, 22, 42, 92, 104, 109–10,
  120, 134, 165
 reduction to ethics (morality) 92, 96,
  99, 100, 147, 152
 reform of 2, 7, 15, 18, 166
 revealed 1, 2, 14–18, 90–4, 100–1,
  114–15, 118–19, 123–4, 165,
  187 n. 49
 sacramental 89
 and science 13
 of service 17, 18, 165
 in Spinoza 22, 116
 spurious 116
 superstitious 113, 117
 true 10, 67, 98, 101, 114–21, 147
 universal 22, 83, 95, 115–18, 134, 136,
  167
 without presupposition of God's
  existence 145, 148
 world 136
Religion-as-Translation 104
republicanism 8
Rescher, Nicholas 177 n. 33, 208
revelation 4, 8, 14, 16–19, 22, 57, 92,
  100–3, 114, 119–20, 123, 167, 169
 divine 17, 103, 119–20
 Christian 22, 109
 critique of. *See* critique
 historical 94, 133–4, 165
 immediate 66
 and reason 13, 59
 scriptural 91, 99, 108, 113, 118, 120–1,
  134

supernatural 119
  as a vehicle (means of propagating rational faith) 115, 120–1
Riem, Andreas 130, 191 n. 15, 208
Robespierre, Maximilian 11
Roëll, Hermann Alexander 184 n. 6
Rossi, Philip J. 128, 185 n. 16, 191 n. 11, 208, 211
Rousseau, Jean Jacques 127, 173 n. 36

S
salvation 22, 46, 101, 106, 117–18, 126, 132, 169
Sauter, Michael 89, 178 n. 24, 184 n. 2, 189 n. 103, 208
Schmidt, James 89, 184 n. 2, 208
Schönfeld, Martin 175 n. 6, 197, 208
Schröder, Winfried 15, 170 n. 6, 172 n. 27, 173 n. 32, 173 n. 35, 174 n. 57, 185 n. 7, 185 n. 14, 187 n. 51, 189 n. 103, 194 n. 22, 201, 204–5, 208
Schulz, Johann Heinrich 'Ponytail' 54, 67, 114, 178 n. 24
Schwärmerei 3, 25, 46, 60–1, 63, 76, 80, 180 n. 35. *See also* enthusiasm
science 1, 2, 8, 9, 11–14, 18, 98, 115, 160
  natural 143
  philosophy as 131
  unity of 69
scientia intuitiva 75–6, 118
Scripture(s) 3, 4, 13, 14, 16, 17, 22, 83, 89, 93, 98, 100, 102–4, 108, 112, 114–21, 134, 185 n. 13
secret societies 8, 63, 89
secularism 4
  political 172 n. 21, 191 n. 6
secularization 1, 2, 90–1, 121, 123, 126, 136, 167–9, 172 n. 30, 190 n. 115
self-knowledge 70–1, 74
self-legislation 42, 86–7, 168. *See also* autonomy
self-positing 159
  practical 5, 21, 153, 158, 160, 168
  theoretical 158
Semler, Johann Salomo 184 n. 6
simple notions 31, 39
Socinians 114
sola Scriptura 116
Solomon (Jewish King) 117

Son of God 107, 110–13, 162, 167
Sorkin, David 1, 170 n. 3, 171 n. 1, 208
space 20, 30–1, 35, 39, 41, 43, 159, 163, 177 n. 36
  and extension 20, 30–1, 39, 40
  moral 159, 161–2
  and time 25, 27, 35–6, 40–1, 43, 156, 158
Sparn, Walter 19, 173 n. 45, 185 n. 11, 209
Spinoza, Baruch (Benedictus de) 3, 4, 10, 13, 14, 16, 18–23, 25–6, 33–5, 38–9, 41, 45–6, 51, 54, 60–1, 63–4, 66–84, 87, 89–92, 97–8, 102–3, 110, 112–19, 121, 161–7, 169, 172 n. 26, 174 n. 52, 176 n. 20, 176 n. 25, 177 n. 30, 177 n. 31, 181 n. 8, 181 n. 14, 181 n. 17, 182 n. 18, 182 n. 21, 182 n. 22, 182 n. 24, 182 n. 27, 182 n. 28, 182 n. 32, 182 n. 35, 182 n. 39, 182 n. 42, 182 n. 44, 182 n. 45, 182 n. 47, 182 n. 50, 183 n. 54, 183 n. 57, 183 n. 61, 183 n. 63, 183 n. 65, 185 n. 13, 186 n. 38, 187 n. 50, 187 n. 51, 189 n. 94, 189 n. 96, 189 n. 110, 190 n. 111, 190 n. 115, 190 n. 116, 190 n. 127, 190 n. 129, 209
  in Bayle's article 45–7
  as contributing to the radical Enlightenment 1, 8, 10, 19, 67–8
  Kant's 3, 21, 46–8, 50, 54, 62, 161, 163
  as a moral (virtuous) atheist 20, 45, 55, 67, 123, 166
Spinoza's circle 16, 91, 174 n. 54
Spinozism 3, 8, 11, 19–21, 25–6, 33–6, 39, 40, 43, 55, 61–3, 68, 90, 114–15, 162, 166
Stang, Nicholas 175 n. 4, 209
Stevenson, Leslie 104, 173 n. 39, 178 n. 11, 187 n. 57, 209
Stilpo 47
Stjernfelt, Frederick 7, 171 n. 2, 209
Stoic 50
Stosch, Friedrich Wilhelm 114
Strauss, Leo 1, 2, 13, 15–18, 22, 170 n. 5, 172 n. 22, 172 n. 25, 172 n. 28, 172 n. 29, 209

Strickland, Lloyd 176 n. 11, 194 n. 15, 194 n. 21, 209
substance
    (an entity) 35, 37, 40, 62, 144–5, 156, 161, 194 n. 15
    (Spinoza's ontology) 3, 25, 38–9, 68, 70, 73, 77–9, 81, 116, 164, 176 n. 80
summa intelligentia 154, 159–60. *See also* God
summum bonum 92, 154, 159–60. *See also* God
supernatural 8, 11, 16, 17, 65, 103, 106, 119
supernaturalism 119, 121
superstition 9, 13, 25, 75, 80, 97–8, 115–17, 123–4, 134
supreme maxim 105–6
Swedenborg, Emanuel 62, 65, 181 n. 49
symbol 109, 188 n. 65

T
taking something to be true (*Fürwahrhalten*) 48, 55
Tampio, Nicholas 135, 192 n. 26, 209
Taylor, Charles 15, 133, 171 n. 10, 172 n. 21, 173 n. 37, 192 n. 21, 206, 209
teleology 8, 131
theism 8, 57, 64, 95
    moral (*theismus moralis*) 92, 145, 148
theist 91
    moral 58–60
Theodorus 47
theology 3, 9, 10, 12, 57, 60, 76, 88–9, 92, 97, 99–101, 109–10, 114–15, 123, 131, 161–2, 164, 196 n. 3
    natural 57, 179 n. 30
    philosophical 2, 91, 145
    post-critical 147–8
    pre-critical 34–6, 42–3
    rational 2, 91, 133, 146
    transcendental 57, 91, 179 n. 30
theonomy 4
theosis 151–2
things in themselves 27, 42, 61–2, 64, 73
Timm, Hermann 179 n. 26, 210
Toland, John 21, 123–4, 165, 191 n. 3, 210
toleration 1, 8, 9, 15
    religious 1, 184 n. 2
Tomasi, Gabriele 50, 178 n. 15, 185 n. 21, 210

Tomaszewska, Anna 25, 170 n. 7, 171 n. 13, 173 n. 39, 192 n. 22, 192 n. 25, 192 n. 27, 200, 205, 207–8, 210
transcendental
    ideal (*prototypon transcendentale*) 109
    philosophy 143–4, 157–8, 160, 162
    realism 36, 40–1, 43
trinitarian 22, 101, 112
Trinity 100–1, 110, 112, 151
Tuschling, Burkhard 162–3, 195 n. 40, 210

U
unbelief 3, 15, 16, 46, 49, 54, 59, 64, 166, 168
    freethinking 25, 48
    moral 108
    of reason 63
unbeliever 50, 52, 57, 67
    righteous (*also* moral, virtuous) 45, 51, 53, 55, 60, 68, 83, 166
unconditioned, the 27
universalism 8, 11
unsociable sociability 128

V
Vaihinger, Hans 147–8, 193 n. 2, 193 n. 12, 210
van Bunge, Wiep 174 n. 57, 190 n. 130, 196 n. 1, 207–8, 210
van Eekert, Geert 172 n. 15, 210
van Hattem, Pontian 114
Vanini, Lucilio 47
vicarious 22, 127
virtue 50–3, 82, 100, 127, 138
    laws of 133–4
Voltaire 9, 11, 13, 15, 21, 173 n. 36
Voysey, Charles 173 n. 31, 210

W
Wachterus, J.C. 15
Walker, Nicholas 47, 198
Walker, Ralph C.S. 85, 183 n. 68, 210
Walther, Manfred 19, 174 n. 46, 210
Watkins, Eric 43, 177 n. 34, 197, 200
Waxman, Wayne 182 n. 34, 210
Weber, Max 9
Werkmeister, Benedikt 15

Wimmer, Reiner 144, 148–9, 158, 160–1, 193 n. 4, 194 n. 14, 195 n. 36, 210
wisdom 131
    divine (*also* of God) 39, 54, 97, 110, 113, 117
    doctrine of 76, 131
    highest 160
    human 116, 131
    study of 69
Wissowatius, Andreas 184 n. 6
Wolff, Christian 62
Wood, Allen W. 2, 92, 104, 109, 119, 169, 170 n. 10, 170 n. 11, 176 n. 15, 184 n. 1, 185 n. 16, 187 n. 56, 188 n. 66, 190 n. 135, 198–9, 210–11
Word of God 22, 83, 102–4, 117
worthiness to be happy 50–2, 157. *See also* virtue
Wöllner, Johann Christoph von 89, 90, 136, 178 n. 24, 184 n. 2

Y
Yong, Peter 29, 39, 175 n. 10, 177 n. 27, 211
Yovel, Yirmiyahu 22, 81, 100, 116, 121, 132, 138, 157, 174 n. 56, 183 n. 52, 183 n. 55, 186 n. 47, 190 n. 115, 190 n. 137, 191 n. 18, 195 n. 30, 211

Z
Zammito, John 211, 180 n. 39
Zoroastrianism 112

www.ingramcontent.com/pod-product-compliance
Lightning Source LLC
Chambersburg PA
CBHW062219300426
44115CB00012BA/2130